If your image does not work,
put a dog in it.

If it still does not work,
put a bandage on the dog.

Norman Rockwell

Big Bang

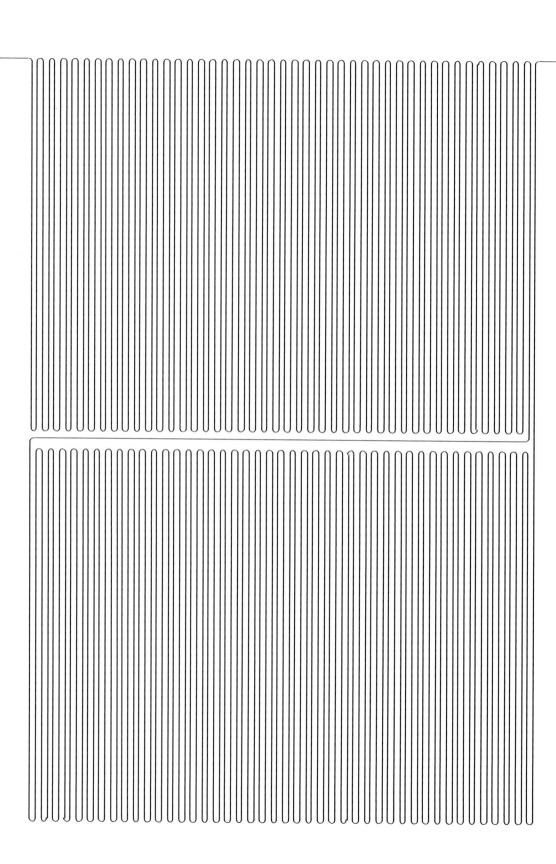

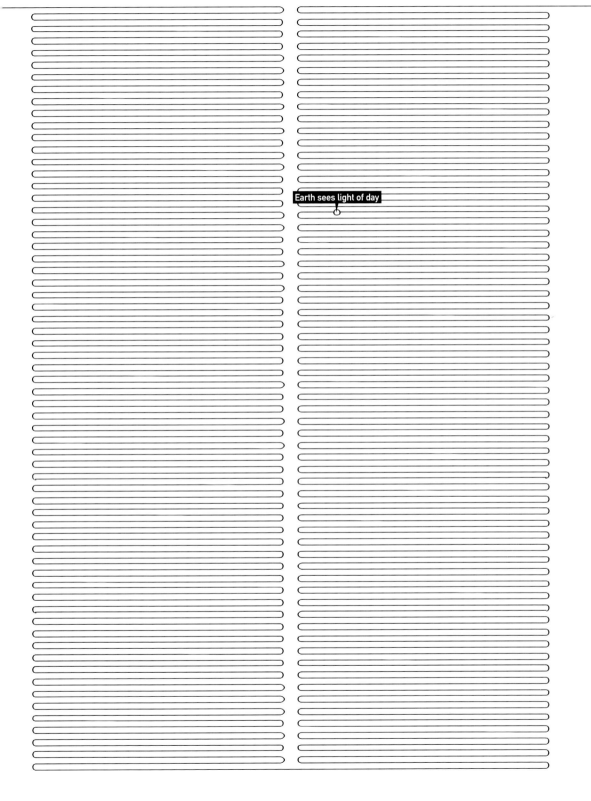
Earth sees light of day

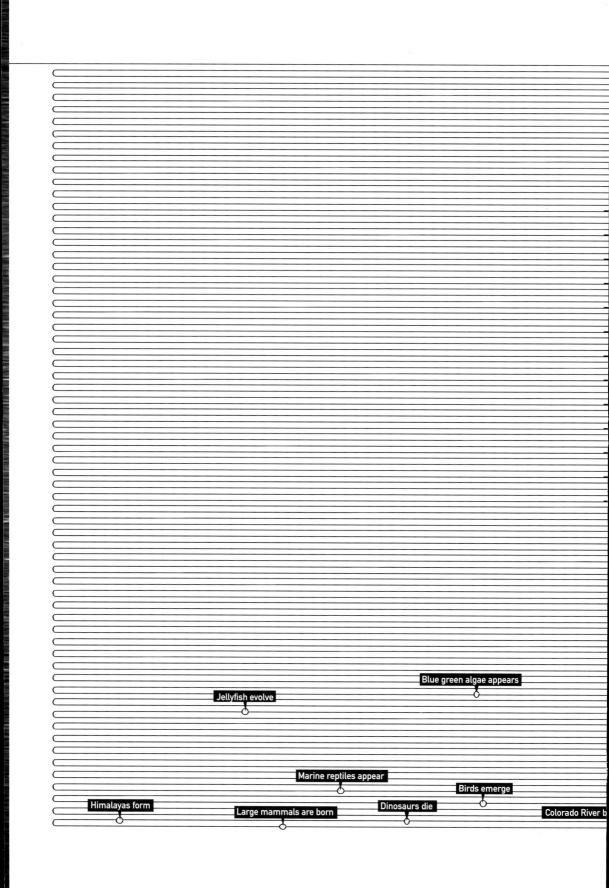

Blue green algae appears

Jellyfish evolve

Marine reptiles appear

Birds emerge

Himalayas form

Large mammals are born

Dinosaurs die

Colorado River b

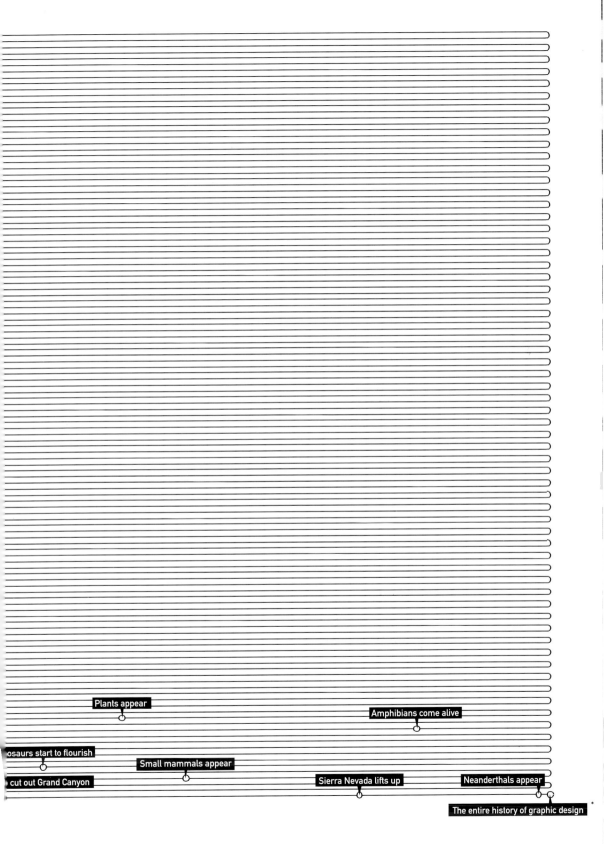

Plants appear

Amphibians come alive

osaurs start to flourish

Small mammals appear

cut out Grand Canyon

Sierra Nevada lifts up

Neanderthals appear

The entire history of graphic design

* The little circle representing the entire history of graphic design is of course shown much too large here: In real life and scale it is about 1/10 000 of an inch, which is a very, very small circle. Now, my whole working life: Too bitsy to think about. That Aerosmith job that went on forever? Oh boy.

Sagmeister

MADE YOU LOOK

ANOTHER SELF-INDULGENT
design mon·graph
(PRACTICALLY EVERYTHING
WE HAVE EVER designed
INCLUDING the BAD STUFF) *

WRITTEN BY PETER HALL
DESIGNED BY SAGMEISTER INC.
IMPROVED BY CHEE PEARLMAN

Booth-Clibborn Editions

* WE INCLUDED THE BAD STUFF BECAUSE
  a.) IT COULD BE VALUABLE FOR STUDENTS OF GRAPHIC DESIGN
  b.) NOT enough GOOD STUFF
  c.) ADMITTING TO BAD WORK MIGHT BE GOOD
  OF COURSE, YOU DECIDE WHICH IS THE GOOD AND WHICH IS THE BAD. HOWEVER, IF YOU
  ARE INTERESTED IN OUR OPINION, CHECK OUT THE LITTLE RATINGS SYSTEM
  IN THE CREDITS SECTION (p 280)

This is a traditional show-and-tell graphic design book.
No revolutions or big theories in here. It does show
most of our work from the last two decades, and none
of it has been created specifically for this book (with the
exception of the "Designer Biographies," pages 138 to
147 which was photographed recently but is based on
an old story, and the cover itself, which is based on a
previous CD packaging project).

Contrary to our expectations, putting it all together
was one of the most enjoyable design experiences
we've ever had.

Stefan Sagmeister

Design by Sagmeister Inc., New York
222 West 14th Street, #15A
New York NY 10011
Fax: 212/647-1788
<stefan@sagmeister.com>
Text by Peter Hall
<peterhall@aol.com>
Improved by Chee Pearlman
Read by Andrea Codrington and Paola Antonelli
Cover & back cover photo: Kevin Knight

First published in 2001 by Booth-Clibborn Editions
12 Percy Street
London W1T 1DW
www.booth-clibborn.com

Reprinted 2004

A catalogue record for this book is available from
the publisher.

ISBN 1-86154-274-7

Printed in Hong Kong

We wrote a letter to a number of designers we like, asking them two simple questions: 1. Which piece of design touched your heart? 2. Why?

→ I HAVE KEPT A
DIARY SINCE I
WAS 14.
ADDITIONALLY,
about 10 YEARS
AGO I STARTED a
BUSINESS DIARY *
(this WAS ONE OF **
my two good BUSINESS IDEAS)
THE HANDWRITTEN
TEXT THROUGHOUT
THIS BOOK
COMES OUT of THAT. ***

Für Mama in Bregenz,
Papa im Himmel
&
Anni in New York

* I NORMALLY WRITE ONCE A WEEK, REFLECTING ON WHAT WENT WELL AND NOT SO WELL.
** THE OTHER ONE IS TO KEEP THE STUDIO SMALL.
*** THE DIARY, OF COURSE, WAS NOT WRITTEN WITH PUBLICATION IN MIND. I TRANSLATED (from GERMAN)
AND EDITED (THE ENTIRE THING IS RATHER BORING) THE DIARY FOR THIS BOOK, CLARIFIED A COUPLE
OF THINGS AND ADDED SOME STORIES. THESE ARE ALL SOMEWHAT TRUE, RETOLD TO THE BEST
OF MY RECOLLECTIONS.

Day 1

Austria

Day 3

in BREGENZ AUSTRIA

THE TRANQUIL ALPINE TOWN of Bregenz, Austria, is a picturesque spot that, with its lake, impressive mountain peak and good sausages, appeals to well-heeled tourists. But beneath the town's polite appearance is a rarely noted vein of brash opportunism. It all started in 15 B.C., when legions of Roman soldiers invaded the area. An enterprising local Celtic tribe—known as the Brigantes—managed to convince the Romans to name their settlement after them, and Brigantium, later Bregenz, was born. A similarly enterprising spirit kicks in every summer during the town's popular opera and orchestral festival, staged on a floating platform on Lake Bodensee. While the inhabitants of nearby ski resorts are milking the cows, the people of Bregenz are hauling in 200,000 tourists, hiking up the hotel rates and milking the profits.

Our story begins at the turn of the last century with the owner of a tiny liquor-making business in Bregenz named Otto Sagmeister ("Uncle Otto") who decided, in the spirit of the Celts, to advertise his business as if it were a formidable international concern. He printed letterheads (right) showing a fictional giant brick edifice (looking suspiciously like an elongated version of the family home with extra chimneys), with text stating that this was the Sagmeister

distillery, with a branch in Cognac, France. The fact that he never even been to France didn't deter him. When it came to on-site advertising, Otto hit his stride. Outside his house, he installed a rotating sign that would chime noisily when the wind blew. Ultimately, the neighbors got so sick of the clanging that they filed a lawsuit against Otto for disturbing the peace.

And so it was, 75 or so years later, with this opportunistic vein and a family trait for inventive advertising that young Stefan Sagmeister—Uncle Otto's grand nephew—sat in the examination hall of the Hochschule für Angewandte Kunst (University of Applied Arts) in Vienna, tapping green paint onto a piece of paper. It was the third and final day of examinations to get into the prestigious school, and the assignment was to design a poster titled "Green in the City." In Sagmeister's hand was a thick, round brush with a rubberband tied around its bristles, which he was dipping into a pot of poster paint and tapping over the paper surface. The technique, which he'd picked up at private art school, didn't work particularly well, but the constant banging of the brush had the useful effect of driving his exam-room neighbors berserk. Sagmeister was accepted into the school, while dozens of others, perhaps driven to distraction by the

tapping, were turned down. Uncle Otto would have been proud.

The passage out of Bregenz had not come easily. Born in 1962, the youngest son of the owners of a fashion-retailing business in Bregenz, Stefan Sagmeister's early encounters with the Austrian educational system were vividly painful. High-school professors were typically old and despotic, according to Sagmeister. The Latin teacher, for instance, preferred to turn his ring around before delivering a disciplinary smack, so that the protruding stone would maximize the blow. Sagmeister entered the local engineering school, fueled mostly by the desire to do something different from his two elder brothers who had gone to business school and become fashion retailers, but the choice was not a good one. As a long-haired revolutionary artsy type surrounded by clean-cut, wannabe engineers, Sagmeister made few friends, and since he was an inattentive and uninterested student, he didn't make much ground with the professors either. "On top of that," recalls Sagmeister, "I was in a band that sucked totally and had a girlfriend who was horrible."

By the end of the third year of engineering school, Sagmeister was more than ready to transfer to a college in a neighboring town, Dornbirn, which lay >

Fol.

FABRIK FEINER LIQUEURE

Otto Sagmeister

TELEGRAMM-ADRESSE
LIQUEUR-FABRIK

DIRECTER IMPORT VON
Französ. Cognac,
Jamaika-Rum,
Thee.

BREGENZ
Römerstrasse 463.
ZWEIGBUREAU: COGNAC, RUE RICHARD 11.

Specialität:
naturreine Fruchtsäfte,
deutsche Weinessig-Essenzen.

CLEARING-VERKEHR-CONTO
No 839.886.

Bregenz den 26./11. 1906 190
Vorarlberg.

Den mir durch **meinen Burschen**
gütigst erteilten Auftrag habe ich sorgfältigst ausgeführt und ersuche, mich für den Betrag nachstehender Rechnung erkennen zu wollen.
Ich bitte um baldige Erneuerung Ihrer schätzbaren Ordres und verharre

hochachtungsvoll

Otto Sagmeister.

Comm.

Factura für Herrn GEBHARD SAGMEISTER,

B R E G E N Z.

Ziel 3 Monate oder per Cassa 2% Skonto.

No	Gattung	Für Ihre werte Ordre, Rechnung u. Gefahr durch	Preis	Zahlbar und klagbar in Bregenz
				Kronen-Währung
A.C. 723		1 Fassl feinster Weisswein 234 Liter		
		10 Liter Schwund		
		224 — 224 Liter	48.—	107.52
		Fass leihweise oder		24.—
		Kronen		131.52

Zahlungen durch Postsparkassa erbeten.

> at the center of the region's giant textile industry. Serendipitously, the town was also home to a small left-wing quarterly publication called *Alphorn*, "the magazine for a rural area," and Sagmeister leapt at the opportunity to join its young, anti-establishment editorial team. Discovering his talent for providing spot illustrations and layout designs, he quickly mastered the available technology (setting type with IBM electric typewriters) and began to give voice to the inventive energy that had been stifled in engineering school. *Alphorn* was a seat-of-the-pants operation, and an invaluable learning experience. For economic reasons, the magazine featured hand-lettered headlines (there were too many missing letters in the donated Letraset sheets) and was even sewn together by hand when budgets didn't permit the printing of larger, folded sheets. Frequently, the pages emerging from the discarded color offset press used by *Alphorn* were unreadable and the people in photographs unrecognizable. Such details were, of course, unimportant. *Alphorn*'s content was the stuff that fired up its editorial team, if not its readers, including articles on the plight of poor Alpine farmers, the impact of bad 1960s architecture in the rural towns and the importance of legalizing marijuana.

The *Alphorn* connection also provided Sagmeister with the chance to get involved with organizing rock and jazz concerts, including the design of the show posters, using professional printers. The poster with the greatest impact, however, was for an *Alphorn* anarchy issue, which Sagmeister designed by convincing his classmates to lie in the school playground in formation to create the letter "A" within a circle and photographing them from the school roof. Shortly after the poster was printed, *Alphorn*'s office was subject to regular visits from the local police, who were trying to establish a connection between the magazine and the sudden appearance of graffiti-sprayed anarchy symbols around the quaint towns of the Vorarlberg region.

At age 19, after graduating from Dornbirn, Sagmeister moved to Vienna, giddy with counter-culture politics and dreams of design greatness, which he was determined to polish off with a degree from the venerable Angewandte. Sagmeister's first application to the Angewandte, likewise, was rewarded with a humbling rejection. "Looking around the examination room it became very clear that just about everybody was better at drawing than I was," he recalls. He tried the conceptual approach that had proven so effective at *Alphorn*, but to

little avail. After two days of examinations, the applicants were asked to design an "imaginary bird." Sagmeister drew a bird walking off the page with a thought balloon that read "fuck imagination." This put a decisive end to his application chances, and the beginning of a year at a private art school. Here, at last, Sagmeister forced himself to learn to draw from nature so that he could apply, with more substantiated confidence— and a memorable paint-tapping technique, a year later. Happily, the strategy paid off.

Angewandte's entrance examinations turned out to be the most demanding part of the entire educational experience at the school. Teaching was based on a "masterclass" system, in which students stayed with the same professor for the four years of the program. If, as might be expected, students began to tire of their professor's esthetic leanings and pedagogical preferences, one course of action was simply to stop showing up for class, which had over the years become quietly tolerated. Sagmeister's professor—Paul Schwarz—was a disciple of A.M. Cassandre, the Ukrainian-born designer whose Art Deco poster designs greatly influenced the century's graphic design development. To zealous New Wave students in the early 1980s, however >

Bologna
Children's Book
Fair
1985

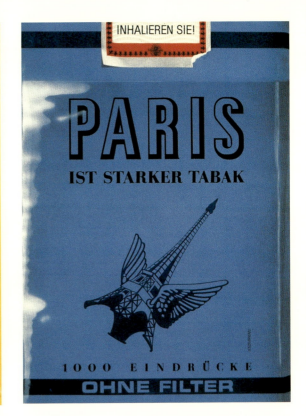

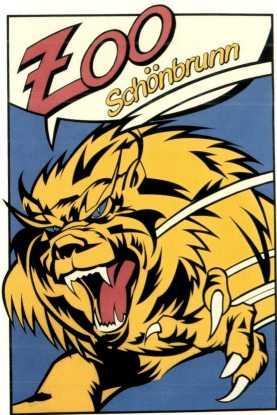

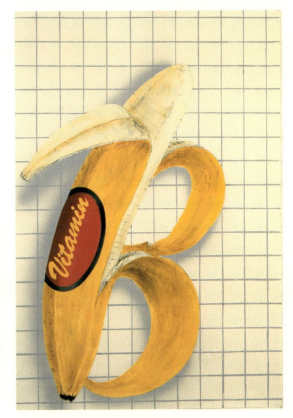

> —during a time when Modernist tenets were being disrupted by more experimental movements, notably from the U.S. and Switzerland—the appeal of Cassandre's bold-but-old geometric posters was limited. "You could learn quite a bit from Professor Schwarz as far as traditional composition was concerned, but for him design stopped with Cassandre," says Sagmeister. "It began with Cassandre too, so there wasn't really much to take in."

More fun, it seemed, could be had with design outside of the curriculum. One particularly useful tool was the screen-printing equipment Sagmeister and his student friends had set up in the bathroom of their digs. Many happy hours were spent amid the toxic fumes of the bathroom press, designing and printing official-looking notices and stickers, then slapping them on strategic spots around the city. It was not quite the politically driven disorder of, say, Jamie Reid's Situationist rebellions, or the subtle humanism of artist True's New York subway sign subversions (see p.277), but it was a rewarding way of sprinkling a little anarchy into the touristy, bourgeoise orderliness of Vienna.

One easy target was Vienna's tabloid newspapers, which had been mounting an abrasive publicity campaign to stop people stealing the paper. On Sundays, when newsstands were closed, customers were supposed to place five Austrian schillings in an insecure vending unit, but since many didn't bother, the papers had begun pasting a warning: "Somebody's watching. Please pay five schillings." When this failed to significantly increase the revenue, the warnings had become harsher, first notifying potential Sunday swipers that "plain clothes controllers" were patrolling the area, and later adding "we hope you will be caught."

● auf jeden , der die 5ös nicht zahlt,hetzen wir den Hackenmörder!

At the same time, the tabloids had been reveling with morbid curiosity in the grisly saga of the Hackenmörder, a deranged inhabitant of the city who had hacked off the hand of a child with an axe. Late one Saturday night, Sagmeister and 24 friends ran out behind the delivery vans, covering the warning stickers with ones of their own design (above). The replacement read:

"For each and every person who doesn't pay five schillings: we will send the Hackenmörder after you!"

The following morning, Sagmeister noticed that one of the stickers had been placed on a wall in the Vienna Museum of Modern Art. The tabloids were less impressed, and posted a reward for information leading to the identity of the culprits.

Familienbild vom 1.6.84

Wir haben . . . .

Gebhard Heidrun Simon Clemens

OCT 9 1983

SITUATION: I AM lying IN BED, SMOKE ALREADY ROLLED, the POLICE ON the HEADPHONES. SAW A VERY BEAUTIFUL, VERY OLD LADY TODAY IN THE SUBWAY. Huge SUNGLASSES WITH ROSES AROUND the LARGE FRAME; FIRE RED LIPS, long grey HAIR. I WANTED to tell HER HOW BEAUTIFUL SHE IS — DID NOT HAVE THE COURAGE in the SUBWAY, — WHEN SHE got OUT IN HITZING I FOLLOWED her THROUGH THE STATION AND FINALLY, AFTER QUITE SOME HESITATION, I did get it out!

"Excuse me, I think you look really beautiful today."

HER FACE JUST LIT UP, IT CAME OUT ALRIGHT, I GUESS THESE THINGS ALWAYS COME OUT ALRIGHT. WHAT A great easy THING it WOULD be IF I COULD DO THESE THINGS ALL the TIME.

23

A flat dimensional form with parallel circles, at top an inverted triangle solidly shaded in bright pinks reds, purples and sometimes the blues. An arrow is stuck through it and two sets of initials are inscribed on it. The letters are F F and I R + Ed Fella

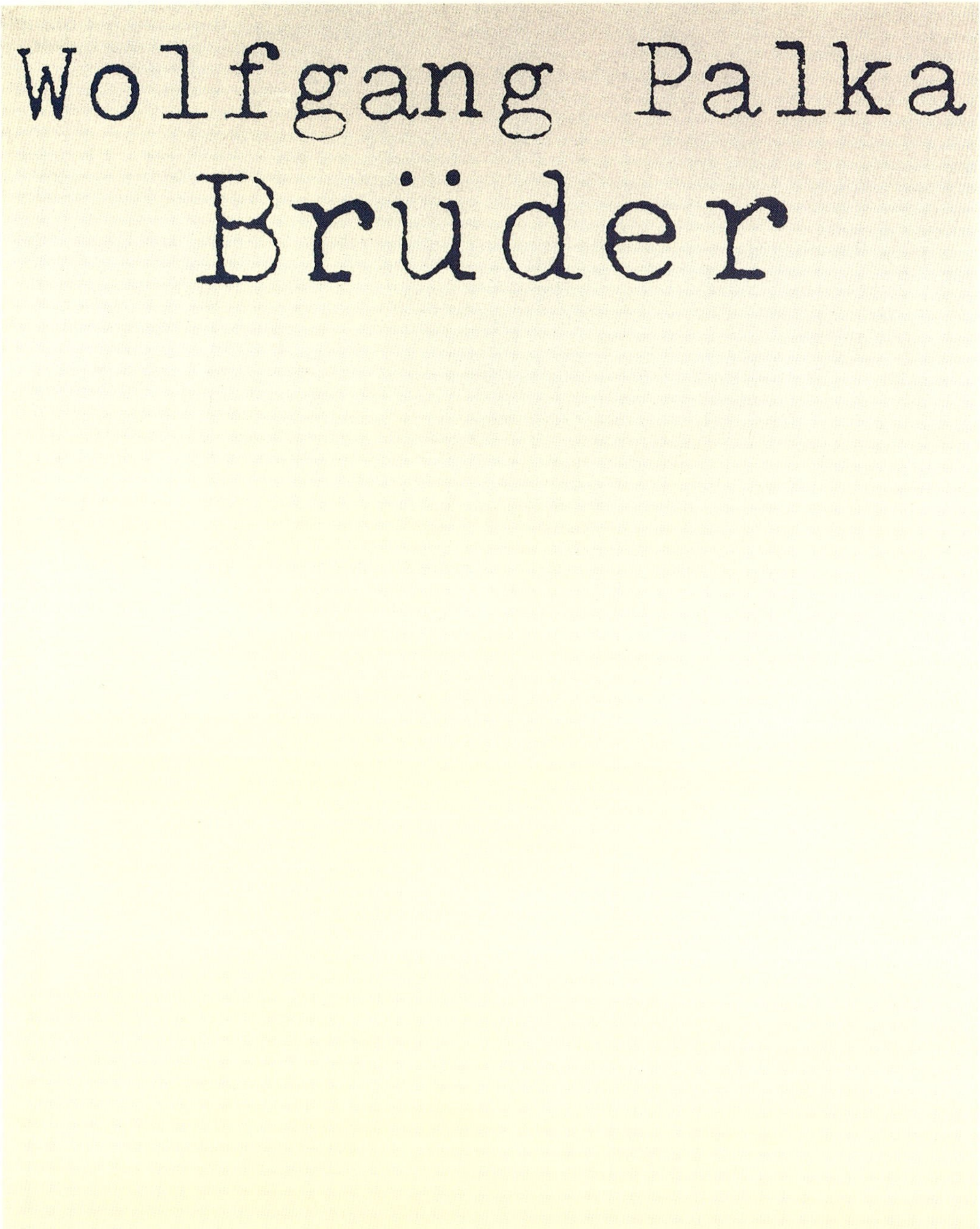

Wolfgang Palka

Brüder

Schauspielhaus

Leitung: Hans Gratzer Tel. 34 01 04

Clara S.

✦ E. JELINEK ✦

Schauspielhaus

Leitung: Hans Gratzer   UK   Tel.: 34 01 01

A CHANCE CONNECTION to the music business in 1982 provided the student Sagmeister with a more practical education than anything the Angewandte classroom could offer. His sister happened to be dating a rock musician named Alexander Goebel, who offered Sagmeister the job of designing his next album cover, titled *Awkward on Top*. Sagmeister's proposal for an awkward parallelogram-shaped sleeve (page 20), was accepted by the record company on the condition that it be straightened out. The designer naturally refused, and the project came to naught except that Goebel, by way of compensation, put Sagmeister in touch with the Schauspielhaus, Vienna's popular modern theater, where Goebel had a part in a production of the *Rocky Horror Picture Show*.

The theater director, Hans Gratzer, agreed to consider using poster designs pitched by Sagmeister and a few classmates for the next production. To cover his bases, Gratzer commissioned a professional designer to develop ideas for the same poster, but he was unsurprisingly content to sample the low-cost services of enthusiastic design students with seemingly unlimited amounts of time. Gratzer ultimately chose Sagmeister's design, leading to a long-term relationship between the theater and the student group, subsequently named "Gruppe Gut."

The assignments offered Gruppe Gut the opportunity to design posters that would appear across the city, their subject matter the acclaimed contemporary productions of the Schauspielhaus. Thespian subjects were deliciously rich: Elfriede Jelinek's play about Robert Schumann and his wife Clara, who watched the composer slowly grow insane, afforded Sagmeister and colleague Jurislav Tscharyiski the trio of perennially-linked themes—music, madness and love—which they distilled into a single image of a piano keyboard with a depressed key (left). >

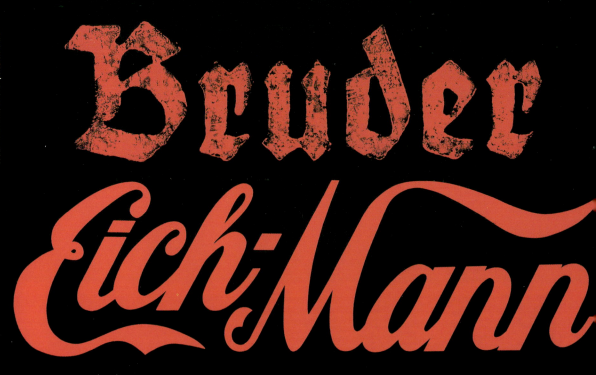

Bruder
Eich-Mann

KIPPHARDT

Schauspielhaus

Leitung: Hans Gratzer ÖB/UK   WIEN KULTUR   Tel.: 34 01 01

The scene: Rehearsal space, old factory, around 1984. A group of students arrives from the Academy to show poster designs. One of them stands out: Stefan. Tall, thin, the eyes, the seriousness, the smile. He understands the problem, circles the subject, grabs it, turns it around, rips out its secret, separates it, forms it into a picture and gives back the secret.

• **Hans Gratzer** director SCHAUSPIELHAUS, Vienna

> Gruppe Gut's method of working was simultaneously competitive and inefficient. All four designers in the studio would have a go at creating the poster for each project, and Gratzer would choose the piece he considered most appropriate. Inevitably, some members of the group found that their work was less likely to be picked than their colleagues'—notably Sagmeister's, whose approach seemed to gel with the director's tastes. Frictions thus developed. "If you want to have a functioning group that stays together it's not a good way of working," says Sagmeister.

The group, which lasted for a year and a half in its initial configuration (two of the founding members eventually relocated the firm to northern Italy) nevertheless provided its members with an extraordinary education in poster design. For technical and typographical advice, the students could consult their professors. Once a poster had been printed, the designer would experience an emotionally thrilling countdown to the day when his or her work would appear on the advertising columns and in the cafés around Vienna. "You knew exactly what day they went up and you couldn't wait to take the subway into the city to check it all out," says Sagmeister. >

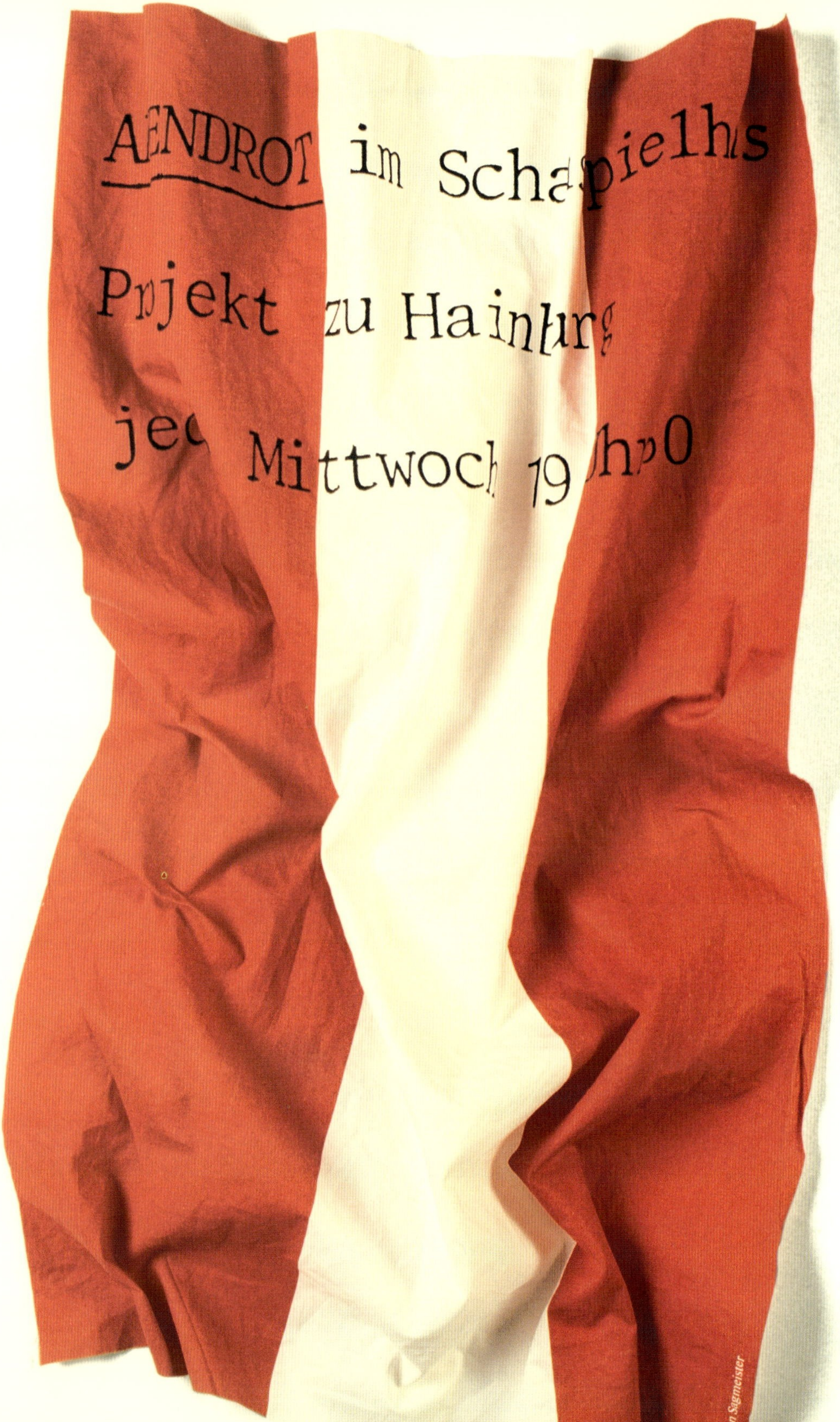

abendrot. theater poster. vienna

> To stand out amid the opulent architecture and pervasive nostalgia of Vienna, posters were often pasted *en masse*, with entire advertising columns carrying notices for one theater performance. Sagmeister's posters often added an interpretive voice to the presentation of the plays, suggesting that the Schauspielhaus wasn't just promoting, but telling its audience what it thought of the show. For *Über die Dörfer*, a play by Peter Handke (writer of *Wings of Desire*), Sagmeister took the director's view that the play sentimentalized life in the Alps and created a poster around a kitschy painting of alpine scenery (see p.24). The theater

was also willing to embrace causes, staging, for example, a play written in just a few days about an ongoing controversial proposal to construct a power station in Hainburg, a small town on the Slovakian border. The play, *Abendrot* ("evening red"), gave voice to the ecological protests against the plan, and Sagmeister designed a poster (left) showing the type printed on a crumpled Austrian flag, as well as screenprinting a number of flags and hanging them in cafés around the city. The ecological campaign was ultimately successful, garnering support from a wide group of Austrians, and the power station was never built.

JUNE 1 '84

SOMEHOW, LATELY I ALWAYS FEEL LOST AT the SCHAUSPIELHAUS. WITH THE EXCEPTION OF A COUPLE OF PEOPLE I FEEL UNACCEPTED BY EVERYBODY THERE. I THINK MOST OF MY FRUSTRATION IS CONNECTED TO MY LACK OF GUTS.

RONAC R

INSZENIEREN.

JULY 21 1984

I AM STONED
AND I'M THINKIN
ABOUT my LIFE.

I WAS DREAMING
ABOUT THE RONACH
OPENING AND HO
I'll BE ON TV AN
HOW THE PARENTS
WILL BE PROUD
(OH BOY).
ON ONE HAND
I'M CONVINCED THA
I'D LIKE TO BE
A FAMOUS designe
ON THE OTHER
HAND THIS DESIR
IS SO SILLY
(AND WILL general
A LOT OF STRESS
THIS IS BULLSHI

I MEAN, ALL THAT MATTERS IS
TO TRY TO BE GOOD, TRY T
BE HONEST. THE BETTER I
FEEL, THE EASIER IT IS.

RONACHER

VIENNA

VIENNA'S 100 YEAR-OLD white rococo palace, the Ronacher music hall, was threatened with demolition in the early 1980s. The plight of this beloved 19th-century vaudeville playhouse caught the attention of Schauspielhaus director Hans Gratzer, and in 1984, Gratzer launched a

"save the Ronacher" campaign, enlisting Sagmeister to design the posters. The crusade presented Sagmeister with a potent mix: a high-profile public arts campaign, a client happy to provide artistic freedom and the colorful tale of the Ronacher.

Named after Anton Ronacher, a local

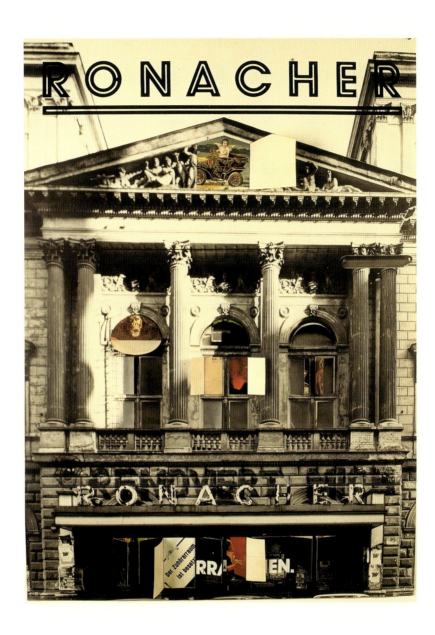

entrepreneur who allegedly built the theater with financial assistance from the composer Johann Strauss, the Ronacher was greeted by the city's bourgeoisie upon its opening in 1888 as a welcome alternative to the élitist Burgtheater. It was launched with a variety show that included a yodeler and an ape woman, and proceeded to enjoy a turbulent history in the succeeding 100 years. Program highlights and lowlights had included Josephine Baker's jungle dance, Yvette Guilbert's torch songs and a bizarre performance by fakir Hadji Soliman, which featured the fakir pulling his eyeball out of its socket on the end of a knife blade and charming a viper to sleep before biting its head off. After World War II, however, the Ronacher had become the temporary home of the Burgtheater, then put to more mundane use as a television studio. Finally, it >

> was left vacant, and by the time Gratzer arrived on the scene, the building was greatly dilapidated.

Sagmeister's poster campaign emerged out of the same populist, playful spirit that had defined the Ronacher's heyday, using mixed media and one-off designs in a 35-poster series around Vienna. The aim was simple: to convey the kind of cultural enrichment the Ronacher would bring as a prominent theater in the city if it were saved. One poster comprised a toy cable car strung across a molded plastic alpine scene, with the words "Ronacher: to set up a scene" (p.32). Another functioned like an advent calendar, showing a picture of the building with doors that could be opened to reveal events inside (p.33). One incorporated perforated tickets with the head-

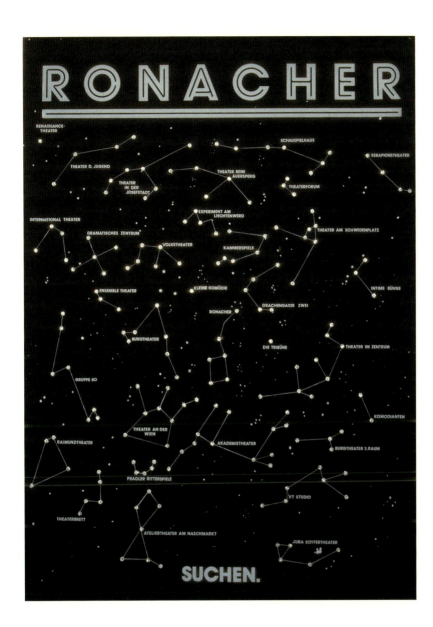

line "to make reservations," (opposite page, below right) and another was a three-inch thick, poster-sized fish tank containing live goldfish and the words "Ronacher: to dip in." Sagmeister had this one installed in a Vienna restaurant, where it required daily feeding by the waiters.

The campaign succeeded in saving the Ronacher from demolition, with the help of the city mayor, but Gratzer's first production was a flop, and he quickly lost control of the building. The city leased the theater to a commercial musical company, which used it to stage productions like Lloyd Weber's *Cats*. In 1983 the Ronacher was adopted by two cultural benefactors and renovated, making it a 1,142-seat theater, now the largest private theater in Austria.

IN 1985, SAGMEISTER was invited back to his old college town, Dornbirn, to mount an exhibition of his work at the Scala gallery. He devised an invitation based on a party favor, featuring tiny balls that had to be rolled into holes. The exhibition poster featured a diagrammatic image of the prodigal designer, portfolio in hand, printed in white on a black background, and again in black on a transparent overlay, so that by moving the overlay, the figure appeared to move.

Sherri knew she needed another drink. "Will you excuse me just a minute?" she asked in a quiet voice. He watched as the stunning blonde got off the bed and went into the other room. He could hear her pouring a drink at the bar. Ted lay back and gripped his throbbing penis.

> *It was Stefan's first exhibition and mine too. We showed his posters for the Schauspielhaus Vienna, his graduation project, a campaign for the revival of the Ronacher in Vienna and specially designed silk screen posters he had made for the exhibition at Scala. The silk screen work was my favorite: the elaborate movable poster impressed me, but also his ability to convey things with a few lines.*
>
> • **Hannes Rothmayer** owner SCALA, Dornbirn, Austria

SAGMEISTER'S THESIS PROJECT at Angewandte University laid the groundwork for many of his subsequent projects. In 1986, he designed and constructed 20 interactive postcards—interactive in the analogue sense of the word, developing many techniques that demonstrated his emerging taste for tricks and inventions. Every design incorporated a triangle, from 3-D pyramid shapes to Escher-like logotypes, and themes covered included the measurement of time—a postcard that folded out into a sundial, adjustable to your time zone (opposite page)—and the weather, in the form of a foldable raincoat.

One postcard glowed in the dark, one became a magic trick and another employed an optical illusion, reused for a Yellow Magic Orchestra CD, designed a decade later (see p.202). "I used a lot of the things I developed in jobs later on, or at least tried to," says Sagmeister. "There's something to be said for doing uncommissioned work like this."

For the Angewandte year-end show, the postcards were handmade and screenprinted in quantities ranging from 10 to 50, then placed in aluminum holders around the exhibition space with posters relating to the themes. The project was so well received—Sagmeister was awarded a first-class honors degree and a prize of $1,000 from the City of Vienna's cultural affairs office—that Sagmeister was encouraged to make a number of attempts in subsequent years to turn the postcard set into a commercial project. The most progress was made with New

York's Museum of Modern Art gift store, which showed a great deal of interest in the early 1990s in producing the set before backing out completely. "Boy was I disappointed," says Sagmeister. "I realized then that with these complicated printing projects you have to produce them yourself. No one else is going to do it." >

sundial postcard. thesis project. university for applied arts. vienna

> The loudest thesis postcard was one that popped up into a manually operated record player. Using a flexidisk, a pin and a fold in the card that formed a speaker cavity, Sagmeister proved that some of the most entertaining multimedia promos have no digital component whatsoever. He revived the idea several years later in a Christmas card commissioned by Aerosmith, for which the band recorded a special rendition of a seasonal tune for the flexidisk, complete with juvenile lyrics.

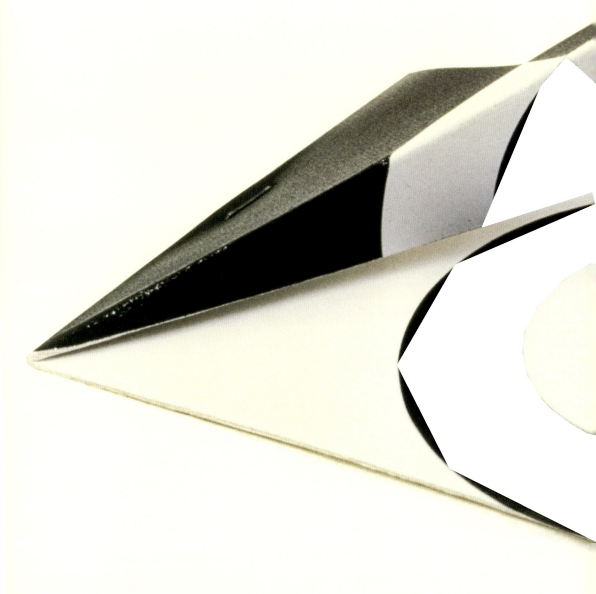

Hello

NEW YORK

goodbye

... packaging, pratt institute, new york

I take EVERY OPPORTUNITY to MAKE PHONE CALLS, FILL OUT FORMS ETC., – anything THAT PREVENTS ME FROM HAVING TO think.

ANOTHER THING: I AM STILL afraid
AND WORKING ON A CONCEPT. I GUESS ITS THE
FEAR OF NOT BEING ABLE TO come UP WITH ANYTHING
– FEAR of FAILING.

Not graphics, but pictures and images of great gestures. For example, Michelangelo's finger of God before it fell into the hands of Hollywood's promotion painters. (E.T.) – Or when Americans have their hands on their wallets while singing their anthem. This gesture originates in the very old welcome and

A NEW RECORD last WEEK:

STARTED WORKING ON SUNDAY MORNING AND WORKED all the WAY UNTIL THE FOLLOWING SATURDAY EVENING WITH A GRAND TOTAL OF 2 HOURS OF SLEEP ON WEDNESDAY.

I HAD ACTUALLY NO PLANS TO DO THIS, IT JUST HAPPENED THAT WAY. BY THE END OF the WEEK IT WAS FUN to SEE HOW FAR I could PUSH IT.

Stefan was an imposing figure of sorts, tall with long hair always getting in the way. He was the kind of student who made the professors work hard; I am sure he makes his clients work hard for him as well. He broke the norm because he knew what the norm was at that time at Pratt. He took his partners in a Memphis furniture book project on a wild ride that I am sure they have not forgotten. As the book slid open, it had Memphis style flying and wrapping its way into your living room. You didn't just sit—you had an experience.

- **Kevin Gatta** Professor, Graduate Communications Design Programs, PRATT INSTITUTE Director, GATTA DESIGN & COMPANY, INC.

S A M E

IN THE MIDST of the frenzy of his final year as a student at Angewandte University, Sagmeister happened to pass a poster advertising the Fulbright program and a chance to study in the U.S. William Fulbright's enlightened scheme—established after World War II—sends students from 50 countries to the U.S., and vice versa. A demanding application process is required for entry. "I was so stressed and busy I thought I couldn't possibly apply for a grant," says Sagmeister, "but I wrote down the number anyway." Sagmeister applied and within months had been offered a place at Pratt Institute in Brooklyn, New York. Apparently, the Fulbright committee had taken the unusual step of awarding a scholarship to a designer, mostly on the basis of his Schauspielhaus work: Many of the members, luckily, were avid theater-goers.

Arriving in New York in 1987, Sagmeister swiftly entered what he later called "post-Modernist heaven." Architects were littering their buildings with neoclassical motifs, and graphic designers were dousing their work with all the motifs and trimmings of the era. Sagmeister adapted the ballsy, concept-driven approach of his Schauspielhaus work to a more mannerist style with self-conscious historical references. Projects at Pratt were typical of the era, including a brochure for Memphis Design (the frivolous Italian-led rebellion against the prevailing austerity of Swiss Modernism), which Sagmeister turned into an interactive "experience," according to his professor, Kevin Gatta. The *piéce de resistance*, however, was a perfume bottle design resembling London's Canary Wharf skyscraper, the bottle a pyramid on wheels perched on top of a skyscraper-like block of empty packaging. "It was highly originally named Cairo," says Sagmeister, "an ugly little sucker."

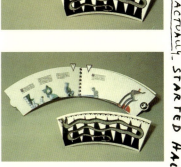

NEEDED to GET some STATS done in Manhattan on FRIDAY and ACTUALLY STARTED HALLUCINAT ING on THE SUBWAY. HAD to GET up FROM MY SEAT AND HELD on to THE POLE AS to Not PASS out. GUESS THIS IS IT FOR MY SLEEP DEPRIVATION RECORDS. NO NEED to TOP THIS ONE.

New York

NEW EXHIBITION

PERMANENT COLLECTION

COLLECTION HIGHLIGHT

PEGGY GUGGENHEIM COLLECTION

MEMBER-SHIP

GENERAL INFORMATION

SPECIAL EVENT

CONTINUING EXHIBITION

TRAVELLING EXHIBITION

FUTURE EXHIBITION

SIGNETS FOR CALENDAR OF EVENT

LIFE IN NEW YORK CITY is marked by its unsettling contrasts—balmy nights and sub-zero mornings, gourmet food in backstreet diners and homeless people sleeping outside swanky hotels. Sagmeister slipped into the lifestyle like a native, experiencing the culturally contrasting mix of a Fulbright-sponsored education—which included free tickets to musical and theatrical events—and a crummy apartment on Manhattan's Lower East Side, then a haven for drug dealers. Summers were spent lounging on the roof of Sagmeister's tenement

it in through the door of my building in a second," recalls Sagmeister, "but I had an old car which they must have seen. They shat on the windshield. The next time I came down I turned on the windscreen wipers and there were these two sausages going back and forth."

Back in the rarefied seclusion of the classroom, Sagmeister was undertaking a redesign of the corporate identity of the Guggenheim Museum. Picking up on the spiral motif of Frank Lloyd Wright's celebrated building (built in the 1940s and 1950s), the identity proposed adapting

Sagmeister called the Guggenheim for an appointment with its director, Thomas Krens. He was granted a meeting, at which he presented his new identity scheme for the museum, then sat back and waited for the director's approval. "I was thinking they'd take my Guggenheim logo and put it on the museum, which didn't happen. I didn't understand why," he says. "They were very supportive and sweet, and boy was I proud of that project. Now I know it was obvious and lame. I also didn't know at the time that one of the oldest rules in design is that

LADIES

MEN

POSTER

POSTER

building on Clinton Street, wallowing in a cheap inflatable pool and eating the fresh pastries baked by his Austrian roommate. Floating up from the street below came the sounds of summer—drug dealers bellowing "roadrunner! roadrunner! brand new works!" and Latin music booming from the jacked-up car stereos. One particularly colorful neighborhood encounter came when Sagmeister found a woman shooting up on his doorstep, asked her to move and was confronted by her boyfriend. "I made

the motif to everything from bathroom signs to restaurant menus, with slight variations in each application. Sagmeister painstakingly redrew Wright's typeface for the building for each use, and made exploratory sketches showing the link between Wright's organic tapering funnel and forms found in nature. A poster design developed the connection between nature and art further with a whelk shell adapted to look like a Mondrian painting (left).

Emboldened by his own virtuosity,

you can't sell anything that the client didn't originate."

Although his professors were impressed with his energy and professionalism, Sagmeister reflects on his output as the product of some naïveté, "I was working really hard at the time but I have difficulty now comparing the work to what my current students do. It think my students are better. They know what's going on in design—they're much more savvy."

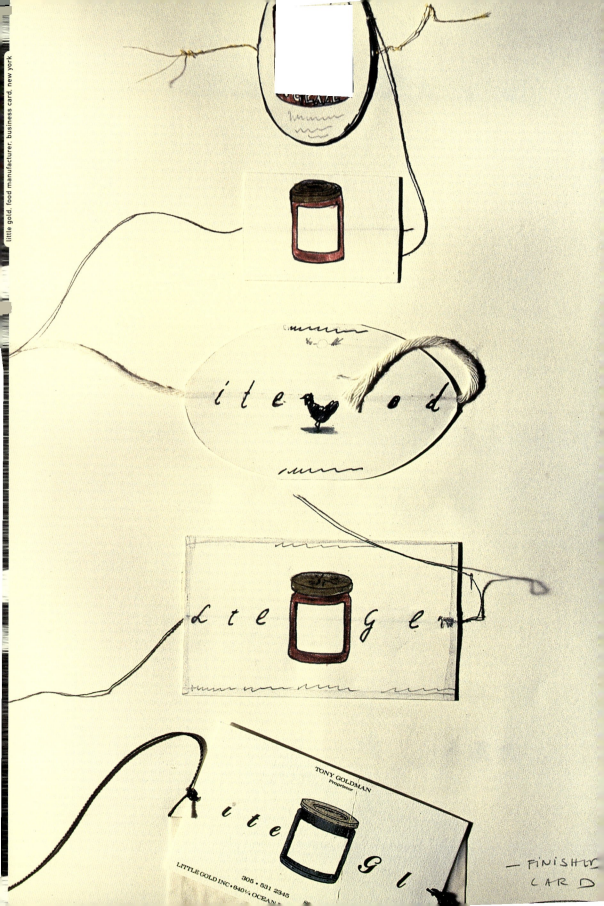

ONE LUXURY OF THE FULBRIGHT scholarship was that Sagmeister didn't need to work to support himself. There were, however, the occasional choice projects that couldn't be turned down. A photographer friend put Sagmeister in touch with Tony Goldman, the real estate tycoon behind the rejuvenation of Miami Beach, who was setting up a food and produce company. The task was to design a business card to stand out at food trade shows, where potential customers would typically amass a pile of business cards and never look at them again. Sagmeister's solution was based on an old party trick in which images printed on each side of a piece of card appear to converge when the card is spun on its axis. By twirling the business card with its attached strings, the company name, Little Gold, formed and a chicken appeared inside a jar. The card proved quite popular at the trade fairs, where fun-starved businessmen would stand around the Little Gold stand, vacantly twirling.

FOR A CLASS ASSIGNMENT at Pratt to originate and design a book, Sagmeister plundered books of symbols and pictograms and constructed a vaguely autobiographical narrative around the images. The protagonist was named *Socko*, one of Sagmeister's childhood nicknames. "It's one of the few school projects I actually like reading now," says Sagmeister. "It benefited from having no strict brief or client" The abridged version of this rambling tale of a hapless, love-lorn hedonist, appears on the following pages.

Hi there.

Yeah, this is my first appearance in an illustrated story.

Well, you have to know,

it's a rather interesting story.

I hang around a bit,

then I lose both buttons of my trousers,

I'm looking for them,

can't see them.

I look on the floor,

upstairs,

can't find them anywhere.

Oh, what shall I say about the story?

I stole the symbols

from a guy named Modley.

Anyway, just came back from Jamaica,

it was horrible.

I tell you, 10.000 wet tourists,

belly dance and party.

Right at the customs

those Germans saw my passport and identified me

as a German-speaking person. I could've hanged myself.

It started immediately: how lucky they were that they got this extremely cheap flight, only $249,

I told them that I had paid $410 and that of course if I'd known

I would've bought a cheap ticket too,

(I had paid only $198— my good deed for the day)

How happy and satisfied they were, jupidu.

Anyway, Montego Bay itself is a short story:

Everybody wants your money.

The Jamaicans,

The Americans,

continuously and constantly, somebody wants your cash.

And, of course, you don't wanna offend anybody,

| so you're nice, | you talk to everybody, | and you wind up sitting with a rastaman | in an unbelievably expensive |

| bamboo hut bar and drink beer. | And as soon as you stop paying for his beer, | you sit alone in an expensive bamboo hut bar | and drink beer. |

| Only my last evening | felt real. | The belly-dancing tourists had just elected | the best bellydancer. |

| So I went to the sea | and played the saxophone. | A storm was coming up. | The sea roars like hell. |

Waves 2 meters high,

splash!

And I press air into the saxophone

and the sea roars

and reggae from the beach-party

and roars

and I go, after long thoughts about

the might and the power of the sea, back to the hotel.

On the way back I have to get rid

of all the kids

who wanna make braids in my hair.

Only for the dull question: "Hey, wanna look like a rastaman?"

I should have twisted their arms backward

for years.

I was pretty glad to go back to NYC.

I got out of the JFK express,

went home,

took a shower

and walked to my coffeeshop.

At the counter stood this wonderful woman.

I placed myself carefully so I could look into her eyes.

How can I approach her?

Shit, she's taking her handbag, she's leaving.

Fast, an idea, she's going!

Shit!

Oh, here she is again. She took the wrong hat.

She is taking her coat off!

Without it she looks fat though.

No matter. Hi, I'm Socko. Wanna go out sometime?

Well, at the moment I'm busy.

Yeah, next week as well,

but thanks so much for asking.

Nothing again. Nothing. Now I was really lonely.	You have to know, I have a split personality	I would just love to be a woman.	I would sculpt ashtrays

paint horses	and collect Kandinsky.	I really can't go on like this.	So I went to get some pizza.

I had had	salami pizza every day.	So I ordered ham and olives.	John Lennon purred from the radio:

"You may say that I'm a dreamer,	but I'm not the only one".	Makes you tired that song.	Finally got up and went to this opening.

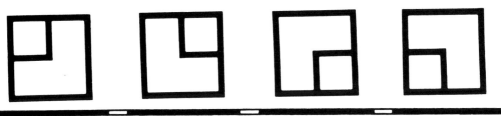

| The paintings | were | rather | boring. |

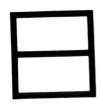 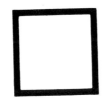  

| All these yuppies stood around, | and talked soapbubbles. | And I was in a bad mood. | "Don't you think that the composition |

| is a bit too heavy in the centre?" | "But the way he addresses issues of gender, | and sexuality. Very interesting. Somehow irresistible." | Assholes! |

| Well, I left, and since I had nothing better in mind | I looked for the buttons which | I lost on page 51. Remember? | A friendly fireman showed me the way: There they fly, the trouser buttons! |

I gave him a nice tip.

He was so happy his trousers wrinkled.

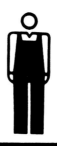
But I still couldn't find the buttons.

And it was terribly cold.

A garbage man froze and starved so incredibly,

that he cut his head off and ate it.

The surgeons left no stone unturned

and utilizing state of the art equipment, tried to sew it on again.

But: Didn't work.

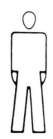
The garbage man turned white,

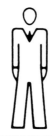
two weeks later, stonedead, laid out at the funeral home.

Oh yeah, New York is a wild city.

Stories are happening, suitcases full.

Like the one when I met this girl at Roseland (she was from BRA-zilia).

Very funny.

I just came back from the loo

and tried to get to the front,

which was quite a hassle.

She took my hand

and followed me to the stage.

The Stranglers start to play.

She rubs herself against me,

I spread my legs,

she spreads hers,

she takes my hand:

Ohh,

and the Stranglers play "Nice and Sleazy,"

I swear, "Nice and Sleazy."

After the concert I gave her the wrong phone number

and disappeared in the streets of NYC.

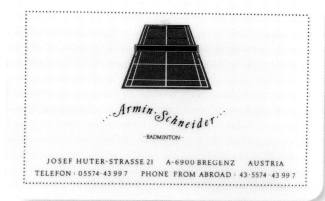

A T-shirt designed by my youngest son, Sam, when he was about 8 years old. It features some characters he invented like "Building Man", "Brick Man", "Screw Man". They are all inhabitants of "Cartoon World". On the back of the shirt he included his two brothers, making it the Matt, Blake & Sam Brand of Apparel. My boys have a saying about sticking together taught to them by their grandfather, "What happens when someone messes with one Anderson boy? They mess with all

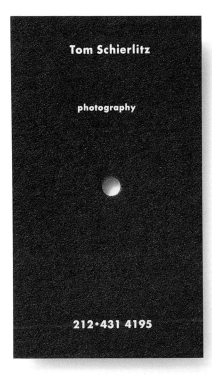

AMONG THE MORE LASTING projects completed while studying at Pratt were Sagmeister's business cards. One for his late brother-in-law, Armin Schneider, a college professor and badminton coach, employed a technique similar to the Little Gold card, with an image separated onto both sides of the card (opposite page.)

A fortuitous business card assignment came in 1988 from the photographer Tom Schierlitz, who was to become Sagmeister's long-term collaborator. After determining that the card should have a pinhole punched through the center, Sagmeister went about different typographical treatments, from International Style to "Neville Brody style." The center-stacked sans serif version worked best, and Schierlitz is still using the card 12 years later.

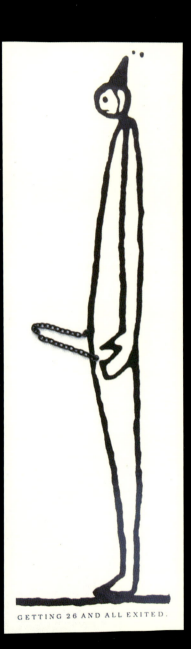

GETTING 26 AND ALL EXITED.

STEFAN SAGMEISTER
8 CLINTONSTREET
NEW YORK, NEW YORK 10002

◆ • ◆

◆ • ◆

◆ • ◆

◆ • ◆

SAGMEISTER'S 26TH BIRTHDAY presented an early—if not the last—opportunity to indulge in a penis joke. The party invitation, which came in a long, thin envelope (all innuendoes intended) featured a black crayon line drawing of a naked man in a party hat (opposite page). The character's penis, however, was depicted with a small piece of black chain, attached at either end, so that with a shake of the card, it would become variously erect, flaccid and oddly shaped.

The design writer Steven Heller noted in his book *Low Budget High Quality Design* that "one of the virtues of low-budget design is that in capable hands it is not necessarily obvious that it was 'done on the cheap.'" In the case of Sagmeister's business card for his then-girlfriend, Lucia Belci, the budget limitations were blatantly obvious (above). "She said whatever you do, one card cannot cost more than a dollar," says Sagmeister. "So we wound up printing them on dollars." The ingenious touch was a folding system that turned the bill into a self-contained envelope, with the stiffness of a business card. Best of all, the card could be used to buy coffee.

Dear Girls!
Please be nice
to Reini.
Dear Girls!
Please be nice
to Reini.

THE PHONE RANG at 9 Clinton Street. It was Sagmeister's old schoolfriend Reini, calling from Vienna. He said he would come to visit New York, but he was concerned, says Sagmeister, that none of New York's famously beautiful-but-ice-cold women would talk to him. Sagmeister told Reini not to worry, reassuring him that Manhattan's beautiful people were occasionally friendly, but decided on impulse to mount a poster campaign. He printed and pasted bills around the Lower East Side with Reini's photograph, and a headline suggesting, "Dear girls! Please be nice to Reini." On the day of Reini's arrival, the mythically hostile city seemed to await him with open arms. "I thought I was dreaming," recalls Reini, "on every corner a poster of me!" A week of *wein, weib und gesang* ensued, culminating in a cocktail party at which Reini found himself talking to an attractive woman about the poster. One thing led to another, and the pair became a couple. "I always call this my one successful ad campaign," says Sagmeister. "It's one of the pieces that's dearest to me."

> *When I came for the first time to New York, my mouth was wide open—impressed and speechless. We drove from JFK airport to the City and I couldn't believe all the things I saw. It felt like I'd been here before—when you grow up in Europe and see all those movies and TV series, somehow you know America. Stefan lived at Clinton Street: we threw my stuff in his apartment and went outside—drug dealers, trunk-sized boomboxes, homeless people and steam coming out of manholes. We crossed Houston Street—there were burned-out buildings and a long wooden fence. And as I stood there, I noticed posters with my face on it and I thought I was dreaming. On every corner a poster with me on it! Asking girls to be nice—that was too much. I think it turned out to be a long night.*
>
> • Reini

CRUNCHY

Vienna

soggy

BACK in Vienna

GURU, ONE HALF
OF THE NEW YORK
RAP DUO GANG STARR
WAS GIVING A
CONCERT IN VIENNA.
BACKSTAGE HE ASKS
the Austrian
MAKE-UP LADY
FOR the german WORD
FOR "PEACE".

→ NEXT PAGE

AUSTRIAN LAW REQUIRES that all males spend eight months in military or community service before they reach age 30. Returning to Vienna to fulfill this obligation after three and a half years in the U.S., Sagmeister pleaded conscientious objection to military service and thus was assigned a job in a refugee center, Jungarbeiterdorf Hochleiten, outside Vienna. The camp was not the most harmonious of places in 1989, despite its magnanimous origins. It had been founded by a rich philanthropist after World War II as a village for young Austrian workers who were taking apprenticeships and could not afford housing. Since there were no longer enough Austrian apprentices to fill the houses, two of the buildings were used by Eastern European and North African refugees. Some of the remaining Austrians were, by Sagmeister's account, dubious characters who had stayed on because they were unable to find their own accommodation and developed extreme right-wing and sometimes neo-Nazi political affiliations. Sagmeister found himself in the middle of a group of refugees and a group of refugee-hating Austrians who also disliked conscientious objectors as a matter of principle. "I was always super happy when a refugee came in and two days later had a great

The make-up lady, thinking that he is asking for the German word for "PIECE" (as in piece of cake) tells him: "STÜCK" instead of the correct "FRIEDEN"

So GURU goes up on stage and raises his fist and shouts: "STÜCK, MAN, STÜCK, STÜCK STÜCK!"

Since GURU is hip and black and from New York the clueless Viennese audience thinks this is really cool.

For months afterwards people greet each other with: "STÜCK, MAN, STÜCK."

job in Vienna," says Sagmeister, "and our stupid Austrian workers were still sitting around."

Sagmeister's official job was to help the refugees get acquainted with Austria, but he quickly found himself doing graphic design jobs for the village, including a local map, meal forms and posters for annual festivals. "I noticed how much I missed graphic design when I wasn't doing it," he says. Fortunately, he was not required to stay in the village, and in the relative refuge of Vienna evenings, Sagmeister worked on freelance design projects.

One of the first such assignments was for the Nickelsdorf jazz festival, which had a strong reputation for commissioning bold, arresting posters. Asked to design a series for the 1990 event, Sagmeister developed an idea based on the surrounding Burgenland region's association among Austrians and tourists as a breeding ground for storks. He sketched designs featuring flying storks and commissioned an entire photoshoot exploiting the visual counterpoint between the form of a stork and a naked saxophonist cavorting under gloomy skies. The bird idea was a big flop. "The organizers hated it," says Sagmeister. "Their response was that it was just not working." >

> Surfacing from a second rejection by the Nickelsdorf organizers, Sagmeister agreed to give the poster one more try. He began mulling over the vague directions he had been given. The client had suggested a theme of "confrontations" within the jazz festival, which that year was marked by the contrast between aggressive and ambient jazz. Sagmeister developed a design based on a schematic, schizoid face that worked as both a lenticular, delivered with two metal rods for cafe interiors, and in a flat orientation for wheatpasting in outside locations, where it took on a disturbing, almost cubist appearance. As a lenticular, it offered the two sides of the festival—calm and combative (pp.72-73). It was the first of several of Sagmeister's schizo-optical tricks.

I remember first meeting with Stefan in our club listening to sophisticated music, smoking cigars, drinking whiskey and later after midnight discussing business. A week later he came back with a Pannonian image of a white bird and a black body and I was quite disappointed. Then he came up with this beautiful idea of the three-dimensional poster, which turned out sensationally. People are still asking for it.

• **Hans Falb** JAZZGALERIE NICKELSDORF Austria

KON FRO NTA TIO NEN '90

JAZZGALERIE
NICKELSDORF
KONFRON
TATIONEN
'90

ENTRITTSPREISE:
Freitag 250,- Samstag 380,-
Sonntag 250,- Festivalpaß 900,-
INFORMATION UND
KARTENVORVERKAUF:
JAZZGALERIE
A-2425 Nickelsdorf · Untere Hauptstraße 12
021 46/23 59
RED OCTOPUS RECORDS
1080 Wien · Josefstädterstraße 99
0222/48 14 22
KATZENMUSIK
1010 Wien · Am Hof nr.schleTg10
0222/535 75 05
AKUT
1010 Wien
Helferstorfer Str. 6
0222/535 73 27

FREITAG
20.JULI ab 18Uhr
Perfekt Trouble
Bailey / Honsinger /
van Bergen
Marilyn Crispell Trio
James Blood Ulmer /
Sirone / R. Ali

SONNTAG
22.JULI ab 16Uhr
Georg Gräwe's
Grubenklangorchester
Michael Moore Quartet
Revolutionary Ensemble
Falaq
Programmänderungen vorbehalten

Welcome To
AUSTRIAN

UKS
Mit Unterstützung der
Burgenländischen Landesregierung

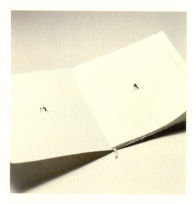

ACCORDING TO THE ORACLE of nuptials, Martha Stewart, the form of a wedding invitation is fixed by tradtion: it should be a stiff letter sheet, classic or embassy size, folded once and double enveloped. Sagmeister's wedding invitation for two of his best friends, Tom Schierlitz and Bettina Budewig, blithely flouted these rules. First, an oversized, square-shaped envelope plopped on the invitee's door-mat. Inside was a cord-bound card, a white silk sheet and a vellum square with a perforated circle, on which was printed a picture of a dancing couple. On the card were details of the wedding and a set of instructions: to place the silk on the sur-face of a tub of warm bathwater, pop out the dancing couple and put the disk on top of the silk. With the heat of the water ris-ing through the silk the disk began to undulate, spin and dance, like the party favor fortune fish that curls in the palm of the hand.

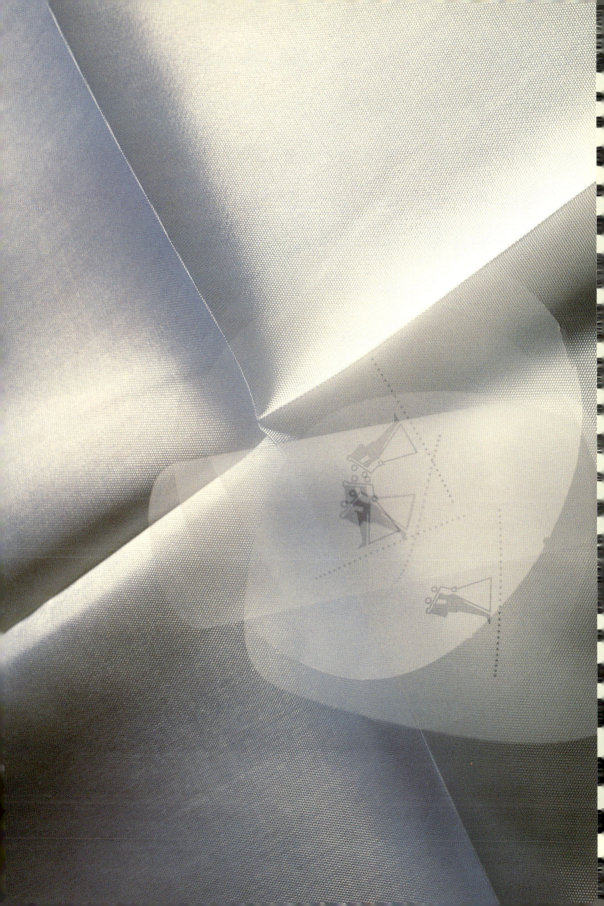

DISASTER ART 1990

FRANK's DISASTER ART Enterprises
Department of agreement
between nations
Thomas F. Sandri
Rauchfangkehrergasse 11/1/1
115o Vienna / Austria
Tel.0222/8337845
PHONE FROM ABROAD : 43/222/8337845

·ENTERPRISES·

FRANK'S DISASTER A
GEGRÜNDET 1986

GEGR.   1990

FRANK'S DISASASTER A
Enterprises

FRANK'S DISASASTER ART ★

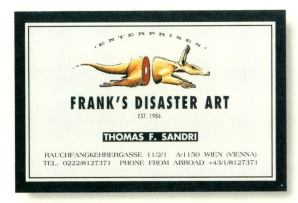

A VIENNESE MAN named Thomas Sandri ran a tiny company that helped artists realize technical problems. He also designed automated "disaster" machines, including a vending unit that, upon receiving ten schillings, would produce a model of Stephan's Cathedral in Vienna on mechanical arms, break off the tower and deposit both pieces in a chute for the pur-chaser. Sandri asked Sagmeister to design him a business card.

After considerable market research and endless focus groups, the rational design solution for Frank's communication problem emerged: An identity based on illustrations of a bifurcated South African ant-eating quadruped. "He liked aardvarks and I liked cutting things in half," explains Sagmeister.

This is my mom Rosa Sandri. She is a very nice person. Sadly, she only gave me one first name: Thomas. So I decided to get one more: Frank. And that's also the name of my company.

• **Thomas Sandri,** FRANK'S DISASTER ART Vienna

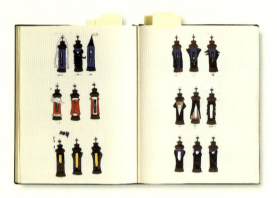

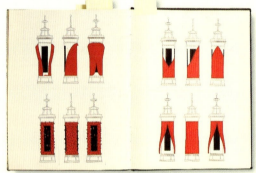

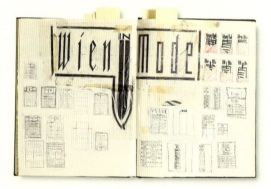

FOR A WEEK OF FASHION shows at Vienna's Palais Lichtenstein, the event organizers commissioned Sagmeister to design a campaign using the city's Litfasssäulen—the distinctive advertising columns. Having used the columns for his theater posters a few years earlier, Sagmeister felt comfortable enough to take the medium a step further and dress up entire columns in fabric. Six weeks before the show opening, however, the organizers informed Sagmeister that their media buyers had left it too late, and failed to purchase a single column in its entirety. "Even the partial spaces that we got for posters were much too few," he says. "We were in a really bad situation."

These giant advertising kiosks were used over a period of two weeks every day from 11.00 am to 7.00 pm in the main plazas of Vienna, around the opera, the Stephansplatz and the Hofburg. We had hired 16 students who got along marvelously and did their job—even though it was actually very hard to maneuver these columns in heavy wind.

I checked up on them every once in a while and saw how each student inside had developed his own way of 'driving' the kiosk. Some chased down pretty girls and tried to get into a conversation through the hidden window. I saw three kiosks, strolling happily down Kärntnerstrasse and forming something of a pedestrian blockade: When the tourists swerved to the right, so did the kiosks. Dogs hated them and immediately started to bark.

• **Günther Hrazdijra** STUDIO MOTIVA, Vienna

The solution, when it struck, turned out to be better than the original. Instead of the existing columns, the campaign would use custom-made portable columns on wheels, putting students inside, and having them roll around the city (p. 80-81). The structures, made of polyester and fabric-covered aluminum, required some tweaking to prevent them from toppling over in the wind, and a seatbelt construction was added to give the operators control, but it was a propitious invention. No building permission was required from the city, because the columns were moving, and the publicity it attracted was boundless: every TV news program, magazine and newspaper seemed to leap on the story. "They looked great on TV," says Sagmeister. "The students liked to shock the tourists by standing for two minutes—then suddenly moving."

before

HONG KONG

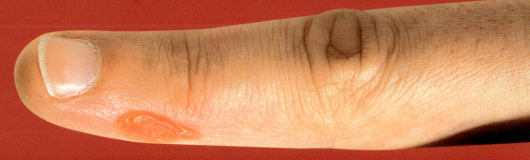

after

THE APPROACH of one's 30th birthday can initiate drastic action. John Lennon quit the Beatles, Elizabeth Taylor left her fourth husband for Richard Burton and Liberace dropped his first two names (Wladziu Valentino) to establish himself as a household brand. Stefan Sagmeister, age 29, went to live in Hong Kong.

Like the British traders who arrived there in the early 19th century, Sagmeister hadn't intended to make a home in Hong Kong when he arrived there in 1991. It was during a vacation with a friend who lived there that he became intrigued by the humid, chaotic, futuristic metropolis, and decided to explore the design scene in the city. To gain access to the studios, he figured it would be best to "pretend to look for a job," and had his portfolio sent over from Vienna. After seeing eight firms, he was offered a position by Leo Burnett, the ad agency. "They asked if I would be interested in being their typographer. I wasn't," he says. "So I made up a high number and said I would do it for that." Unperturbed, Leo Burnett met the figure and, shortly thereafter, Sagmeister was back (briefly) in Vienna, packing his bags for the East. >

Robert Rauschenberg's "Overseas Culture Interchange-Project," as put down in his 'Roci' book. For me, the concept of his manifesto is as brilliant and courageous as the output. Arts meet society in a perfect *pas-de-deux*. - **Jaques Koeweiden**

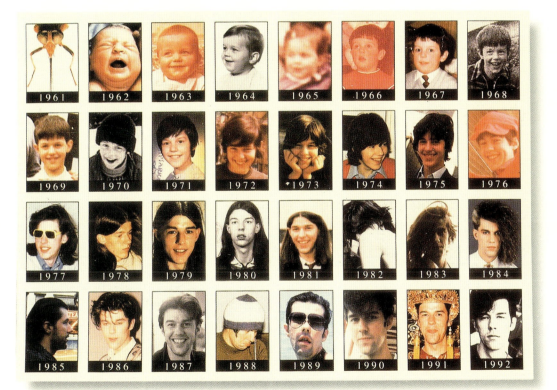

JAN 22 1991

STARTED WORK THIS WEEK. YESTERDAY WAS COMPANY DINNER. 220 PEOPLE, FANCY HOTEL,
THE GRAND BALLROOM. I AM PLACED AT THE BURNETT MANAGEMENT TABLE. I HARDLY KNOW
ANYBODY. IT'S SHIT BORING. NOBODY REALLY KNOWS ANYTHING TO SAY. WHITE & GOLD UNIFORMED
WAITERS SERVE HUGE STEAKS WITH ENORMOUS FOIL-WRAPPED BAKED POTATOES. GARY, my NEW BOSS,
LEANS OVER AND WHISPERS: "I'll PAY YOU HK$ 500.- OF my OWN MONEY IF you TAKE THIS
POTATO AND THROW IT ACROSS the ROOM. I do.
A POOR WAITER, LADDEN WITH SILVER TRAYS, BOWLS, PLATES WALKS STRAIGHT
INTO THE POTATO'S FLIGHT-PATH: HE IS HIT. SMACK ON THE FOREHEAD.
HE GOES DOWN. TRAYS FLY.

I AM SO SORRY.

THE TABLE SNICKERS. SUDDENLY THERE'S CONVERSATION,
DRINKING STARTS. HEAVILY, FOUR HOURS LATER MEDICS ARE PUSHING
DRUNK PEOPLE OUT IN WHEELCHAIRS. ⟶

> Hong Kong in 1991 was in the last bloom of its days as a colonial outpost of the British Empire, an efflorescence of exaggerated capitalism on the edge of Communist China. Wealthy Japanese and European tourists were still flocking to the island to stay in overpriced luxury hotel rooms, eat gourmet meals and shop. The powerful economy had spawned a thriving design and marketing industry, predominantly small sweatshops that supplied local businesses with cheap, fast services, turning out annual reports and collateral at a per-page rate. Studios specializing in more lavish, sophisticated design, however, were less widespread, and Leo Burnett, which had offices around the world, recognized a gap in the market. Two weeks after hiring Sagmeister, the agency suggested he start the Leo Burnett Hong Kong Design Group, granting him

autonomy (including the right to turn down projects) on the condition that the studio remained profitable.

A steady stream of work began to pour into the studio on Taikoo Wan Road almost as soon as it opened. Brochures and promotions for airlines, hotels and department stores, all with sizeable production budgets, made up the bulk of the work, but the more interesting projects often proved to be those aimed at the creative community. For Creasia, a conference in Bangkok, Thailand for art directors and designers working in Asia, the group was asked to design the conference graphics. Sagmeister, working with his Leo Burnett colleagues Peter Rae and Andrew Pogson, first developed a logo using the motif of the human eye, then decided that every attendee should have a personalized notebook, contacting each one in advance to

find out their eye color. Arriving at the conference, attendees opened their notebooks to find themselves caught in the Cyclopean gaze of a real glass eyeball, matched to their own color, nestled in a die cut hole beneath the notebook's cover (pp.88-89). The group managing director at Leo Burnett, initially horrified at the production costs for this project, was subsequently placated when the graphics won the Hong Kong Design Award, the prize for which was a shipment of Apple Macintosh computers.

> *You looked at the book. It looked back. It was a huge success and was talked about for a very long time.*
> • **Gary Conway** Executive Creative Director LEO BURNETT, Hong Kong

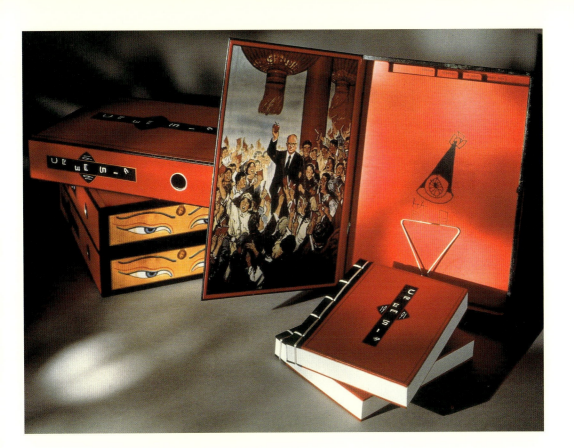

→ MOST OF MY TABLE REGROUPS IN
a SUITE UPSTAIRS FOR MORE DRINKING.
SOMEBODY HAS SOME HASH BUT NO PAPERS.
I, PROUD TO FINALLY BE of
SOME HELP, OFFER KNOWLEDGE OF a TECHNIQUE
WHEREIN A SMALL PIECE OF HASH IS PLACED ON A
CARDBOARD MOUNTED PIN, LIT, – THE SMOKE CAUGHT WITH
AN OVERTURNED GLASS AND INHALED. WHEN I ASK:
"DOES anybody have a needle #2" THE ROOM goes SILENT.
MORE DRINKING. I'm GONE,

MONTH LATER I FIND OUT : ENGLISH NOT BEING MY FIRST LANGUAGE I HAD WANTED A PIN BUT ASKED FOR
A NEEDLE. MANAGEMENT THOUGHT I WAS ABOUT TO SHOOT UP, THAT THEY HAD HIRED THEMSELVES
A HEROIN ADDICT.

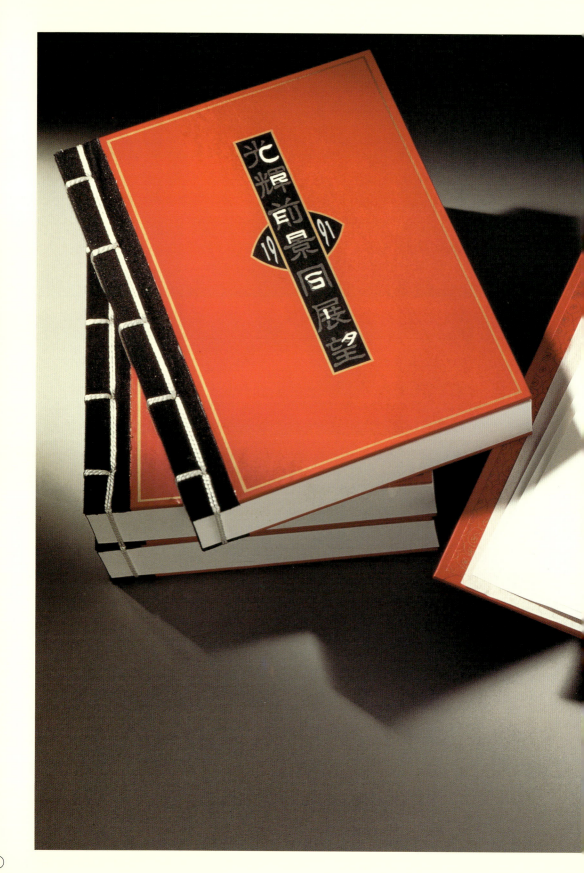

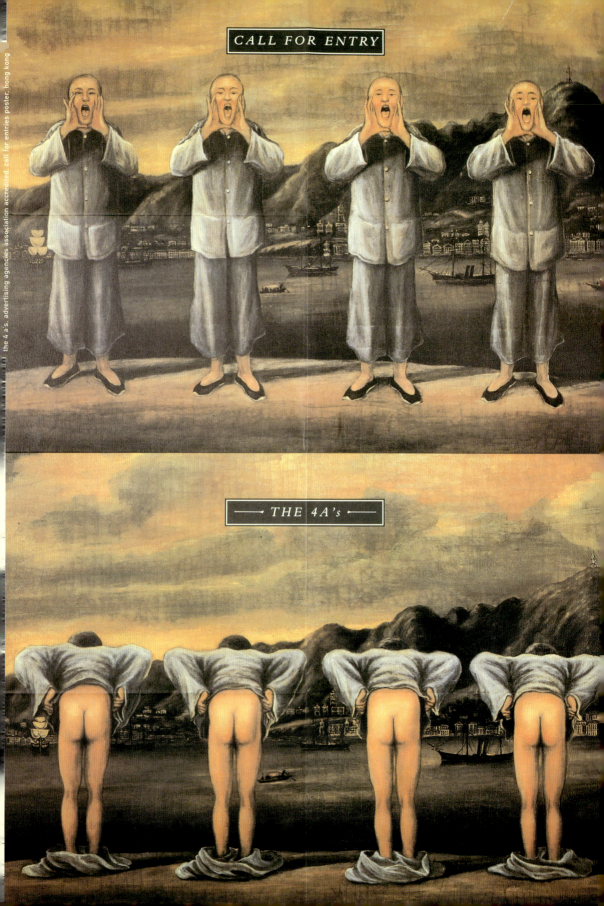

HONG KONG CULTURE, it has been noted, represents a convergence, but not quite a blend, of Chinese restraint and British snobbery, brought together by a citywide desire to make lots of money—an agenda that crosses all classes. The city's birth is firmly rooted in commerce—if not greed.

Hong Kong island became British after the Opium Wars. The Chinese had taken exception to the British practice of running opium into China—a cynical move by the British to redress the imbalance of trade that accompanied Europe's insatiable taste for Chinese silk and tea. War broke out and China was forced to cede the island after it was captured by a British commodore in 1841. When the Communists came to power in China in 1949, many feared Hong Kong would be reclaimed by military force. But the Communists also recognized the city's economic importance to China—and the territory retained its unbridled capitalist trappings even beyond its return to Chinese control in 1997. There are more Rolls Royces per head in Hong Kong than in any other country.

In the early 1990s, the strange mix of manners and mercantile motives manifested itself in design work that was almost universally conservative—from the brashly commercial "buy one now"—to the upscale, but formal and controlled work of respected designers like Alan Chan and Kan Tai Keung. So when Leo Burnett Design Group was offered the chance to design a call for entries poster for the annual competition of the Advertising Agency Association Accredited (AAAA) in Hong Kong, Sagmeister recognized an opportunity to stir things up. "It was a rebellion against the bullshit that everything has to be nice and sweet in Hong Kong," he says. His cue was the unintended anal innuendo in the poster copy. "When the title for this project "The 4 A's, Call for Entries" came out of the fax machine, the entire thing practically designed itself," he says.

With the four "A's" as the poster's focal point, the only remaining question was how to present them. "We first tried different famous behinds throughout history," says Sagmeister. "Marilyn Monroe, Michelangelo's David, anatomical behinds, and so on, but this direction had a real advertisingy look." At the same time, Sagmeister had been looking into the Cantonese trade painting styles that emerged when English oil painters moved to Hong Kong and Canton in the late 19th century and began to influence local Chinese artists. "It became obvious that this was the best way to do it," says Sagmeister.

Preparations included exploratory photographs from which an illustrator could render a sketch. For the sake of his art, Sagmeister insists, he pulled down his pants and let a colleague take a Polaroid of the view. The Design Group then took the illustration to one of Hong Kong's giant "painting factories," a local industry borne out of the demand among luxury hotel chains for copies of old paintings. Customers can choose the imagery and style and even the number of cracks required in a painting, and have the copies made—often at a lower cost than a same-size photographic reproduction.

All went according to plan except that the result—printed in four colors on uncoated paper for authenticity (not a common practice in lavishly-inclined Hong Kong) was devastatingly light on ink, despite the fact that a Leo Burnett staff member had approved the project on press. Sagmeister's team coaxed the printer into running the same sheet back through the press for another four-color run (the posters were still uncut) and—contrary to most expectations—the poster came out perfectly.

The public response to the four bared behinds, carefully depicted in the Cantonese painting style, was predictably bilious. A rival agency, Dentsu, Young and Rubicam, refused to attend the award ceremony, and tried to organize an industry-wide boycott of the entire competition—unsuccessfully, in fact, since the poster had stimulated a 25 percent increase in entries. A copy of half of the poster (the polite part) appeared with a front page article in the *South China Morning Post,* Hong Kong's largest English-speaking newspaper. There were letters to the editor "for weeks," says Sagmeister. "My favorite simply read: 'Who's the asshole who designed this poster?'"

AND ANOTHER HOTEL SHOOT IN BANGKOK:
THE CLIENT SELECTED THE PHOTOGRAPHER
(SEEMED GOOD ENOUGH, - WE SAW THE BOOK)
UPON ARRIVAL HE IS TOTALLY, UTTERLY
& COMPLETELY STONED - OUT OF HIS MIND.
1st DAY : SHOOTING THE LOBBY; AFTER QUITE
SOME ARGUMENTS, HOTEL MANAGEMENT AGREES
TO CLOSE IT OFF FOR A COUPLE OF HOURS.
IT'S A STRAIGHT FORWARD LONG-EXPOSURE SHOT

WITH A BELLBOY (= OUT OF FOCUS → STREAKS) RUNNING THROUGH.
THE BELLBOY STARTS GOING, HE GOES, HE GOES, HE'S GONE,
OUT OF THE FRAME, - THE CAMERA CLICKS.
BOB IS STONED. THIS REPEATS 4-5 TIMES UNTIL FINALLY
HIS ASSISTANT TAKES THE SHOT. GARY ARRIVES FROM
HONG KONG IN ORDER TO HELP. HE TRIES TO ENGAGE
BOB IN A FRIENDLY CONVERSATION:
"SO BOB, HOW'S THE DOPE AROUND HERE ?" WHICH PUTS BOB
INTO DEEP THINKING MODE, - HE CRUNCHES DOWN AND REALLY

REALLY DIGS IN.   "GREAT MAN, JUST great." * THIS IS ALL HIS ANSWER.

THE 4A'S CREATIVe AWARDS DINNER HONG 19 92 KONG

* HALF A YEAR LATER THERE IS AN ITEM IN THE SOUTH CHINA
MORNING POST ABOUT THE ROYAL WEDDING IN THAILAND AND
THE PRINCESS' WEDDING CAKE. THE CAKE, A 10 FOOT MULTI-
TEARED AFFAIR, IS TO BE PHOTOGRAPHED ON THE
DAY OF THE WEDDING. THE PHOTOGRAPHER APPARENTLY
GOT ON A LADDER AND MANAGED TO FALL INTO THE CAKE (!)
THE PHOTOGRAPHER - YOU GUESSED IT - WAS BOB.

** BALI - IT SEEMS - HAS THE SHORTEST SUN RISES AND SETS.
10 MINUTES AND ITS ALL OVER
*** NOW I CANT BELIEVE HOW MUCH ENERGY WE PUT INTO THESE THINGS.
WE WORKED OUR ASSES OFF AND AT THE END ALL WE HAD
WAS ANOTHER HOTEL BROCHURE.

> *The intent was to be arresting, artful and, yes, provocative. And provoke it did.*
> • Gary Conway Executive Creative Director LEO BURNETT, Hong Kong

SHOOTING IN BALI JVL 14 1992

KEVIN ORPIN, OUR CLIENT AND I ARE SINCE 5 DAYS HERE TRYING TO PHOTOGRAPH ANOTHER HOTEL BROCHURE.

THE HOTEL IS IN ITS EARLY CONSTRUCTION PHASE, THIS IS ONE GIANT SITE, ABOUT 5000 WORKERS AND N HERE AND WE ARE SUPPOSED TO MAKE IT LOOK LIKE A FINISHED THRIVING, HIGH-END LUXURY RESORT. BOY OH BOY.

THERE IS NO KITCHEN, NO RESOURCES ON SITE WHATSOEVER AND OF COURSE NO PRODUCER, NO STYLIST. EVEN FOR SIMPLE PROPS LIKE COFFEE & CROISSANTS TO USE IN AN EARLY MORNING INTERIOR ROOM SHOT, WE HAVE TO GO ALL THE WAY DOWN TO DENPASAR.

THE PROTOTYPE ROOM WE ARE SHOOTING IN WAS SUPPOSED TO BE FINISHED BUT OF COURSE IS NOT.

THIS IS GOING TO BE ONE CRAZY HOTEL THOUGH: THE SMALLEST 'ROOM' IS OVER 2000 SF, EACH AND EVERY ONE HAS ITS OWN PRIVATE POOL! THE RATIO OF EMPLOYEES TO GUEST IS 4:1 (A REGULAR 5 STAR IN THE USA HAS A MAXIMUM OF 1:1) THERE WILL BE 1 GARDENER PER GUEST, - ALL MADE POSSIBLE BY SALERIES OF $50/MONTH. ROOM RATES ON THE OTHER HAND WILL START AT $220/DAY. THE CLIMATE HERE IS SO CONDUCTIVE TO GROWTH AND THE SOIL SO FERTILE, THEY LITERALLY JUST STICK A LOG INTO THE GROUND, IT SPROUTS LEAVES IMMEDIATELY AND A SEASON LATER YOU HAVE A REGULAR TREE.

BECAUSE OF THE ON GOING CONSTRUCTION EVERY SET-UP BECOMES THIS MAJOR PRODUCTION, HUNDREDS OF PLANTS HAVE TO BE LOGGED ALONG TO HIDE CONSTRUCTION DEBRIS

I FIND MYSELF SHOUTING SILLY THINGS LIKE: "I NEED 10 MORE MEN" AT 5 O'CLOCK IN THE MORNING. MY CIGAR SMOKING IS COMPLETELY OUT OF HAND, I CHECKED MY SUPPLY TODAY AT 6 AM

left margin, top: ON CONSTRUCTION SITE AND START 4 DAYS WORK IN EARNEST... BACK TO WE CONSTRUCTION SITE

left margin, lower: "GET THE FUCK OUT OF HERE" I'M GONNA THROW YOU OFF THE FUCKING CLIFF" THEY UNDERSTAND, BELIEVE AND RETREAT.

right margin: I HAD ACTUALLY GONE THROUGH 5 VILLIGERS ALREADY, THE MODELS ARRIVED YESTERDAY, THE WOMAN WAS SMART ENOUGH TO SLEEP WITH AN OPEN WINDOW AND NO PROTECTION, TODAY HER FACE FEATURED A DOZEN OR SO MOSQUITO BITES WHICH WE PROCEEDED TO SCRATCH RESULTING IN BLOTCHES ALL OVER HER CHEEKS & FOREHEAD. A SMALL VILCANO IS FORMING ON HER FAT CHEEKS & FOREHEAD WHICH IS JUST AS WELL, I HAD ALL PROJECTS IN WITH SHE

LEO BURNETT DESIGN GROUP swiftly gained recognition, and Sagmeister found himself running a busy studio with as many as 125 projects on the go. The work ethic in Hong Kong, driven by the city's insatiable desire for money, was unforgiving. A typical day would begin with a 7:00 am taxi ride along the harbor to the office—and end with a taxi ride back from the office at 10:00 pm. "The first year and a half were grueling," says Peter Rae, who was hired by Sagmeister in early 1991. "We were working every holiday, weekend and doing late nights all the time. But at the same time we were trying to get a reputation, so it seemed necessary."

The fast turnover of projects also provided a number of valuable lessons. Work was scheduled with giant flow charts: If there were three hours to come up with nine concepts, then each was timed at 20 minutes. Although this factory-like approach yielded an undesirably large proportion of conceptually weak output, the various explorations into processes would provide useful information for stronger projects. The Cantonese-painting style in the 4 A's call for entries, for instance, was first discovered during research for an airline brochure.

Increased productivity had the cumulative effect of reiterating the need for good ideas. "You're constantly confronted by the fact that your salvation is not in the production," says Sagmeister. "Six-color printing doesn't save a bad idea." Some of the group's best work, in fact, used the cheapest printing methods and lowest quality papers—it gave the projects a certain freshness, local color, and on the *pro bono* work, kept the budget low. Local silkscreening, however, was so cheap that the second four A's poster, could be printed in 14 colors. A moving announcement for the agency (pp.96-97), meanwhile, uses the sepia effect more commonly associ-ated with cheesy wedding photographs. The image, of a pair of legs and hands carrying a portrait painting of Leo Burnett past an indigenous-looking store, had a slapstick comedy feel.

With the uproar following the first four A's poster, the Design Group was obliged to tone down the follow-up material. A variation was developed for the second poster, with the "A's" representing the four elements of an art director's emotional cycle—from anxiety to applause. But elsewhere, the asses were surreptitiously worked back in. The "famous behinds" idea was used for the event program, and the stationery label featured a tiny photograph of a Hong Kong skyscraper with hundreds of round windows, known popularly as the "building of 1,000 assholes"—retouched so that only four were visible.

bottom margin: TO SHOOT AT 6 AM SUNRISE, ENOUGH TIME TO DRIVE INTO THE CRATER TO SEE IF WE CAN FIND BREAKFAST. THE PROPRIETOR OF A TINY SHACK NOT ONLY SERVES COFFEE & ALSO PREPARES A DELICIOUS VERSION OF BANANA PANCAKE. I AM SO HAPPY. WHILE SAVOURING THIS UNEXPECTED TREAT THE FIRST RAYS OF SUNLIGHT APPEAR, WE PAIR INTO THE JEEP FRANTICALLY, RACE UP THE CRATER PHOTOGEAR GOES OUT, KEVIN SETS UP & CAMERAS, I RUN UP A CLIFF TO LOOK FOR A BETTER LOCATION TO SHOOT FROM, A BREATH-TAKIN PANTING, WE HAVE 5 MINUTES BEFORE

DRIVE IN PITCH BLACK NIGHT INTO THE IMPONDERABLE SUNRISE. ON THE SEARCH FOR LANDSCAPE SHOTS TO BE USED IN THE BEGINNING OF THE BROCHURE. KEVIN HAD HEARD ABOUT THIS SITE WHEREIN A SMALL VOLCANO IS LOCATED WITHIN ANOTHER, LARGER VOLCANO, BOTH OF THEM PRESENTLY INACTIVE. THEY BUILT A VILLAGE INSIDE THE BIG ONE, IT'S SAW WHEN WE GET THERE

HOTEL SHOOTS ANYWAY, WE GOT UP AT 2 AM EVERYDAY

PARTICULARLY FORMALIST take on the theme of East–West integration was the Design Group's modular corporate identity for Cheney, a media company, which was based on a tangram—the Chinese geometrical puzzle. On each stationery application, the tangram (a square dissected into five triangles, a square and a rhomboid) was recombined to form a different figure.

The Design Group was winning plenty of local design awards, but the pace was exhausting. "The first year was just madness," Sagmeister says. "Part of that madness was Hong Kong. You could have a printer come in at 3 am and get the proofs back to you by 7 am. Everyone works so hard. You would get in around 7 am and wake up the people who were sleeping at their monitors. They'd go to the bathroom to brush their teeth, get back to their desks and resume working."

DELIVERY NOTE

INVOICE

FAX TRANSMISSION FORM

COPY INSTRUCTIONS

ADVERTISING CONTRACT AND INSERTION ORDER

DATE: _____   CONTRACT NO: _____

PUBLICATION _____

ADVERTISER _____

_____

PRODUCT _____

ADVERTISING AGENCY _____

_____

NUMBER OF INSERTIONS _____   SIZE _____

COST PER INSERTION _____   TOTAL _____

INSERTION DATES _____

ARTWORK DEADLINE _____

REMARKS _____

_____

C. CHENEY & ASSOCIATES LIMITED   WE AGREE TO PAY THE AMOUNT
                                        DUE PER INSERTION PER PUBLICATION.

FOR AND ON BEHALF OF THE PUBLISHERS   FOR AND ON BEHALF OF THE ADVERTISER

C. CHENEY & ASSOCIATES LIMITED

LEO BURNETT HAS MOVED TO 6th FLOOR CITYPLAZA 3. 14

OO WAN RD., HONG KONG. TEL: 567 4333 FAX: 885 3209

JUNE 1 1992

THAT GIFT CATALOGUE I REALLY DID
NOT DO AS WELL AS I COULD HAVE.
I HAVE TO TRY A PROJECT LIKE
THIS FROM A TOTALLY
DIFFERENT ANGLE
NEXT TIME.

...tural ...li... becon... sultry clim... for business me... ing and shopping–ma... are connected to large reta... tainment complexes. They also p... some of the harbor's more interesting... architecture. For the new Island Shangri-La hotel, which opened in 1991 as part of a fashionable shopping complex, the Design Group's task was to design a series of brochures emphasizing the range of facilities, and highlighting features like a 60 meter-high painting visible from the glass elevators in the 41st floor atrium. Each brochure featured an icon appropriate to its theme (an abacus, for example, for the hotel business center).

Shangri-La, incidentally, has little to do with Chinese culture: The word was invented by a British novelist James Hilton in 1933 for a fictional Utopia in Tibet, free from the worries of modern civilization ...Despite their rebellious inclinations, ...n Group's work most frequently ...Kong's strange cultural ...ny and Eastern trading ...dern status ...fashioned ...hig t... assist... that their b... see cleaners wit... the cathedrals and bra... Hong Kong.") A Christmas g... Lane Crawford–a local equivalen... London's Harrods—has the clean, ups... look of a cosmetics brochure. The Island Shangri-La material has a no-expense-spared ambience."The photoshoot went on for about six weeks," says Rae, "the pho-tographer was unhappy with the flowers, so he flew in his flower arranger—a huge, butch guy– from New York."

The Hong Kong weather in summer is unbearably humid, to the extent that failing to hail a cab within 10 minutes obliges the by-now sweat-soaked hailer to go back home, take a shower and change. The writer Jan Morris, among others, has speculated that the near-tropical climate had something to do with Hong Kong's quickly earned reputation as a lascivious ...rurient place. Early settlers were ...their vigorous appetites and ...d today the city seems to ...ip. Morris notes the ...cal newspaper ...between ...rothel, c... second... employees–

→ ALMOST LOST CONTROL OF
THIS CATHAY JOB, WENT
ON HOLIDAY AND LOTS OF SHIT
WENT OUT. THE CHINESE, THE
INDIAN AND THE JAPANESE PAINTINGS
WERE PARTIALLY OR EVEN TOTALLY WRONG.
  ALSO: I HAVE TO GET RID OF my HATRED FOR ACCOUNT EXECUTIVES.
  IF I HAVE A PROBLEM, SPEAK CALMLY WITH them, BUT
    DO NOT BADMOUTH BEHIND THEIR BACK. AND FINALLY,
  STOP BLAMING THE CLIENT.
    ONCE AND FOR ALL. I MEAN, THAT
  GATEFOLD AD WAS REALLY MY
FUCK-UP AND AFTER HE
    FORCED ME TO CHANGE IT IT DID
    LOOK BETTER.
      OH BOY.

...g styles redolent
... the Design
... Pacific
... that
wa... added, with one of those singular smiles

Like... which did not escape the young man,
was initially ... I have completed my affairs in
nariness–and the ... ll go and die in the East; and
real underground cultu... to see me again, you
ally lured into its ways. "I go... Bagdad, or or
the money culture much more tha...
thought I would. At the end of the secon... be the
year I felt I was becoming a person I didn't ... le's
really like.

"And you are right," said his host; "it
shows you have a tendency for an Oriental
life. Ah, those Orientals; they are the only
men who know how to live. As for me," he
added, with one of those singular smiles

with those wings I could make a tour of
the world in four and twenty hours."

"Ah, yes, the hashish is beginning its
work. Well, unfurl your wings, and fly into
superhuman regions; fear nothing, there
is a watch over you; and if your wings, like
those of Icarus, melt before the sun, we
are here to ease your fall."

I THINK I'll do THIS J..
FOR A YEAR AND A HALF,
SAVE a TON OF MONEY and then
MOVE ON TO AN ISLAND OR WRITE
a book OR DRAW A CARTOON OR...
I MEAN THE WORK is ALMOST
too MUCH FOR ME HERE, BUT
THIS time I'll follow IT THROUGH.
→ I AM NOT QUITTING
they'll HAVE to FIRE me
to get RID of me
IT'S JUST TOO FUCKING FAST.
EVERYDAY I GET up IN THE MORNING THINKING:
OK, ANOTHER DAY AT WAR.
AT THE MOMENT, I'M JUST ABOUT TO LOSE CONTROL
OF THE WHOLE THING. ┬┬┬┬

ART-DIRECTED PHOTOSHOOT INSIDE 747-400 THIS WEEK. WHAT STRESS.
WE HAD THE PLANE, COMING FROM BANGKOK AND LEAVING FOR LAX
FOR EXACTLY 18 MINUTES TO SHOOT VIDEO AND STILLS. EVERY
MOVEMENT WAS REHEARSED TO the last DETAIL 2 WEEKS ago IN
the CABIN MOCK-UP NORMALLY USED FOR CABIN CREW TRAINING.
FOUR GUYS WENT IN AND DISMANTLED THE FIRST 6 ROWS
of SEATS CREATING SPACE FOR CAMERAS ETC.
DURING THE ENTIRE SHOOT ONE GUY SHOUTED A
COUNTDOWN: "14 MINUTES LEFT, 13 MINUTES LEFT,
12 MINUTES LEFT" UNTIL EVERYTHING
IS DONE, CLEANED UP AND THE
PLANE IS OFF AGAIN.

POLAROIDS looked
BLAND & CHEESY,
but that WAS THE IDEA.

HEARD THAT my BRITISH PREDECESSOR TWO YEARS AGO INSISTED ON
SHOOTING WITH A PHOTOGRAPHER FRIEND OF HIS FLOWN IN FROM ENGLAND
WITH NO PREVIOUS AIRLINE EXPERIENCE. WHEN HE LIT THE CABIN FROM
OUTSIDE THROUGH THE WINDOWS (TO GET THAT MID-AIR SUNRISE LOOK)
ONE OF THE FILM LIGHTS WAS PLACED TOO CLOSE TO A WINDOW AND
BURNED A HOLE IN IT! THE 747 HAD TO BE TAKEN OUT OF SERVICE
FLIGHT CANCELED, PASSENGERS STRANDED UNTIL REPLACEMENT WINDOW
ARRIVED.

AFTER REVAMPING ITS FIRST-CLASS service, the Hong Kong airline Cathay Pacific
was looking for a new brochure appropriate to the price of a ticket. The Design
Group gave them a lavish hardcover
book, printed in six colors with a 300 line
screen, complete with vellum overlays
and an embossed slip case.

The distance between the life of advertising and the Eastern culture of China
was sometimes frustratingly vast. Though
Sagmeister had determined to assimilate
rather than become another rigid imperi-
alist who yelled in English to be understood, this proved nearly impossible in the
circumstances. He tried several times t
learn Cantonese, but each effort w
scuppered by the the exces
at Leo Burnett and the
language (the first
ed how same
mean

"It's very seductive lifestyle, but it is a
claustrophobic place." says Rae, who
stayed for three more years after
Sagmeister's departure to lead the Design
Group. "I stayed too long. Once you've
been there for about seven years, you
become very regionally specific and it's
quite difficult to move anywhere
eventually moved back to
for Siegelgale.

Then the three
towards him
approa
re

ow-
itudes
sist, but which
ooks inflexible and
with which the serpent
bird; and then he gave way
ooks that held him in a torturing
asp and delighted his senses as with a
voluptuous kiss. It seemed to Franz that
he closed his eyes, and in a last look

about him saw the visio
pletely veiled; and
of passion li
Proph
t

ne
, love was
ss a torture, as
pressed to his
e was held in cool ser-
mbraces. The more he strove
st this unhallowed passion the more
s senses yielded to its thrall, and at
length, weary of a struggle that taxed his
very soul, he gave way and sank back
breathless and exhausted beneath the
kisses of these marble goddesses, and
the enchantment of his marvellous dream.

Half-way through his second year in Hong Kong, Sagmeister quit the Design Group to move over to advertising at Leo Burnett. In the back of his mind, the act of detaching himself from the group he had helped found was the first step toward leaving. The excessive work load was taking its toll, but so too was the ex-pat's fear of becoming one of those once-talented but now "sad and cynical" foreigners who had stayed for too long because of the money and the perks (old-timer ex-pats in Hong Kong boasted personal drivers and three housekeepers). "It's a very well-to-do life there, but not a very happy life," says Sagmeister.

One possibility was to relocate to London. While researching a series of ads for the London Regent Hotel, part of the international Regent chain, Sagmeister and a copywriter were sent to London to check out competing hotels. The campaign, which stressed comfort and friendliness over the die-hard habits of old London hotels (antiquated customs, snobbery and formal house rules) was based on an actual experience. At one venerable establishment with a typically cobwebby dress code, Sagmeister's visiting superior—the Leo Burnett executive creative director—was turned away at the hotel door with the words, "We would love to have you here sir, the next time you have a jacket on."

The experience also helped Sagmeister settle on a destination for his future career—New York, a city where outsiders (even sans jackets) are widely welcomed. Back in Hong Kong, he began making arrangements to leave. "I was happy I went," he says of his Eastern excursion, "but even happier that I left."

FOUND A FAT RINGBINDER CONTAINING THE LAST SIX MONTH'S WORTH OF CORRESPONDENCE OF THE PREVIOUS HEAD OF THE DESIGN GROUP (HIS ENTIRE DEPARTMENT GOT FIRED BEFORE I ARRIVED). GOING THROUGH ALL THE FAXES AND LETTERS IS AN ABSOLUT HOOT, — DRAMAS UNFOLD AND STORIES ARE TOLD. APPARENTLY HE WAS ART-DIRECTING A HOTEL PHOTO SHOOT IN KUALA LUMPUR. THE CLIENT THOUGHT THAT A PARTICULAR SCENE SHOT IN THE SPA WHEREIN TWO MALE MODELS LOUNGE AROUND IN A JACUZZI WAS TOO HOMOSEXUAL IN FLAVOUR. IT WAS AGREED TO RETOUCH ONE GUY OUT IN PAINT BOX. THE BROCHURE WENT TO THE PRINTER DEPICTING A SINGLE MAN IN THE JACUZZI. AFTER THE ENTIRE RUN WAS PRINTED, BOUND AND SHIPPED AROUND THE WORLD, IT WAS DISCOVERED THAT THE DEPICTED HEALTH SPA FEATURES A MIRRORED CEILING WHEREIN BOTH MALE MODELS WERE STILL FROLICKING HAPPILY. THE GAY GHOST THAT CAME TO HAUNT THEM.

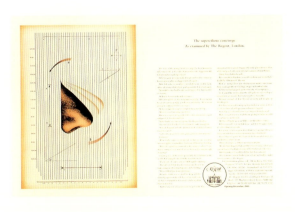

NOV 1 1992

WELL, IT'S GOING EXTREMELY WELL,
WELL, I'VE QUIT AND NOW everything IS A OK,
I AM NOT ANGRY NO MORE, EVERYTHING FUNCTIONS
BY ITSELF, I AM WORKING WITHOUT STRESS OR WORK
I SUDDENLY REALIZED, THIS JOB IS ACTUALLY PRETTY
EASY. I MEAN NOW THAT IT'S ALL BEHIND me
IT JUST became clear
HOW
EASY IT
WAS.

/ SRI LANKA /

In Spring 1993, Sagmeister left Hong Kong for the last time and hopped on a plane to Sri Lanka. He stayed for nearly three months, working on a self-commissioned book project in the mornings and enjoying the subtropical island and its scenery in the afternoons and evenings. Since the country had been torn apart by the civil war (the long-running Sinhalese–Tamil conflict), it had fallen off the international tourist map and, in this respect, was unscathed by cultural imperialism.

Setting up office in a beach hut, Sagmeister took advantage of the many artisans in the area, and commissioned a sign painter to create a sign for his business (opposite page). The book was never published, and no clients came seeking work, but Sagmeister emerged from the sojourn feeling refreshed and ready for New York.

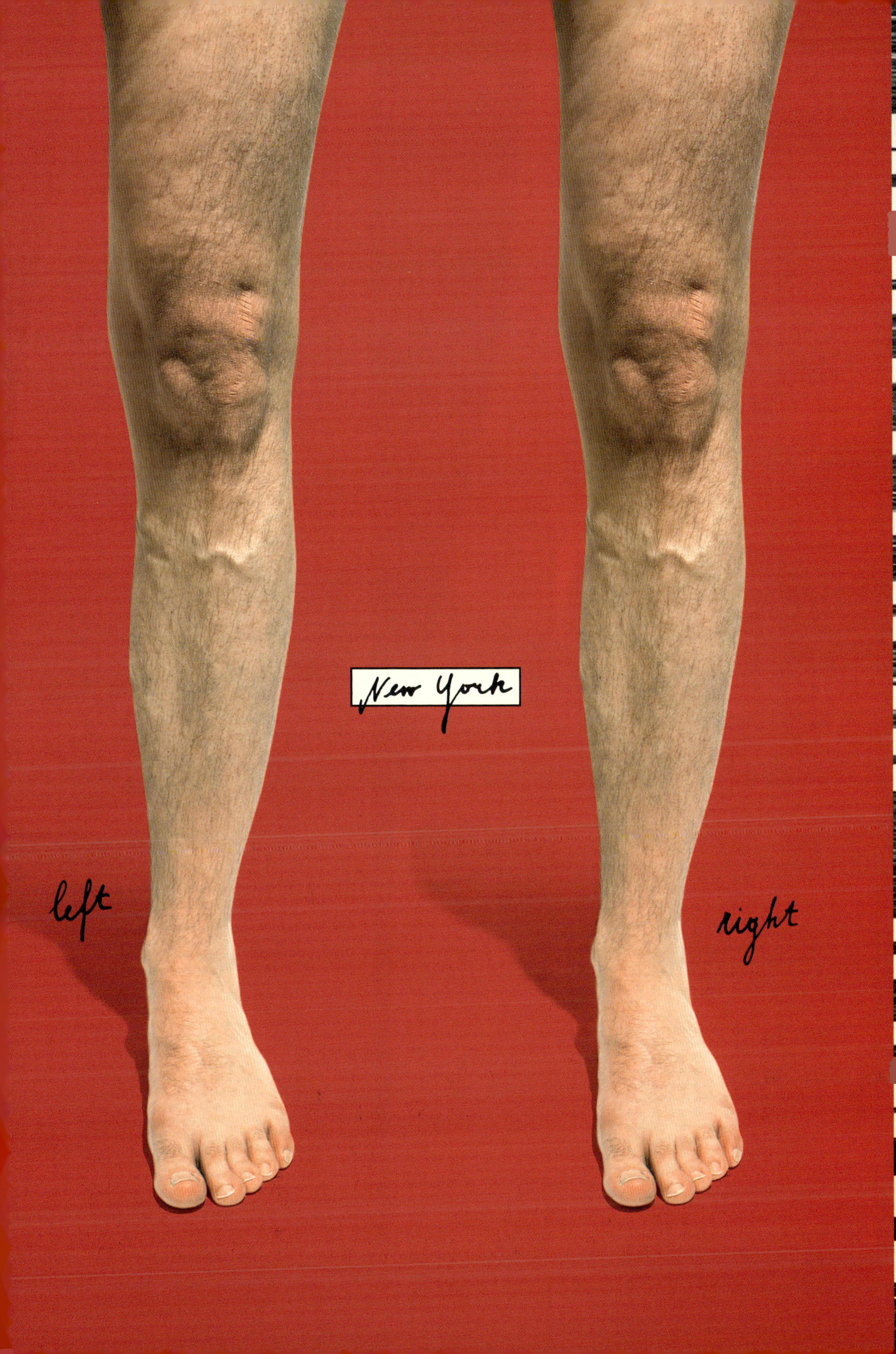

left

New York

right

During the late 1980s, the dream destination for most New York design students was M&Co, the studio of the legendary controversialist and design-entrepreneur Tibor Kalman. Sagmeister, while a student at Pratt Institute, had been no exception: In 1989 he had phoned the M&Co office "around 25 times in two months" in the hope of getting a job. Eventually, Kalman had returned the call, and the two had become acquainted, leading eventually to Kalman's offer to sponsor Sagmeister's green card application for US residency.

Four years later, while visiting New York from Hong Kong for a wedding, Sagmeister paid a visit to his long-time hero. Fortune, Kalman, and the Immigration and Naturalization Service were smiling: The green card application had been approved, and Kalman, heavily involved with Benetton's new *Colors* magazine, was looking for someone to run the studio. In the early spring of 1993, Sagmeister arrived at M&Co to take up the reins.

A few weeks into the job, it dawned on him that Kalman wasn't as willing to hand over control of his dearly beloved firm as he'd first appeared. "He didn't quite know how to give it to me and I didn't quite

know how to take it," says Sagmeister, who found himself working as a senior designer under Kalman's jurisdiction—a somewhat frustrating transition from the automony of Leo Burnett Design Group. There was much to learn at M&Co, however, including the production perils of Sagmeister's first job: To design the invitation for a Gay and Lesbian Taskforce gala.

Sagmeister had decided to spruce up the whole invitation process by designing an elaborate package: a box containing tissue-wrapped fresh fruit (a banana and a plum) which made for a juicy pun on the slang word for homosexual and a visual innuendo. The card was printed with the Biblical quotation "By their fruits ye shall know them" (Matthew 7:20).

The only thing that couldn't be designed was the weather. M&Co's producer, Keira Alexandra, lined up a fulfillment house to wrap the fruit in the specially-printed tissue paper and dispatch the boxes to the invited guests in one day. Unfortunately, the plums, caught between seasons, didn't show up in time. A New York heatwave kicked in, and the 5,000 bananas, already wrapped and boxed, went black. When the plums finally did arrive, two days later, along with a new batch of fresh bananas, there was only enough tissue paper left to wrap 2,500 of

them. Two more days went by until the freshly printed tissue paper arrived, by which time the plums were rotten. "There were tears involved, Tibor went around screaming—this was a *bro bono* project so it was on M&Co's time—and there were times when half of the studio staff were involved in it," says Sagmeister. "It was a real nightmare."

Eventually, the various components converged, the invitation was hand-delivered, and the event was a surprising success. Sagmeister went on to complete one more M&Co project (see pp.202-203) before Kalman announced that he would close the studio and move to Rome to edit *Colors* full-time. For Sagmeister this was a cue to go solo. They parted on good terms (a contrast to many M&Co departures) and Sagmeister emerged after six months with a number of well-learned M&Co lessons, including a variation on the old adage: never work with children, animals or fresh fruit.

MAY 8 1993
TIBOR SAID HE'L SHUT DOWN M&Co.
AND I WAS HAPPY!
NOW I HAVE THREE TIMES THE REASON TO FINALLY FIX
my OLD DREAM and open UP A DESIGN STUDIO
FOR CD COVERS. YES!
→ I WENT THROUGH THE GRAPHIC DESIGN NEW YORK BOOK
AND HAVE TO SAY: SO MANY BROCHURES, SO MUCH RUN OF THE MILL STUFF
THE IDEA OF WORKING ON THESE THINGS JUST DOES NOT FEEL EXCITING AT ALL.

SAGMEISTER LAUNCHED his New York studio with a card and party invitation showing two photographs of himself standing
naked in a crummy-looking office.
Captions implied that the left image was
taken before launching his own studio and
the right was taken after. Subtly placed
strips of masking tape of varying lengths
indicated, as Sagmeister put it, "that it
takes bigger balls to open your own
place." Extra-curious recipients could tear
off the tape and try to establish which
image had been digitally manipulated.

QUICKLY THOUGHT ABOUT
WHAT I ACTUALLY
WANT TO DO WITH THE
STUDIO :
• DESIGN GOOD CD COVERS
• EARN A LITTLE MONEY
• DO NOT GROW
AND OF COURSE : HAVE much FUN

The Beatles' Sgt. Pepper cover, for the following reasons. – 1. Timing — I was 18 at the time I saw the cover. I was in art school (Tyler School of Art). I was smart enough to know that the cover was a piece of graphic design but innocent enough to be overwhelmed by it (I'd be too jaded now). – 2. Identification — the cover was a "concept album". The album was a "concept album". Concepts at that point were cool, and the things that didn't have concepts weren't (Right now the reverse may be true). I identified with the cover stylistically. – The Victorian outfits were very groovy and timely in that psychedelic period. The Beatles had appropriately identified with the style of the time and culture, so I could identify with it. – 3. Complication and involvement — there was a game to play. Who's in the picture? There was Dylan, there was Marilyn or Jane Mansfield. How many people can you name? Are they all famous? Do you get the joke? The complication keeps me there and

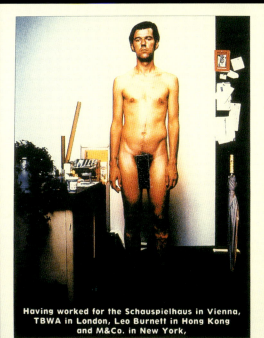

Having worked for the Schauspielhaus in Vienna, TBWA in London, Leo Burnett in Hong Kong and M&Co. in New York,

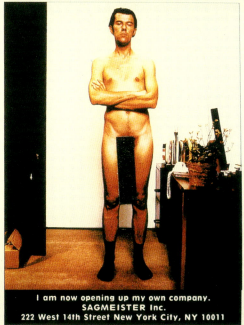

**I am now opening up my own company.
SAGMEISTER Inc.
222 West 14th Street New York City, NY 10011**

Having worked for the Schauspielhaus in Vienna, TBWA in London, Leo Burnett in Hong Kong and M&Co. in New York,

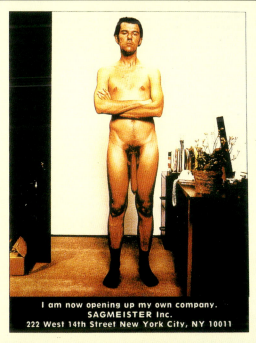

**I am now opening up my own company.
SAGMEISTER Inc.
222 West 14th Street New York City, NY 10011**

A PARTY TO BAPTIZE Sagmeister Inc. was thrown at the designer's home studio on January 14, 1994. From the start, Sagmeister's aim was to specialize in music business graphics: On the reverse side of the penis card were three copylines, "Style = Fart," "We will do anything for design," and "Design for the music industry." The first was a motto emphasizing ideas over form, a creed to which the studio would try to adhere. The second, though it sounded a little extreme, identified Sagmeister's unfailing love for his profession, and the third was, at the time, wishful thinking. The music industry didn't immediately come running with assignments.

The company business card, however, hinted at the optical trickery that the studio would eventually bring to CD cover design. The card appears inside an acrylic slipcase as a simple "S" in a circle. When the card is removed from the case, the company name and address magically appear on the white outer ring of the circle. The trick was simple—the card simply covers up the lettering, but like a magician's illusion, the pizzazz of the movement distracts the eye from the deception.

RECEIVING A PIECE of GRAPHIC DESIGN IS ~~almost~~ LIKE GOING VERY WELL (=HAS STYLE) ON A DATE. IF MY DATE TURNS OUT TO BE DRESSED VERY WELL (= GREAT FORM) I AM MOST CERTAINLY HAPPY. AND IF SHE IS BEAUTIFUL (= GREAT FORM) WELL, ALL THE better. BUT IF IT turns OUT SHE HAS NOTHING TO SAY (= BAD CONTENT, NO CONCEPT) OR HAS A MEAN HEART, IT IS going TO BE A VERY SHORT RELATIONSHIP ANYWAY.

WE ARE HAPPY TO GUARANTEE 100% PHILLIPPE STARCK FREE OFFICES.

The business card turned out to be the studio's most useful promotion. Reprinted three times over the years, it had a covetable aspect that seemed to prevent people from throwing it away, and thus initiated a number of useful leads.

With the help of the money he had accumulated during his well-compensated years in Hong Kong advertising, Sagmeister purchased a penthouse apartment in downtown Manhattan and had it converted into live/work premises (pp.112-113). Behind the move to contain office and home in one place was a strategy based on both his experience of running an overbooked studio in Hong Kong and subsequent advice from Kalman. "Tibor said the toughest thing with running your own studio is not to grow, but if I hadn't had the Hong Kong experience that wouldn't have sunk in," says Sagmeister. "The higher your overhead, the more freedom you give up: You don't have the option to say no to a well-paying client."

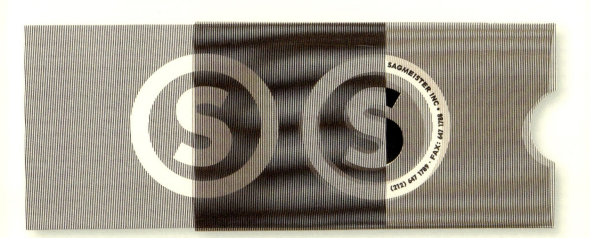

THE FIRST SPRING of Sagmeister Inc. brought a meager trickle of work, and studio time was mostly devoted to research and sending out cards in the hope of drumming up assignments from the music business. When Sagmeister's brother Martin telephoned with an identity project for his new retail business, Sagmeister was initially relieved. When Martin told him the name of his firm, a chain of fashion stores for young people selling blue jeans, "Blue," Sagmeister was crestfallen. "I was looking for a nice way of telling him on the phone what a lame name that is," he says. "Then I had this other idea, and stopped myself."

Sagmeister's thought pattern began with a negative: Why make a stupid blue logo for a company called Blue? The question provoked a Dadaist solution: an orange logo for a blue company, stamped with bold black type. The idea was extended to the

20-image advertising campaign, for which the firm had a humble $5,000 photoshoot budget. Instead of gorgeous models they would use Sagmeister's ordinary-looking friends, with paper bags over their heads.

The four-part design process that Sagmeister developed in Hong Kong was the foundation of Blue's brand development. The process follows a strict methodology adapted from a 1930s manual titled *A Technique for Producing Ideas*.

1. Think about the project from any point of view—your mom's, yours, from the point of view of color, or form—and write each response down on a single index card.

2. Spread all the index cards out on a big table and see if you can find the relationship between the different thoughts.

3. Forget about the whole thing.

4. The idea will strike you miraculously when you least expect it.

A similarly exhaustive approach was used to develop the design approaches to the Blue campaign. Sagmeister tried around 20 typefaces, from script faces to Futura, and drew endless sketches to devise applications for the identity. To develop the quirky personality of the brand, he made exploratory drawings of "blue people" and tried arranging the letters to make a face—"not the most original idea in the world," he admits.

The design solutions gradually revealed themselves. A customized typeface, derived from Futura and Spartan, solved the problem of the typographic hole between the "L" and "U" that emerged when "Blue" was set in a sans serif. The face-shaped logotype was appropriate for the paper bags used to obscure his friends' faces in the photoshoot, especially when hand-lettered. Likewise, the blue people sketches looked funkiest in their >

BLUE | VELVET

LEATHER JACKET
heavy duty
at BLUE ös2,998.-

BLUE Clothing
in Dornbirn, Marktplatz
Bregenz, Bahnhofstraße
and Feldkirch, Marktgasse

B L U E

Designed by Sagmeister, Inc. New York; Photography by Tom Schierlitz, New York.

121

THIS COLOR IS BLUE!

Look at the small black point in the center of the cross in the orange field for 20 seconds. Then look at the small black point in the grey field. The orange field will appear blue. And that's the way it's meant to be.

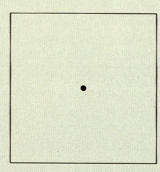

On Thursday 3.3.1994 we will open BLUE Clothing stores in Bregenz, Dornbirn, and Feldkirch.

The cover for the CD Rei Momo by David Byrne, from Doublespace, 1989. When the album came out, I was in my junior year at art school for graphic design. I remember being completely blown away by that image of David Byrne peeking through the polka dots into a heart. It is viscerally beautiful and disturbingly creepy at the same time. If you stare at it, the angles of the face change like a Picasso. You don't know what came first, the face or the heart. You just can't stop looking at it. – **Todd Tarhan**

In our regular (Sagmeister) stores, we sell rather upscale clothing to fashionable customers who spend a great deal of money on their outfits. To appeal to younger and sportier types, the best idea was to launch a new chain—the Blue stores. The Blue customer is not only young (some only at heart) but has a more unconventional way of life.
When Stefan first proposed his design for Blue, the partners were speechless. But we grew to like the idea and the unconventional approach. Needless to say, the stores are doing quite well.
• **Martin Sagmeister** OWNER BLUE, Bregenz

> rough form, applied throughout the merchandise and collateral material.

Various tactics were adopted to persuade his brother that the Dadaist Blue would be the most immediately memo-rable, hip and versatile solution to the identity, including a dummy newspaper with a Blue ad shot by Tom Schierlitz showing his wife Bettina Budewig (a fashion designer) posing on a stool as a "blue angel," paper bag on head. For additional credibility, Sagmeister enclosed a copy of an Irving Penn photo-graph in which Saul Steinberg appears with a piece of cardboard covering his face. It was not what Martin Sagmeister had expected, but after some discussion, his firm decided to take a chance on the design.

Sagmeister also worked with the store architect to apply the identity to three locations in the Voralberg region of Austria. The opening day began with local students parading the streets wearing sandwich boards, handing out fliers and oranges outside schools. Free breakfasts, including copious quantities of orange juice, were served in the stores. A local TV station covered the opening, and with-in three weeks, the stores had sold out of almost all of their merchandise.

Random Bus

Telephone 212 355 2227
Facsimile 212 755 1737

305 East 46 Street, New York City, New York, 10017-3058

A MUSIC PRODUCTION STUDIO named
after the serial buses used to transmit
data between equipment, Random Bus
commissioned Sagmeister to design
its business cards. The resulting design
featured buses driving in different
directions on each application. To get
the required swoosh, Sagmeister used a
toy bus, photographed in motion. It was
also much cheaper than a real one.

"Oh, doctor," cried Barrois. "the
fit is coming on again. Oh, do something for me."

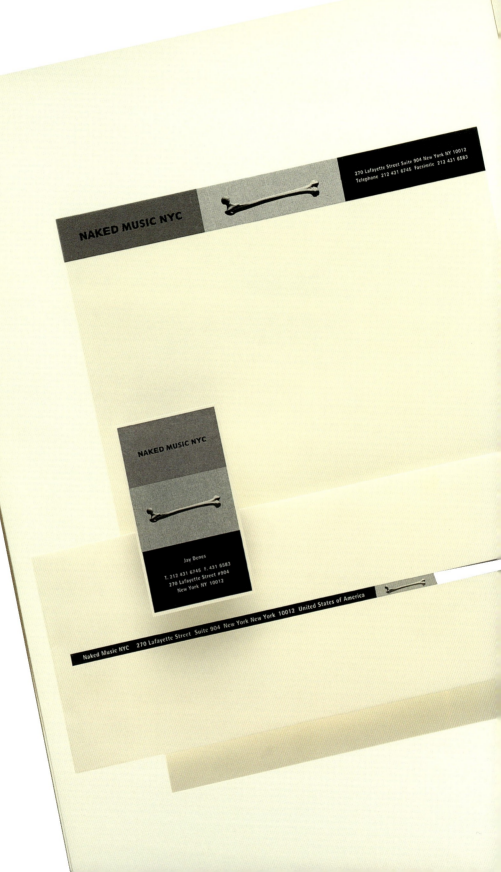

NAKED MUSIC NYC

270 Lafayette Street Suite 904 New York NY 10012
Telephone 212 431 6745 Facsimile 212 431 6583

NAKED MUSIC NYC

Jay Denes

T. 212 431 6745 F. 431 6583
270 Lafayette Street #904
New York NY 10012

Naked Music NYC   270 Lafayette Street Suite 904 New York New York 10012 United States of America

IN THE SUMMER OF 1994, Sagmeister hired his first employee, Veronica Oh (right), after seeing her senior show at Parsons School of Art. "I was going to turn down his offer," says Oh, a Korean-born designer. "But then I found out he had been an art director at M&Co—I was their biggest fan."

Yet Sagmeister was not, Oh quickly learned, the free-form, laid back artiste one might have expected from his work. "The way Stefan did a business plan was really impressive. He kept a time sheet every day, even though there were only two of us," says Oh. "In terms of promoting the studio it was nicely planned and followed through. I didn't expect that at all from a creative crazy person."

In the early days, Sagmeister and Oh, short of work, spent hours visiting museums and brainstorming. When a project came in, they pounced on it.

Naked Music, a music production company, was one of the first. The company needed a logo, and to Sagmeister and Oh, its name seemed irrefutably to suggest the phrase "naked to the bone," A local archeological store supplied the necessary goods.

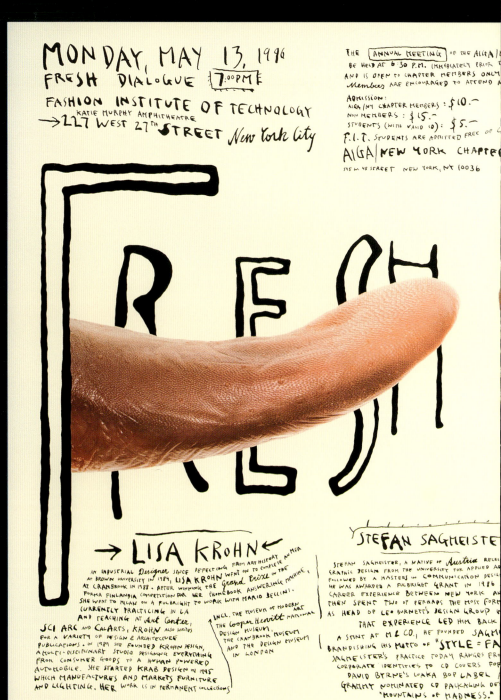

IF THERE IS ONE ASSIGNMENT that calls for an adventurous response, it is the self-promotional poster. The publicity for *Fresh Dialogue*, a series of talks organized by the New York chapter of the AIGA was offered to Sagmeister as a *pro bono* job, which in his mind granted a degree of creative freedom, and, since it was for an audience of designers, necessitated something startling, or at least fresh. Riffing on the lecture series theme of young up-and-coming designers in conversation, Sagmeister chose a metaphor of wagging tongues. While the rest of the mediated world was moving into the synthetic and digital, everything about the *Fresh Dialogue* poster was made organic, from the hand rendered type to the pink, protuberances that licked over the lettering.

The event organizers flew into a panic

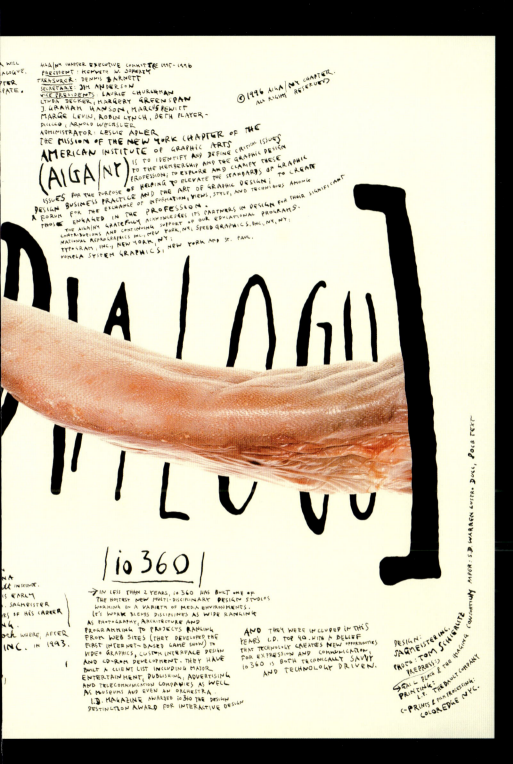

THE MISSION OF THE NEW YORK CHAPTER OF THE
AMERICAN INSTITUTE OF GRAPHIC ARTS
(AIGA|NY) IS TO IDENTIFY AND DEFINE CRITICAL ISSUES
TO THE MEMBERSHIP AND THE GRAPHIC DESIGN
PROFESSION; TO EXPLORE AND CLARIFY THESE
ISSUES FOR THE PURPOSE OF HELPING TO ELEVATE THE STANDARDS OF GRAPHIC
DESIGN BUSINESS PRACTICE AND THE ART OF GRAPHIC DESIGN; TO CREATE
A FORUM FOR THE EXCHANGE OF INFORMATION, VIEWS, STYLE, AND TECHNIQUES AMONG
THOSE ENGAGED IN THE PROFESSION.
THE AIGA|NY GRATEFULLY ACKNOWLEDGES ITS PARTNERS IN DESIGN FOR THEIR SIGNIFICANT
CONTRIBUTIONS AND CONTINUING SUPPORT OF OUR EDUCATIONAL PROGRAMS.
NATIONAL REPROGRAPHICS INC, NEW YORK, NY; SPEED GRAPHICS, INC, NY, NY;
TYPOGRAM, INC., NEW YORK, NY;
VOMELA SYSTEM GRAPHICS, NEW YORK AND ST. PAUL.

/ io 360 /

→ IN LESS THAN 2 YEARS, io 360 HAS BUILT ONE OF
THE HOTTEST NEW MULTI-DISCIPLINARY DESIGN STUDIOS
WORKING IN A VARIETY OF MEDIA ENVIRONMENTS.
IT'S WORK BLENDS DISCIPLINES AS WIDE RANGING
AS PHOTOGRAPHY, ARCHITECTURE AND
PROGRAMMING TO PROJECTS RANGING
FROM WEB SITES (THEY DEVELOPED THE
FIRST INTERNET-BASED GAME SHOW) TO
VIDEO GRAPHICS, CUSTOM INTERFACE DESIGN
AND CD-ROM DEVELOPMENT. THEY HAVE
BUILT A CLIENT LIST INCLUDING MAJOR
ENTERTAINMENT, PUBLISHING, ADVERTISING
AND TELECOMMUNICATION COMPANIES AS WELL
AS MUSEUMS AND EVEN AN ORCHESTRA.
I.D. MAGAZINE AWARDED io 360 THE DESIGN
DISTINCTION AWARD FOR INTERACTIVE DESIGN

AND THEY WERE INCLUDED IN THIS
YEAR'S I.D. TOP 40. WITH A BELIEF
THAT TECHNOLOGY CREATES NEW OPPORTUNITIES
FOR EXPRESSION AND COMMUNICATION,
io 360 IS BOTH TECHNICALLY SAVVY
AND TECHNOLOGY DRIVEN.

DESIGN:
SAGMEISTER INC.
PHOTO: TOM SCHIERLITZ
PREPRESS:
SCALL BLOCK & THE IMAGING CONSORTIUM
PRINTING:
L.T. THEBAULT COMPANY
C-PRINTS & FILM PROCESSING:
COLOREDGE NYC.
PAPER: S.D. WARREN LUSTRO DULL, POCA TEXT

on receiving the design. The problem, as they put it, was that this distinctly Sagmeister poster was meant not for a one-man show, but for a three way event—and wasn't it a bit phallic-looking for a mixed-gender panel? After tentatively requesting an alternative, the AIGA took Sagmeister's suggestion that the design instead should be sent to the other speakers for approval, or replacement. It received a thumbs up from all parties, including the one non-male speaker on the panel, Lisa Krohn. "I thought it was hilarious," she says, "distinctly European."

The little production secret of the piece is that the flesh was not in fact human. "Our own tongues weren't long enough," says Sagmeister, "so (photographer) Tom Schierlitz went to the meat market and came back with cow's tongues. They looked great."

SAGMEISTER'S ONLY FRIEND from his years at Bregenz engineering school, Stephan Schertler, had, since leaving college, invented an acoustic pick-up for amplifying stringed instruments. The unit, targeted at professional musicians, was considerably more sophisticated and accordingly more expensive than rival devices, and required packaging and advertising to reflect its position. Schertler, an audio perfectionist with a completely open design brief, was the definitive dream client. The pick-up came in a special wooden carrying case, with a meticulously cut and fitted rubber foam interior. When Sagmeister proposed printing the graphic identity in silver on the lid and engraving the housing of the pick-up, Schertler changed the housing of the actual pick-up from brass to aluminum so that it would fit in the color scheme, even though it required a complete change in the manufacturing.

Strangely, responding to a *carte* >

AUDIO TRANS DUCERS · SYSTEM WEANA ISCHD SERTI SLER· · **SCHERTLER** · INVOICE / FACTURA · STAHLSTRASSE 1 · 9000 ST. GALLEN · SWITZERLAND · TEL: 071 27 99 12 · FAX: 071 28 36 40

TO

INVOICE NO.

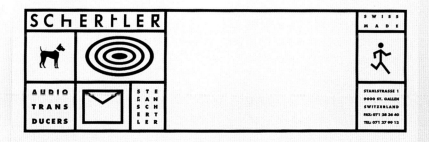

SCHERTLER · SWISS MADE · AUDIO TRANS DUCERS · STE AN CH ERT LER · STAHLSTRASSE 1 · 9000 ST. GALLEN · SWITZERLAND · FAX: 071 28 36 40 · TEL: 071 27 99 12

AUDIO TRANS DUCERS · SWISS STE AN CH ERT LER MADE · **SCHERTLER** · STAHLSTRASSE 1 · 9000 ST. GALLEN · SWITZERLAND · TEL: 071 27 9912 · FAX: 071 28 36 40

schertler audio transducers. stationery system. switzeriana

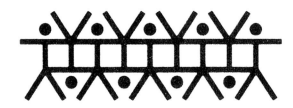

What comes most immediately to my mind is the first time that I visited the Vietnam Memorial. It was Memorial Day. There were thousands of Vets, wives, children, relatives and visitors from around the world. When I entered the dark granite sculpture and walked down the incline I was overwhelmed by the the spacial relation-

APRIL 23 1997

WATCH out, I'm on my best way to become a MEDIOCRE Graphic DESIGNER.

I DID not open THE Studio TO ~~do~~ MEDIOCRE design

I have TO find the POINT AGAIN WHERE I AM ACTUALLY enjoying THIS WHOLE THING.

I HAVE 3 good JOBS TO work ON AND I'M STILL unhappy,

ITS a joke.

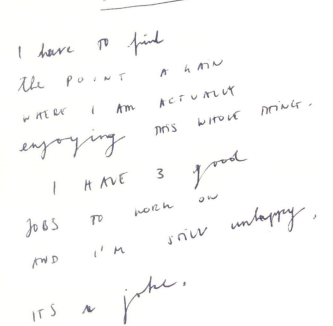

> *blanche* design brief proved quite a challenge to Sagmeister, who eventually came up with a series of obtusely allusive icons contained in a framework of boxes. An icon of concentric rings "seemed to have something to do with sound," says Sagmeister, and the theme was extended to the product literature, which included photographs of concentric rings that appear in nature. The mailing label featured a dog and an envelope icon, suggesting a comedy routine involving a mail delivery person. To complete the theme of fastidious design to the point of absurdity, Sagmeister devised a folder for the product information sheets, featuring a sequence of informative-looking icons: nine stick figures running, a train, and nine stick figures flattened on a train track. It was completely irrelevant to the product, but it looked good.

THE PROJECT to design *Nothingness*, a book of Japanese calligraphy and verse, simmered away for many seasons. It began when Mikio Shinagawa, the son of a well-known Japanese poet and calligrapher, came to the studio. Shinagawa, despite being a successful entrepreneur—owning a restaurant, a gallery and a language school—never appeared hurried. "You would give him a suggestion," says Sagmeister, "and he would say "Stefan, I have to meditate on that. I'll give you an answer in two weeks." Sure enough, he would come back in two weeks and say it was ok."

The driving design theme in the book was that it would be printed on both sides of thin, almost translucent French-folded paper, so that words written in reverse on the back side could be read as if through a veil. Producing it, however, was a lesson in the Buddhist virtues of patience and perseverance, since the poems were delivered to the studio as pictures, making corrections—along with everything

else—painstakingly slow. On top of this, client decisions were a long time coming. "It seemed like a three year project," says Veronica Oh, whose tenure at Sagmeister was outlasted by this assignment. Producing mechanicals in reverse was "extremely complicated," adds Hjalti Karlsson, who took over the oddly counter-intuitive process from Oh. "If you wanted to move something to the right, you actually had to move it to the left," he says, mystically. Amidst all the studio craziness, Mikio Shinagawa would frequently appear with a bottle of water and some flowers for the designers, and breathe equanimity on the proceedings. "He was always unbelievably calm and relaxed," says Karlsson.

Once printed, with a foreword by the Dalai Lama, the book sold out so quickly that the official launch was postponed for a second print run the following year. In retrospect, Sagmeister regretted the somewhat conservative and reverent design. "We spent so much time on it

that I was quite disappointed we ended up with quite a traditional-looking thing," he says. "It could have been much more interesting if we'd seen it from a contemporary level."

Two years later however, the experience was continuing to reveal wisdoms. "The first 60 pages are about nothingness," says Sagmeister, "but I really only understood the concept about half a year ago. That if you understand that life is really nothingness what unbelievable freedom that creates. If life is empty and with no meaning, then you really can start to build whatever you want to build, that nothing holds you back."

A paragraph of explanation at the end of the book by the author, Tetsuzan Shinagawa, highlights a great similarity between the art of the designer and the art of the calligrapher. "In my case, I believe, the transcendental desire—that bubbles up like a fountain to write down what touches my heart—turns into calligraphy."

I am never bothered by bad design. There is too much of it. Graphic design can't save the world as they tried to make me believe in art school. Top design is a rare joy.
• **Joost Elffers**, JOOST ELFFERS BOOKS, New York

Working with Stefan is like getting a ride to somewhere unknown.
• **Mikio Shinagawa** Editor, New York

MEETING WITH MIKIO today
HIM: WHO DO YOU THINK SHOULD WRITE THE FOREWORD FOR OUR BOOK?
ME: I DONT KNOW, WHO DO YOU THINK WE COULD GET?
HIM: MAYBE A WESTERN ARTIST LIKE RAUSCHENBERG OR LICHTENSTEIN
ME: WELL, RAUSCHENBERG WOULD BE FANTASTIC.
HIM: HOW ABOUT THE DALAI LAMA?
ME: WELL, IT BE RATHER DIFFICULT TO GET HIM?
HIM: (HUMBLY) OH NO, MAYBE NO PROBLEM, OLD FRIEND OF FAMILY.
ME: WOULDN'T

NOTHINGNESS

石と語る

TALK TO A STONE

TETSUZAN SHINAGAWA

ONE OF THE GREAT BONUSES of the design vocation is that it exposes its practitioners to the traditions and accomplishments of other cultures. The giant Japanese bathroom fixtures manufacturer Toto, for example, has a catalogue of 20,000 products, including a toilet seat that doubles as a bidet and odor remover. The company came to Sagmeister on the recommendation of one of its consultants, Ayse Birsel—a former classmate from Pratt—to design a new identity for its U.S. arm.

Sagmeister proposed a water-based solution, in which a different photograph of an aqueous body was used for every employee business card. Each image was designed in an extended wide-screen format, making it rather difficult to crop stock photographs to fit, so the studio had a photographer shoot each scene. The ambitious strategy incurred at least two problems, as Veronica Oh recalls: The quantity of images required an unprecedented number of color separations and, on completion, the project was greeted with fights among Toto employees who were envious of their colleagues' particular water scene. "It was good that the corporation was Japanese," she says. "If they were American it would never have flown. It was very expensive but the client loved it."

The studio went on to produce packaging and several brochures for the company (including one for the aforementioned toilet seat). The relationship continued for nearly two years, providing Sagmeister with a steady stream of well-paid and solid work, until Sagmeister's contact, a German marketing manager, parted company with the parent group, and the Toto connection, sadly, evaporated.

MARCH 21 1995

FEDEX called TODAY, SAID THAT THERE MUST HAVE been A MISTAKE MADE: THERE ARE TWO PACKAGES, - CONTENTS GIVEN: TOILET SEATS - TO BE DELIVERED TODAY FROM JAPAN, ONE INSURED FOR $18.000.- THE OTHER ONE FOR $45.000.- I TOLD THEM IT'S O.K.- ONE is FOR THE MASTER BATHROOM, the OTHER ONE FOR THE KIDS.

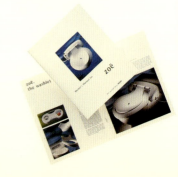

I had just come back from Japan where I had spent a year designing products for TOTO. Stefan was designing all of the printed materials for one of these products, the zoë washlet, and had Tom Vack, the great product photographer, shoot it. The second day of the shoot, just when I am about to leave my apartment to go to the photo studio, Stefan calls me and says that Tom is in jail in Brooklyn, arrested for indecent exposure. Apparently he had had a few drinks and then started running around naked. I can't believe it but Stefan is serious and needs 30 grand to bail him out. I tell him I don't have that kind of money, he tells me he doesn't either, so we worry about who to ask, what's going to happen to the shoot, and how are we going to tell our Japanese client about it. Finally I say OK, let's go at least visit him for starters, and take him some food or something. Stefan says good idea and asks me, "And what day are we?" Thinking he wants to enter it into his calendar I tell him "April 1." As I utter the words I realize that I had just been his April's Fool. I tell him he is an idiot and we hang up and go meet at the photo studio half hour later. We tell Tom Vack of Stefan's joke and he gets pissed off at me for believing that he would run around naked. Oh, well, why not?

The rest of the day Tom and his assistants painstakingly build a set around zoë, lifting it up on glass so that it'll look like it is floating in air. Stefan and I hang out, and to pass time, plan other phone jokes, one of which is to call the product manager for zoë, who is in Germany at the time, and tell him that our one and only zoë prototype, which cost a lot of money, just broke because Tom put it up on a glass platform that fell down. Knowing the product manager well, and that it would give him a heart attack, we decide not to call him. Half an hour later, there is an enormous bang and we turn around to see the zoë prototype on the ground, lying in the middle of a lot of broken glass. The set had come undone under the weight of the glass, and crashed to the ground. I think that was an April's fool joke from up above.

• **Ayse Birsel** OLIVE 1:1 New York

▸ TOTO HAD TWO HAND BUILT PROTOTYPES MADE FOR PHOTOGRAPHIC & EXHIBITION PURPOSES, THE MORE EXPENSIVE ONE ACTUALLY WORKING AND FEATURING THE FAMOUS SPRITE FEATURE.

(1.

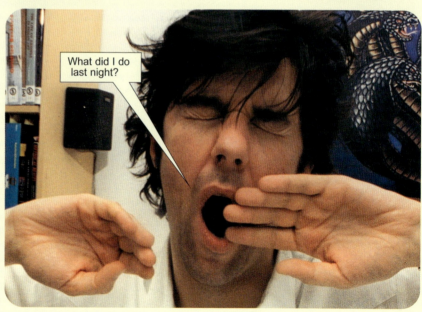

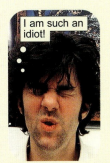

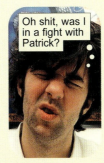

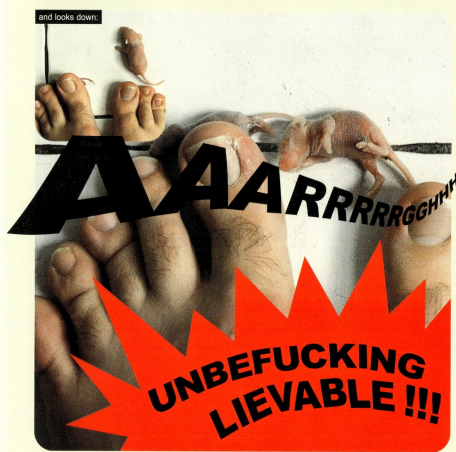

FLASH BACK

One week earlier:

Whats going on? Mice? Rats?

ed Hospital Scenes

Better put some rat poison out.

A couple of days later Stefan found an enormous dead rat in the apartment. It must have been pregnant.

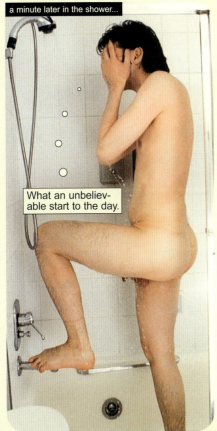

a minute later in the shower...

What an unbelievable start to the day.

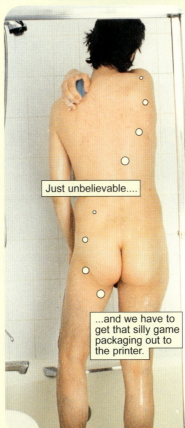

Just unbelievable....

...and we have to get that silly game packaging out to the printer.

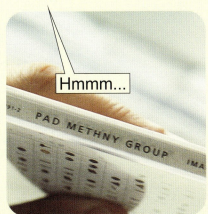

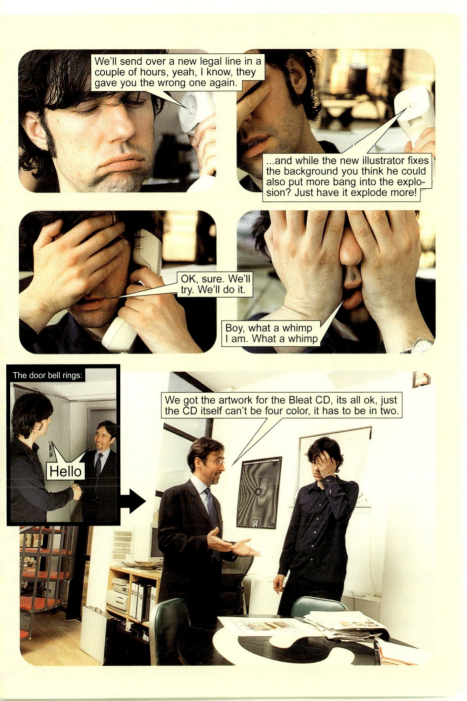

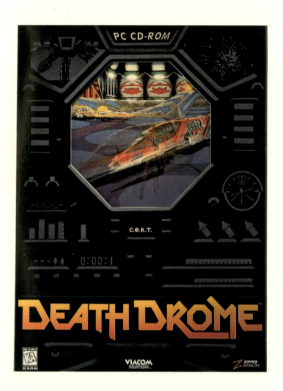

THE WORST DESIGNS to come out of the Sagmeister studio were arguably its CD-ROM packaging schemes for a collection of computer games from Viacom. To beef up their shelf presence, the CD-ROMs were to be double-packaged inside elaborate "cereal boxes"—much as early audio CDs were put in useless cardboard "longboxes" to make them appear as substantial as the 12-inch vinyl records they replaced. Sagmeister took on the project despite deep misgivings. "I hate deceptive packaging," he says. "And I'm not into computer games, particularly not shoot 'em up games."

Sagmeister's next wrong move was to present several alternative designs. One commonly held law of graphic design is that, much as the laser printer always jams when the user is late for a meeting, a client always picks the

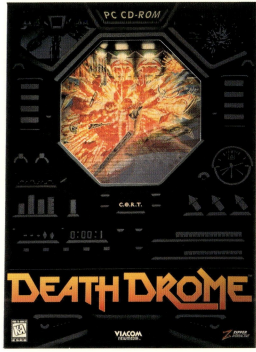

SEPT 14 1996
DONT TAKE ON
ANYMORE BAD JOBS,
I HAVE DONE ENOUGH BULLSHIT
LATELY, I JUST HAVE TO
MAKE TIME FOR SOMETHING
BETTER. SOMETHING GOOD.

designer's least favorite concept. In this case it was a spectacularly overblown scheme using a five-way lenticular picture of an explosion. Bad wasn't quite bad enough, however, and a series of alterations followed, to add a touch more clutter. "Viacom is a huge corporation and behaved like one, with many changes coming out of meetings that you were not part of," says Sagmeister. "The back cover was redesigned probably a dozen times."

Happily, computer games have a short shelf life, and *Death Drome*—along with its ugly sister, *Slamscape* (too awful even to reprint in this book)—have been consigned to the garbage bins of software history.

ANNI KUAN

242 W 38TH ST NEW YORK NY 10018 PHONE 212 704 4038 FAX 704 0651

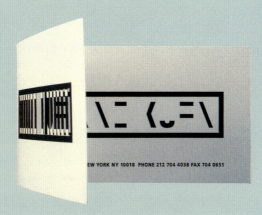

EW YORK NY 10018 PHONE 212 704 4038 FAX 704 0651

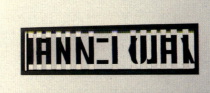

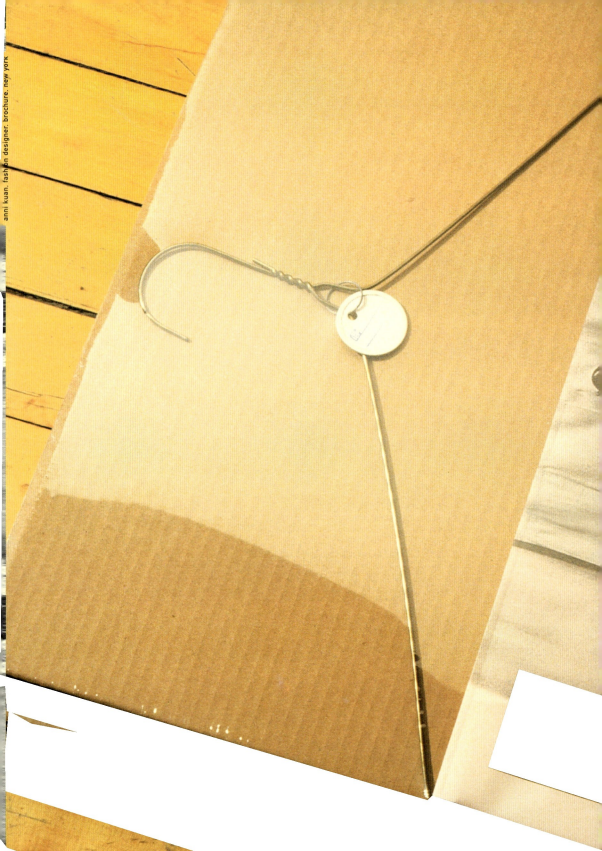

Before the coat hanger mailer I was using a very cliché approach to publicity. The photography was good but I always used a postcard or catalogue format showing a girl in my clothing. I asked Stefan if he would do my mailer, and he said he would, but that I had to leave it all up to him. He requested 12 outfits, and told me they would all be destroyed, run over by cars and splashed by paint. He even wanted to set some on fire. I thought it was a cool concept. My clothes are not super trendy: I have clients from, say, eight years ago still wearing the same thing, so it's just the opposite to the way be presented them—as clothes having a short life. It is making fun of the idea that my clothes are classic. I thought, Why not? Why put clothes on a beautiful model?.

• **Anni Kuan** president
ANNI KUAN DESIGN

SAGMEISTER WAS FIRST INTRODUCED to fashion designer Anni Kuan in the early 1990s. In 1998, they became an item. Kuan's laser-cut folding business card, which forms her name only when completely closed, developed at a similarly leisurely pace. Unbeknownst to Kuan, in the early days of their coupledom, the incurably romantic Sagmeister had been designing her a logo. His criteria were that it work in vertical and horizontal format, and have a slightly Asian feel. (Kuan is a

Chinese middle name: Anni dropped her last name, Huang, because, as she puts it, "In English 'designed by Anni Huang' sounds like it's designed by anyone.")

The next, time-consuming step, was a period of idle experimentation at cutting the logo in two. The typographic effect — illegible lines resembling an ideograph-based language—was pleasing, but getting the two halves to then reform required a perforated fold, and a fastidious and precise print job. It was so tricky, in

fact, that the first batch of business cards came back from the printer with mis-aligned registration. The second run was more successful, and Sagmeister finally had the finished product delivered to Kuan's studio. "It was a big surprise, I had no idea that he was working on it," she says. "He has this child-like desire to deliver surprises."

Since the business card, their client–designer relationship has blossomed, with Sagmeister designing

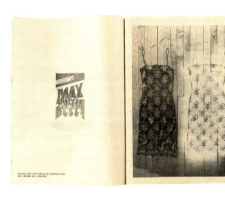

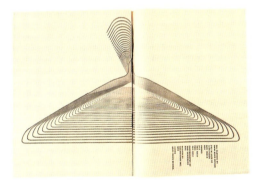

the mailer for each season's Anni Kuan show. The first, cannily incorporating a coat hanger, was deceptively elaborate in light of its simple budget. Taking the form of a newspaper, printed at a Korean-owned printing firm in Manhattan that specialized in cheap, tiny-circulation newsprint publications, the invitation left ink on the fingers, a feature that helped determine the dirty theme inside– photographs of Kuan clothes destroyed by paint and puppy pee, washing powder poured in the shape of a dress and a show announcement in type made of torn pieces of fabric. The coat hanger binding cost somewhat more than a postcard (Kuan's traditional medium) to send in the mail, but Sagmeister and Kuan countered this by streamlining the mailing list. "The mailer included a little postcard that we stamped so that people could return with their opinions," adds Kuan. "We sent out 600 and quite a lot came back. The most popular comments were remarks about the mailer, and requests for an appointment."

The next two mailers took completely different tacks: the first was a tiny four-by-five folded sheet, tied with rubber bands and shrink wrapped. "The next one," says Kuan, "was more extreme, with no pho-tographs at all. It had blank spaces with words like "photograph of NYC skyline reflected in rain puddle," so you just had to imagine the photographs." She adds, "I have no idea what he's going to do next."

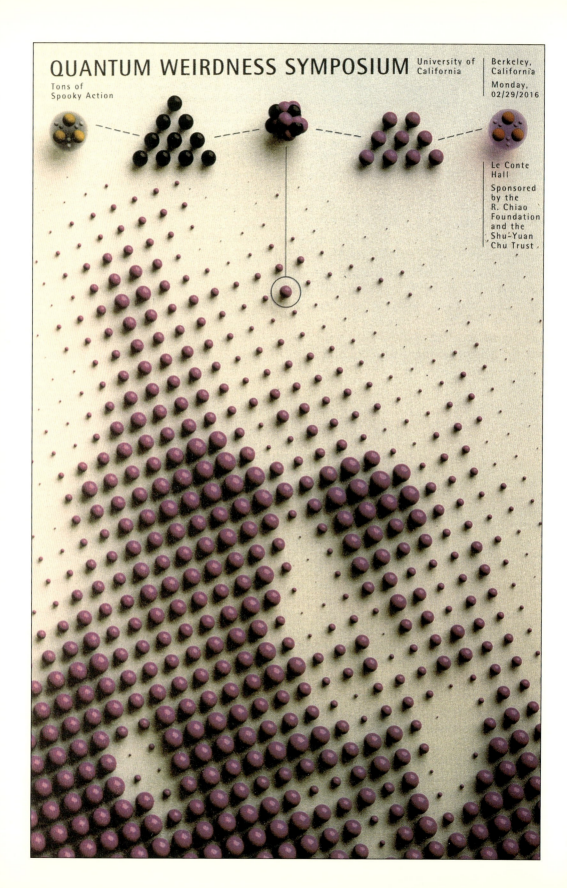

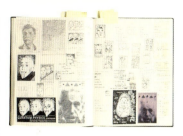

QUANTUM WEIRDNESS is scientific slang for the mysterious "nonlocal" behavior of subatomic particles, a subject that has preoccupied physicists for the last 75 years. One of the prevailing concepts surrounding the quantum conundrum is that subatomic particles are affected by how we observe them. Briefed by the *New York Times Magazine* to create a poster to accompany an article on this subject, Sagmeister came up with a design incorporating an optical shift, whereby squinting the eyes causes a pattern of three-dimensional balls representing particles to form an image. In this way, under our observation, the particles in the image also "take you to another place," as the *Times Magazine* creative director Janet Froelich puts it. The poster was produced with the help of some high-powered proprietary computer software at Blue Sky Studios in New York, for the September 29, 1996 issue.

For a 100th anniversary special issue of the New York Times Magazine *devoted to the future, we asked several artists to create powerful, propagandistic posters to illustrate our various themes. We asked Stefan to illustrate an essay on the future of quantum physics—the strange subatomic mysteries the next Einstein will have to solve. Stefan took the challenge literally; he created a poster for a 'Quantum Weirdness Symposium' in the year 2016. When you look at the poster up close it's just purple balls tastefully arranged in space, but when you step back, changing your point of focus, you see Einstein's face clearly made up of all the tiny little molecules.*

• **Janet Froelich** creative director
NEW YORK TIMES MAGAZINE

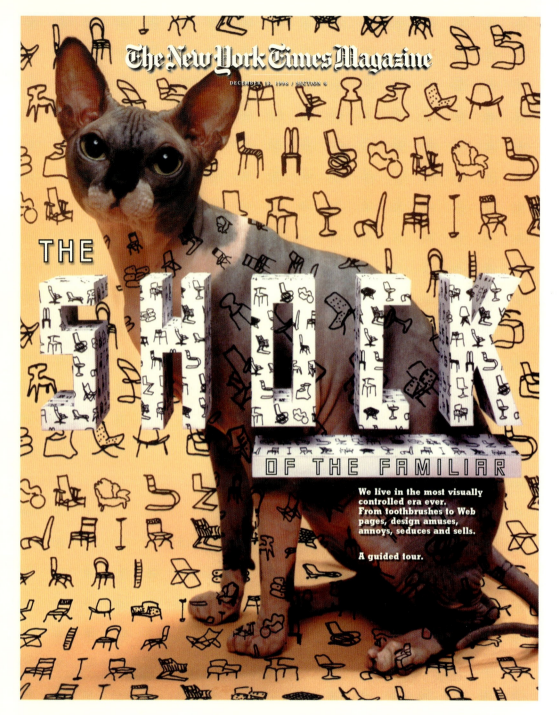

THE NEW YORK TIMES MAGAZINE commissioned six design studios to create a cover for its special design issue, on December 13, 1998, using the headline "Shock of the Familiar." The best of the six would be used for the cover, and the rest featured inside. Sagmeister's submission was a densely-layered futuristic designer world, featuring a hairless cat covered with Sagmeister's sketches of 40 classic chairs. The pet symbolized "living design in many people's homes," according to Sagmeister, while the chair was "the epitome of 20th century object design." Though arrestingly bizarre, the window into a designer world seemed to require written explanation, and didn't win the *Times*'s vote–or Sagmeister's, for that matter. "It was one of those few cases when more time would have helped," he says. "It wasn't massive or crowded enough for my taste." The prize went to Morla Design's type-only, inverted design (right).

DEC 11 1998

JUST SAW THE
JENNIFER Morla
COVER FOR THE NEW YORK TIMES
AND HAVE TO ADMIT THAT IT'S
much BETTER THAN OURS,
THIS IS ALL my FAULT, I REALLY
SHOULD HAVE COME UP WITH a
better CONCEPT,
AND I KNEW AND JUST COULD
NOT DO IT,
I WAS JUST TOO LAZY TO COME
up WITH Something BETTER, JUST
DID NOT THINK ABOUT IT
from A DIFFERENT point OF VIEW.
RIGID CREATIVE THINKING,
EDWARD de BONO WOULD call it.
I AM JUST THINKING TOO STRAIGHT.

familiar

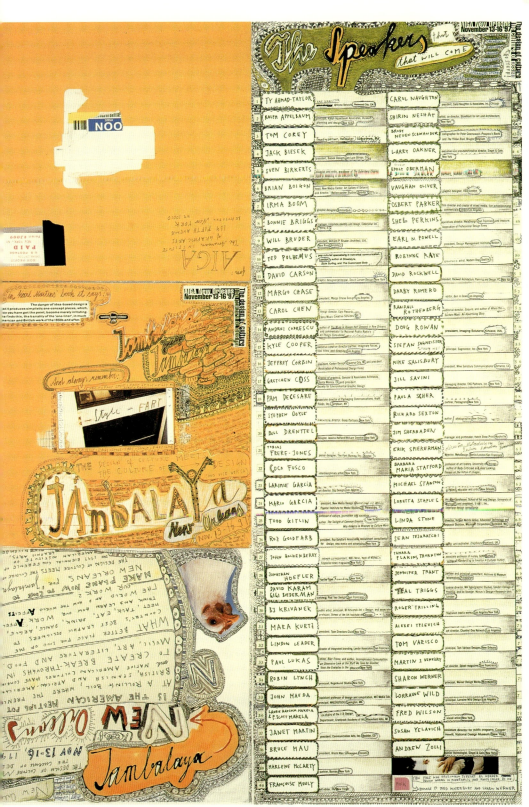

THE TASK—to design a poster for the AIGA's 1997 Biennial conference in the legendary steamy southern port of New Orleans—cried out for something evocative. Yet for Sagmeister the location seemed to inspire only a litany of clichés: crawfish, striptease, gumbo, voodoo, Mississippi steamboats, and so on. When the conference organizer, Janet Abrams, faxed over a boat-load of copy to be included in the poster, the assignment seemed all the more overwhelming. Unsure if it was even physically possible to incorporate all the text, Sagmeister began taking an "information architecture" approach to organizing the data, with thin and thick borders and color-coded elements.

Then he threw it all out. "I was trying to make sense of the copy and how it would all work," he says. "It became clear that with 80 speakers in two and a half days in eight auditoriums and four things going on at the same time, this conference would be a happy chaos. I decided it might be more interesting for readers if the poster were also chaotic–as well as fun for us to do." An image appeared before him that both symbolized chaos and hinted at voodoo in one fell swoop: the headless chicken (pp.160-161).

The process of creating the poster was perhaps closer to painting than digital design-making. Every evening, having spent the evening working for his paying clients, Sagmeister unfolded the giant sheet of poster artwork and resumed the pro bono task. A chicken was decapitated and a chicken foot typeface was designed (both in Photoshop), and the entire studio including two interns, assisted with the doodles. As Abrams sent over alterations to the text, the studio squeezed them in or stuck them over the originals; when Abrams pointed out that certain speakers needed to be highlighted, the designers added hand-drawn doodads for extra emphasis. Finally, in the last remaining gaps, Sagmeister hand-wrote little stories he had heard, including an Adam and Eve joke and a memorable printer story (opposite).

The finished poster sat amid a long-standing debate in graphic design. On one side were those who felt that the "big idea" approach to design was dated. Sagmeister gave voice to this contingent by incorporating a quote from design critic Karel Martens: "The danger of idea-based design is that it produces simplistic one-concept pieces which, once you have got the point, become merely irritating." On the other side were those —including Sagmeister—who felt that design driven by style (for instance, Brody-esque in the 1980s, Carson-esque in the 1990s) was vacuous. Hence the prominent Sagmeister slogan, style=fart.

Sagmeister's chicken poster, though related to the "big idea" school of design (the conference theme is distilled into a singular, bold concept: a chicken) was an anarchic expression of the author's sensibility closer in spirit to the hand-crafted experimentation of practitioners like Ed Fella than the one-concept design that

A LITTLE STORY THAT my PRINTER TOLD ME:
MY PRINTER IN NEW JERSEY WORKS ON this VERY LARGE JOB FOR A FANCY FOOD FAIR in NEW ORLEANS. HIS CLIENT IS THE MARKET LEADER IN THAT SEGMENT, A MAGAZINE CALLED "FROZEN VEGETABLES". IT WAS A rush JOB, THEY HAD WORKED SEVERAL NIGHT SHIFTS TO get A SPECIAL FOOD FAIR ISSUE DOWN TO NEW ORLEANS in TIME for THE SHOW OPENING (LOTS & LOTS OF BOXES) WERE ON FRIDAY. THE MAGAZINES delivered by COURIER TO THE HOTEL WHERE the client STAYED. BUT THE BOXES could NOT be FOUND. THE COURIER COMPANY HAD A DELIVERY SIGNATURE that WAS UNREADABLE. No magazines Friday's SHOW OPENING: NO MAGAZINES. THESE GUYS HAD 10 PEOPLE SATURDAY: NO MAGAZINES AND NO MAGAZINES ANYWHERE. DOWN THERE TO MAN THE STAND WITHOUT GIVING ONE MAGAZINE AWAY! TWO WEEKS LATER THEY FOUND THEM IN THE WALK-IN REFRIGERATOR OF THE hotel. THE BOXES WERE LABELED: "FROZEN VEGETABLES".

Martens had derided. The poster suggested that the issue was more about the obviousness-versus-originality than truly conflicting ideologies. Sagmeister went on to explore the potency of hand-rendered traces in vivid detail (see p.190).

An homage to the poster appeared three years later when a London advertising agency blithely scanned the front chicken image and used it for a film flier. Unable to contain its delight, the plagiaristic agency sent in the poster to London's *Creative Review* magazine as one of their best pieces of the year.

The "headless chicken poster" was the final piece in a series of mailings designed to advertise the American Institute of Graphic Arts' 1997 Biennial Conference in New Orleans. It was crucial that this poster be arresting, informative and a humorous kick in the ribs, to rally the crowds. Thankfully, this task fell to Stefan.

When he sent me his first sketches, I remember chuckling as the decapitated poultry emerged from my fax machine, but also worrying that this image—an apt metaphor for the graphics profession, and a sly reference to New Orleans voodoo—might prove too controversial for the AIGA. Happily, that wasn't the case, though the poster did attract outraged letters from a couple of San Diego chapter animal rights advocates who clearly failed to read the small print (left).

The poster was a handcrafted cannibalization of the previous mailing: Stefan simply chopped up Werner Design Werks' poster, and repositioned the speaker descriptions in microscopically reduced point-size (there's an explanation of that, too, if you hunt for it). Then embroidered the surroundings with manic pencil and ballpoint doodles, obscene tales, shaggy dog stories and in-jokes ("White Space dedicated with love to Massimo Vignelli" next to an empty postage-stamp patch, below the monkey's balls...or are they?). The "STYLE=FART" declaration on the front caused hours of agonized debate. But it, too, finally passed...

While proofreading (yes, just imagine), I discovered that Stefan had gone to work, laboriously hand-pasting text he'd output from the disc for the previous poster. AAAAAGGGGHHH! Where were we going to put the eleventh keynote speaker, recently signed up? And what about speakers who had since dropped out, and new ones who'd joined the line-up? Meticulously placed, there was no way to unstick eighty-odd names and shuffle the sequence. Answer: simply put new names in the gaps, alphabetical order be damned, and finesse room for extra info by sheer force of will, unconstrained by the normal laws of designerly decorum.

All speakers were sent Avery labels and asked to make a 30-second self-portrait for the "chicken" side. Most of them obliged—under threat that an image of a certain portion of Stefan's anatomy would be substituted, if they didn't deliver. In the end, he copped out, and simply typed the absentees' names. When credits for the poster's design and production team were noted missing, Stefan simply wrote them onto a Post-it note and slapped it down near the chicken's leg.

A spirit of rampant improvisation suffuses the poster, which rewards hours of careful scrutiny, takes a magnifying glass to enjoy fully, and was instrumental in luring a record attendance of 2,500 to the conference. Best of all, it produces alarmed guffaws in every first-time viewer, graphic designer or not. That's what I call effective. Strong meat.

• **Janet Abrams** LEADING QUESTIONS
New York

WHEN THE United States Mint announced a special program to replace the bald eagle on 25-cent pieces with a symbol specific to each state, the *New York Post* invited designers to come up with ideas for New York's quarter. The Sagmeister studio proposed seven different designs, its best being the Donald Trump quarter, which would be issued with the cooperation of the multi-millionaire property magnate. "We would ask Mr. Trump to sponsor every quarter with five cents, and in return he would get his picture on it," explains Sagmeister. "So you would actually get five quarters for a dollar."

The studio's other numismatic notions were for a hot dog quarter, a homeless quarter (to be given away) and an elaborate Empire State Building quarter. For the latter, the world-famous Depression-era skyscraper by Shreve Lamb & Harmon is stretched across four quarters to convey its length, each quarter representing a chunk of roughly 300 feet. By adding a couple more of the midriff section quarters, New Yorkers could "trump" the Chicago Sears tower and regain the city's status as home of North America's tallest building.

ABOUT A HALF-INCH in diameter, the little Move Our Money lapel pin has a large message; a conversation piece that veils a big political punch. Designed in 1998 for the non-profit group Business Leaders for Sensible Priorities, its colorful pattern is in fact a pie chart representing the amount of the $540 billion discretionary budget allocated by Congress each year to health, education, housing, defense, and so on. The portion in red is the amount given to the Pentagon—in 1998, $271 billion— about half of the pie. The tiny "x" indicates the amount–15 per cent–that the Move Our Money campaign is dedicated to redirecting toward health and education. The button thus provides an opportunity for the wearer to bend the ears of casual inquir- ers with a diatribe on the glaring imbal- ance in how the U.S. taxpayer's money is spent by the Government.

As part of an armory of props designed by Sagmeister in 1998, and still used by the campaign (see next page), the pin is a good example of how when ideas are strong, style comes second. >

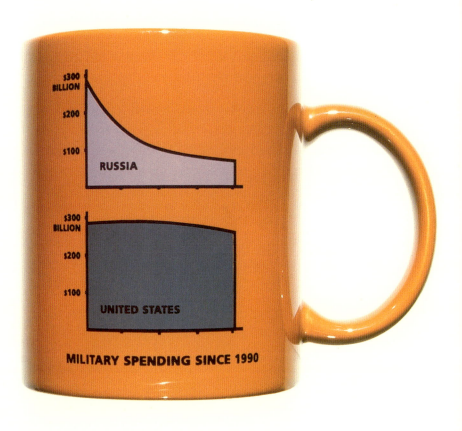

$300 BILLION

$200

$100

RUSSIA

$300 BILLION

$200

$100

UNITED STATES

MILITARY SPENDING SINCE 1990

> Sagmeister's involvement with American politics began in 1988 at the Technology Entertainment and Design (TED) conference in Monterey, where Ben Cohen, the self-named "ice cream guy" and co-founder of Ben & Jerry's ice cream, gave a presentation about his new non-profit group, Business Leaders for Sensible Priorities. Sagmeister, speaking

at the same conference, was impressed by the fact that Cohen's group was "not the usual bunch of left-wing Democrat hippies with a laudable idea that will go nowhere, but people in business who you would normally associate with Republican causes." The non-partisan organization's roll call of members includes hundreds of successful business leaders, even a few

retired generals and admirals. Cohen explained to the TED audience the organization's concerns: that current defense spending is close to 90 percent of the Cold War average —despite the fact that the Cold War is over. By reducing the Pentagon budget to a "rational" level (where there would still be enough nuclear firepower to destroy all the cities

in the world four times over), Cohen argued, America could improve its slipping educational and healthcare standards and better ensure its future world leadership.

Cohen and Sagmeister met at an after-conference gathering. "I was incredibly impressed with the way Stefan was able to present information," recalls Cohen of the designer's TED talk. Sagmeister, in turn, was impressed by Cohen's geniality. "He offered me a ride, and I thought it was pretty nice of a captain of industry to drive me home," he says.

They agreed to work together, and shortly after returning to New York, Sagmeister received from Cohen a giant folder stuffed with information and statis-tics, along with a brief to design the "Move our Money" campaign logo. The process of coming up with a suitable solution was not so agreeable. "I went through the icon stage with all sorts of cheesy ideas like drawings of people holding hands and dollar bills changing hands," says Sagmeister.

The answer finally popped out. "I >

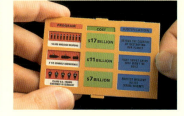
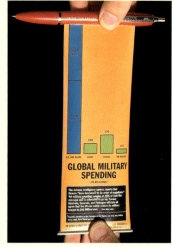

IN NEW YORK WE TEND TO GET SO CAUGHT UP IN APPEARANCES) IT'S EASY TO LOSE SIGHT OF THE CONTEXT.

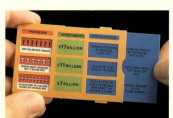

> thought it would be stupid to do a logo when we have facts like this to play with," says Sagmeister. "So I looked for a formal design that would keep these numbers incredibly clear." The studio developed a series of simply stated, brightly presented information graphics, which were adapted to T-shirts, mugs and "advertising novelties." The novelties were a pen with a

> *This was an effort to take some very serious, dry, complex data and present it in a simplified, fun, interesting, and entertaining way. Much of what we were doing was adapting advertising novelties to communicate our message. Probably the most frustrating part of the assignment was that we were in the process of refining our message at the same time that we were working on creating the marketing materials. I kept on feeling guilty about all the changes. We must have gone through three different concepts and 15 different versions of the slide card alone.*
>
> • **Ben Cohen** founder BEN & JERRY'S, BUSINESS LEADERS FOR SENSIBLE PRIORITIES

retractable bar chart, a credit-card sized lenticular "winkie" that doubled as a membership card, a pocket-sized sliding card, and the pie chart lapel pin. By tilting the winkie, a graphic showing an F-22 fighter jet and the figure $200,000,000 changed to a diagram of 20 school buildings. (The original design choice, a B-2 bomber, cost so much that all the schools it could buy wouldn't fit on one card.) The sliding card showed how funding for seemingly irrelevant parts of the arsenal—$11 billion for seawolf submarines to "fight Soviet ships that won't be built," for instance—could be spent on providing health insurance for 11 million children. The pie chart proved particularly versatile. After being blown up to the size of an inflatable, it was adapted to edible cookies that were distributed at primary events in Iowa and New Hampshire by a "Cookie Lady" who ended up in a TV spot. It also became a projection applied to the walls of buildings and a 20–inch diameter chalk stamp for sidewalks.

The campaign took to the road in the form of a "moneymobile": a bus decorated with dollar bills that followed the presidential campaign trail. At strategic points along

the route, three actors would jump out, dragging a family of giant inflatable graphics, and give a show—titled "U Slice the Pie"—to audiences on university campuses, at local fairs and speaker gatherings. The inflatables featured the same style of information graphics developed by the studio for the novelties and merchandise, blown up to giant scale.

As the election build-up took hold, the Move Our Money campaign generated considerable publicity. The moneymobile toured throughout 1999 and 2000, heralding its appearance in every town with a liberal dousing of the advertising novelties. For jaded reporters covering lackluster candidates, the campaign was a welcome splash of color. "What really gets people are the winkie, slide card and pen," says Cohen. "These things are unique in political circles."

move our money, collateral material, bus and inflatable sculptures, burlington, vermont

Dr. HUBERT SALDEN   Tel: 05223/58 45 16

TIROL

MONEY HAS RARELY been in short supply in the conservative Tyrolean town of Hall. In the 15th century, Hall was Austria's third largest city, prospering from the trading of salt mined from the mountains to the north. It is also the birthplace of the taler, Europe's standard currency in the 15th century, which lent its name to the modern dollar. Five hundred or so years later, in 1998, the powerful Tyrolean fathers who control Hall poured thousands of dollars into the renovation of a vast 19th-century salt warehouse, then, rather typically, argued about what to do with it. Finally, after seeing the success of the contemporary art museum in Bregenz, they agreed that art should be the destiny of the renovated warehouse, and appointed a German contemporary art professor, Hubert Salden, to oversee the transformation.

Somewhat to the surprise of the city's fathers, Salden took the word contemporary and ran with it, turning the giant salt hall into a multi-function Internet cafe, electronica dance club, roller-skating hall, movie theater and exhibition space. He

named the institution the Kunsthalle Tirol (the German spelling of "Tyrol"), and opened it with an exhibition on cosmic radiation, followed by a show on the British director Alfred Hitchcock and the American inventor, thinker and designer Buckminster Fuller.

During the planning stages of the museum, Hubert also contacted

Sagmeister in New York with a view to staging an exhibition of the studio's work. Out of this initial contact came the assignment to design the museum's identity, which Sagmeister proposed should be a logotype on white reflecting the idea of a stately art museum in a salt warehouse, counterbalanced with a slab of iridescent Day-Glo orange, more in keeping with the

Kunsthalle's cyber-rave culture alter-ego. On the business card, the studio put the orange color on the reverse side of a die-cut folded card, which reflects a strangely unearthly orange glow on the white backdrop, "a much smoother glow than you could ever try to print," notes Sagmeister. The exhibition, to date, is still waiting to happen.

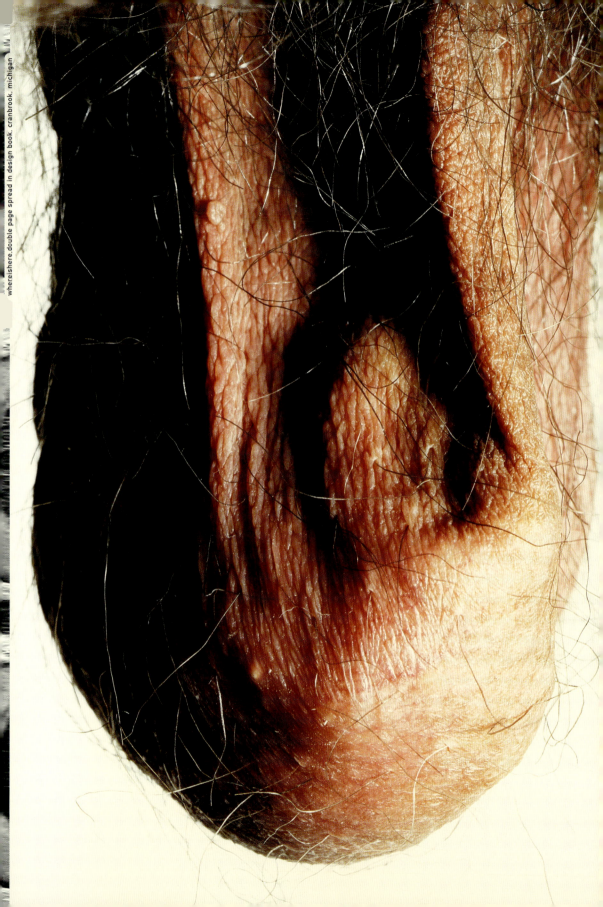

IN THE 1998 BOOK *Whereishere*—a chaotic amalgamation of work by different contemporary designers—Western techno-fetishism and exhibitionist tendencies converge with the Buddhist notion of mindfulness in a kind of high-energy frenzy. The book was compiled by design writer Lewis Blackwell with Laurie Haycock Makela and the late P. Scott Makela, co-chairs of 2-D design at Cranbrook Academy of Art. The Makelas and Sagmeister were kindred spirits,

sharing a belief in producing work that is personal and physically engaging. The authors solicited double-page spreads from various designers whose work they considered important, encouraging them to be loud, free and experimental.

Sagmeister's three contributions—the "monkey's balls" from the AIGA chicken poster (pp.162-165), this time revealed as a human testicle, a surreal photocomposition, and type scratched in

blood—drew fire from design critic Rick Poynor in *Graphis* magazine, who criticized what he saw as an increasingly self-indulgent vein in contemporary graphic design. "Few images better encapsulate the profession's, indeed the culture's, obsession with the self," wrote Poynor.

Sagmeister's defense is that the book was targeted at designers and therefore warranted personal work. "If you're doing work for other designers

you'd better talk about either design or yourself," he says. The testicle, he adds, was his public approbation of "ballsy design." The photomontage was a symbol of the antagonistic relationship between design and art, as Sagmeister sees it, "why art fucks design and vice versa: Artists look down on designers and designers don't care about artists."

The book was not, however, particularly well received. It tended to confuse rather than enlighten or invigorate readers, and sales were sluggish.

The publication of *Whereishere* was shortly followed by the sudden death of P. Scott Makela. For the school, it was a tragic loss. The Makelas had been hitting a stride, winning prestigious jobs, trying new directions, and at Cranbrook, sending out the first waves of influence, with their first class of students nearing graduation. "The program was unbelievable when I saw it," says Sagmeister, "because the students were truly mature—some of them had five years of work behind them and could do honest experimentation."

Sagmeister's most recent visit to the campus left him resolved to take a hiatus from commercial work for a year beginning in June, 2000. "Two or three days there definitely had something to do with my plan for a year without clients. I felt that what the students were doing was very healthy for themselves."

NET WEIGHT
1.7oz 50ml

NET WEIGHT
1.7oz 50ml

THE IDEA OF THE "Unavailable" fragrance, developed by author Karen Salmansohn, revolved around the allure of a woman who plays hard-to-get—or even better, impossible-to-get. The perfume manu-facturer, Blue Q (maker of "Dirty Girl" brand soap), asked Sagmeister to design the packaging, which would incorporate a text by Salmansohn providing a how-to guide to the "philosophy."

The design plays, with deadpan cool-ness, on the catch-me-if-you-can theme. A black strip, similar to the censoring mark used to hide a person's identity in a prize-winning or scandalous photograph,

CONTENTS

partially obscures the perfume name, and is read from the inside of the glass on the opposite side of the bottle. The entire package is sold as a book, which opens to reveal the "unavailable" philoso-phy, and, nestled like a revolver in a die cut, the bottle itself. A surrounding slip-case also features a black rectangle, effectively obscuring the title.

On the accompanying soap, the word "unavailable" was embossed at two dif-ferent depths, so that the first two letters wash away with use. Thus the more the soap is used, the more the soap and its user become "available."

DEC 23 1997

WORKING WITH HJALTI TURNS out NICELY, HE'S A REAL GIFT (AND A CENTER FOR CALMNESS in THE STUDIO)

DESPITE AN INCREASING INFLUX of offers, Sagmeister adhered to the advice offered by Tibor Kalman and kept the business small, turning down work rather than having to hire more staff and raise the overhead. With the departure of Veronica Oh from the studio in 1996, Sagmeister trawled through the names he had kept on file, and fished up that of the Icelander Hjalti Karlsson, who had expressed an interest in joining the

studio six months earlier. Karlsson, a Parsons graduate, had freelanced at various New York design firms—including Siegel & Gale, Pentagram, Arnell Group and Comedy Central—but had been fixating on a seat in Sagmeister's office since seeing the studio's first CD designs.

The Karlsson–Sagmeister collaboration, a harmonious combo of Nordic calm and Teutonic obsessiveness, lasted four years, surviving an encounter with a

decapitated chicken, the Rolling Stones and a body scarification episode—as well as the demands of working within three feet of each other for nearly 1,000 days. "When I started working with Stefan my plan was to stay for a year-and-a-half, max two," says Karlsson. "I can hardly believe that I stayed four years in the studio and we never really argued."

While talking to the editor of the

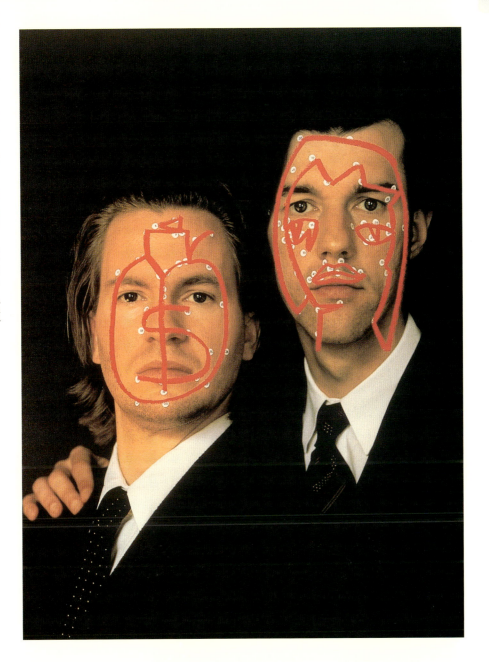

FOR NEXT YEAR : ONLY GOOD CD COVERS, ALL NON MUSIC JOBS HAVE TO PAY WELL, DON'T WORK ON WEEKENDS, MAKE 6 WEEKS HOLIDAY AND HAVE loats OF FUN & JOY.

Japanese design magazine *IDEA* about the possibilities for the cover of its special New York issue, Sagmeister and Karlsson had suggested a self-portrait with a connect-the-dots puzzle, the numbers and dots actually stuck on their faces. The question remained as to what should be revealed when the dots were joined. The conversation drifted to cultural design differences, and how the New York design scene was inextricably tied to commerce. "All we New Yorkers think about," suggested Sagmeister, "is girls and money."

The remark provided the obvious solution: the lusty, money-hungry Manhattan designers should have "money and women" written all over their faces. To give the cover a sense of authority, they commissioned from Tom Schierlitz a portrait in the style of a formal business magazine photo. "We tried to look as if we weren't aware of the dots on our faces," says Sagmeister, "with nice lighting to make us good looking." A few weeks later, Karlsson arrived at an *IDEA* magazine party where people were clutching copies of the issue bearing his image. When a young woman approached Karlsson for his autograph, his dreams of design fame came true. Fortune surely couldn't be far behind.

THE "FIVE YEARS OF STYLE=FART" party invitation, celebrating the studio's fifth anniversary, was appropriately printed on a whoopee cushion. On one side of the cushion was the tagline "when anyone sits down it emits a real Bronx cheer." The other side featured three design variations with matching packaging: a clean, Swiss style design, with appropriately reverential press quotes on the studio's work; a Gothic/party favor design; and a hand-scrawled version, on which Sagmeister projects were reduced to single icons.

print magazine. cover. new york

$7.50

AMERICA'S GRAPHIC DESIGN MAGAZINE
MARCH/APRIL 1996
PRINT L:II

Print

TWO YEARS' WORTH OF LOST HAIR

I LOVE being IN
MY OWN DESIGN STUDIO.
I ENJOY THE TIME much
BETTER THAN
AT M&CO OR AT BURNETT.
SOMEHOW IT SEEMS I'M
IN CONTROL OF my LIFE AGAIN.

TO COINCIDE WITH A FEATURE article on the Sagmeister studio, *Print* magazine asked for a cover design. A few months earlier, Veronica Oh, working at the studio, had asked Sagmeister why he kept a dirty hairbrush lying around. "She called me a pig for not cleaning it," says Sagmeister. "As an excuse I said it's going to be a design project."

Print presented the perfect opportunity. "It struck me that lost hair illustrates the agony of the creative process," says Oh.

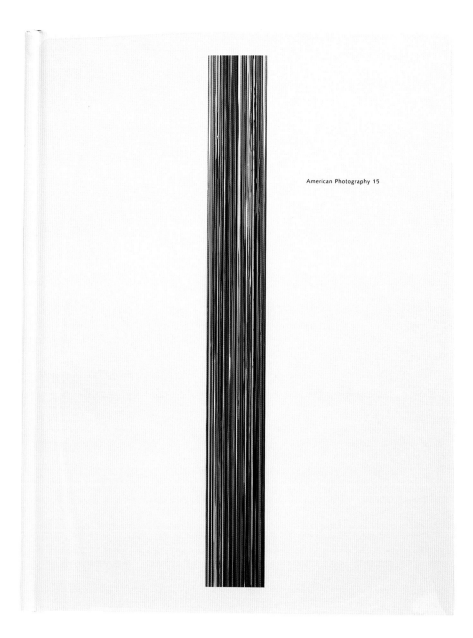

American Photography 15

TRADITIONALLY, the *American Photography* annual would sport one of the strongest images from its competition on its cover. In 1998, however, when Sagmeister was given the job of designing the volume, no single image seemed powerful enough. So the studio decided to use them all. Each picture was digitally compressed into a thin stripe and assembled into a multicolored block resembling a book's fore-edge, running from top to bottom on the cover, back cover and inside endpapers. The actual fore-edge of the book was printed with a panoramic stock photo of an American landscape—to complete the picture, as it were.

Applying pictures to a book's fore-edge was not uncommon in the 17th century, when Dutch and German book designers would simply paint the edge of the closed volume, but today, high print runs make hand-painting unfeasible. Sagmeister's solution involved printing a portion of the picture on the fore-edge of each page, with the portion shifting in tiny increments on each successive page. Since this was not possible with the prevailing software, Karlsson was obliged to work with a test application downloaded from the Internet. When the completed pages began to emerge from the studio printer bearing giant crosses and the words "this is a demo," panic kicked in. Karlsson phoned the client, Mark Heflin, to explain that the project would not meet the deadline. "It sounded like a 'dog ate my homework' excuse," recalls Karlsson. "He was amazingly understanding." The technical hitch was eventually surmounted, and the fore-edge printed successfully. The studio even tried it again with this book *(see fore-edge).*

Michael Lavine

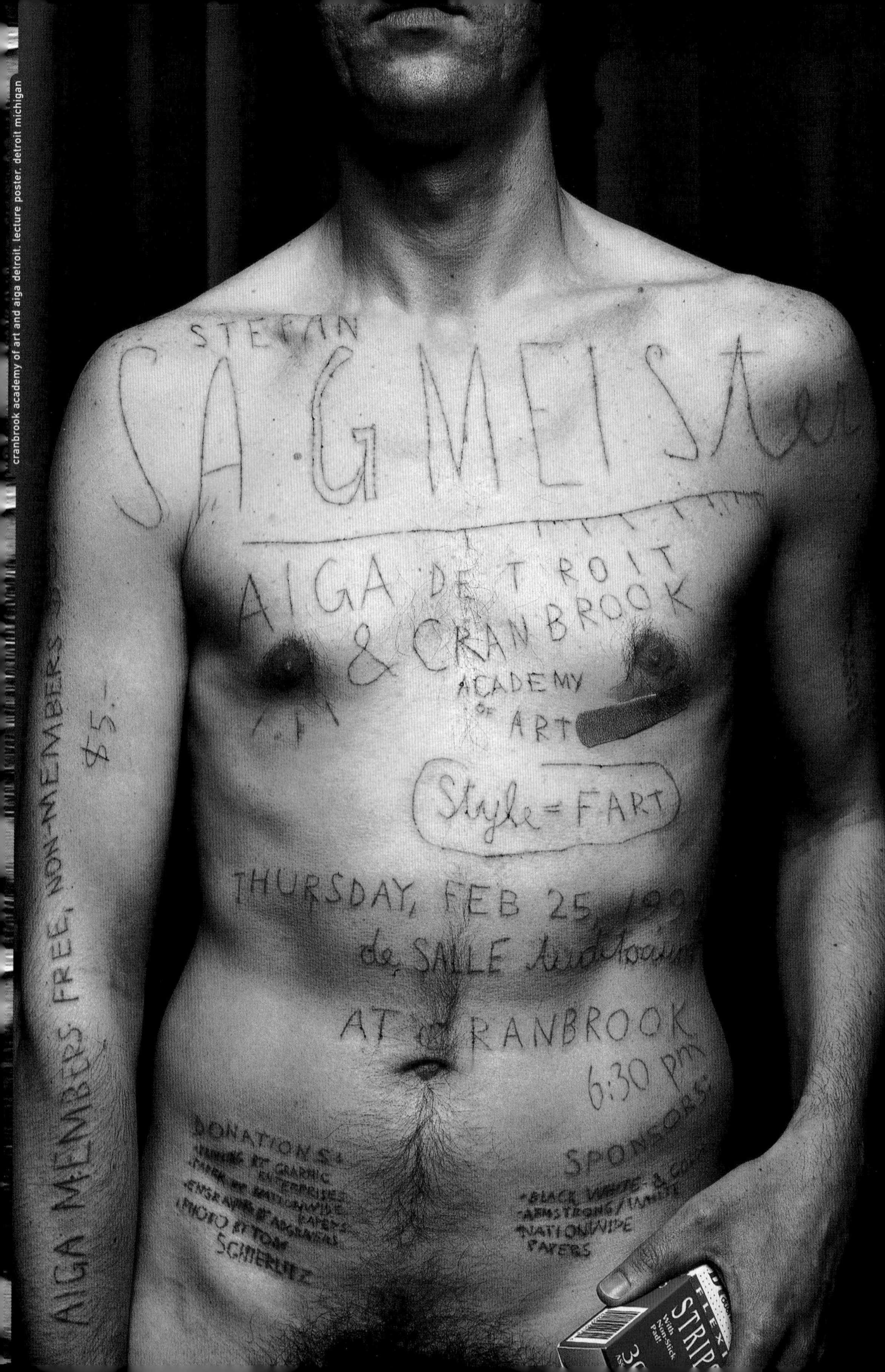

cranbrook academy of art and aiga detroit. lecture poster. detroit michigan

PROBABLY THE MOST NOTORIOUS poster to have emerged from Sagmeister's studio, the advertisement for a talk hosted by the Detroit chapter of the AIGA in 1999, was intended to reflect the ordeals of the design profession. Or, as Sagmeister put it, "the anxious periods, the fighting and the pain." Having experimented with cutting a small amount of text into his skin for the *Whereishere* project (p.176), Sagmeister reasoned that doing it again on a larger scale would be relatively painless.

He was wrong. Sagmeister stood in front of the mirror with a blade at 9:00 am on the day of the photoshoot, and found himself unable to make a single incision. Part of the problem was cutting in reverse, part of the problem was cutting accurately and part of the problem was cutting. He emerged, humbled, from the bathroom, blade in hand, in search of a willing surgeon. Sagmeister's normally loyal accomplice Hjalti Karlsson looked at the amount of copy and bluntly refused. Karlsson gestured to the studio intern, the Swiss designer Martin Woodtli. Being something of a precision-obsessed engineer (with a background in silk-screened fliers with tiny type sizes), Woodtli obliged.

"Eight hours of cutting," recalls Woodtli calmly, "it was very strange." The process began slowly and got slower, Woodtli having to ensure that the incisions were minimal, but deep enough for the letters to be legible. Half way through, the initially irritating scratches began to accumulate into recognizable pain. "I began to have serious doubts," Sagmeister says, "but there was no going back—I had no other ideas." The worst hour was the last, when Woodtli began carving the "stupid" tiny credits around the pelvis.

The poster did its job, and the talk in Detroit was well-attended, though whether Sagmeister lived up to its publicity is in some doubt. "Probably some people were disappointed at what a tame guy I am," he says. The scars, which took a month or so to disappear, had an unexpected resurgence one summer's afternoon when Sagmeister was lying on a beach. As the sun's rays triggered the skin's melanin, Sagmeister noticed the faint, but irrefutable trace of his name, rising in pink to the surface of his chest.

The poster, like the AIGA chicken piece (pp.160-165), signalled a turning point for the design profession, away from aspirations of digital perfection toward a higher appreciation for a designer's personal

mark. Twelve years of computer-driven design had initiated a backlash in favor of the tactile and hand-hewn—anything that showed physical evidence of a creator and evoked an equally physical response, even repulsion. That it was related to a parallel movement in architecture was subsequently documented in the 2000 Triennial exhibition at the Cooper Hewitt National Design Museum, where Sagmeister's poster was juxtaposed with architect Steven Holl's sponge-like MIT residence in a section titled "Physical."

FEB 10 1999
THE FIRST THING I SHOULD BE THINKING ABOUT IS DESIGN THAT TOUCHES. THAT COULD ALSO INCLUDE PURELY FORMAL SOLUTIONS. THE WHOLE THING HAS to be BEAUTIFUL. BEAUTIFUL.

ANAMORPHIC—or optically distorted—art has been used for centuries as a device for concealing images. By looking at an elongated image with a convex cylindrical mirror—an anamorphoscope—the distortion can be corrected. The technique was used by aristocrats in 18th and 19th century Europe to pass around pornography. In the 1980s, the psychology professor and conspiracy theorist Wilson Bryan Key held up for analysis a photograph of a Martini glass, in which, he claimed, someone armed with an anamorphoscope could plainly see a man with an erect penis.

The New York–based multimedia firm Studio SGP presented Sagmeister with an opportunity to deploy this now-neglected optical trick. The company needed packaging for its new presentation CD-ROM, and since its business was interactive media, an interactive anamorphoscope seemed to fit the bill. The firm needed only a short run of the CDs, so silk screening was feasible, making the idea (one that had been in Sagmeister's sketchbook since his thesis project) possible within budget. The cover of the CD was printed on a square of Mylar which came with a set of instructions. By rolling the Mylar into a cylinder and placing it in the center of the CD, the viewer could see the distorted lines on the CD surface reflected as a pair of spectacles, the SGP logo.

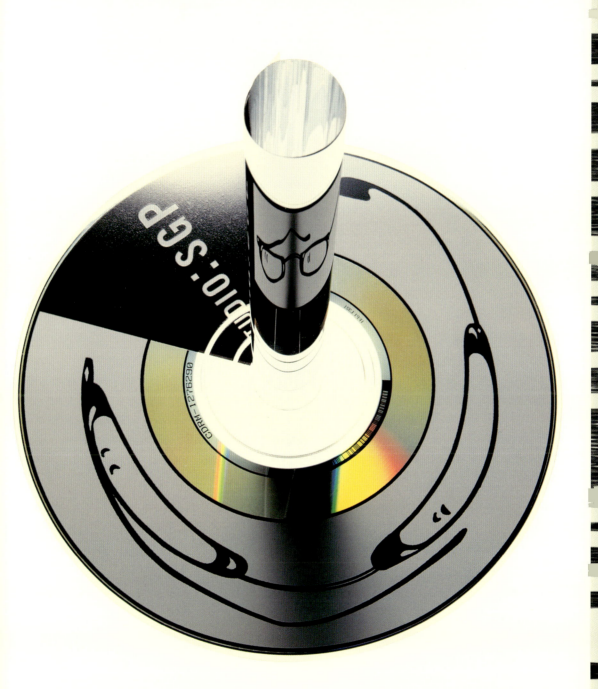

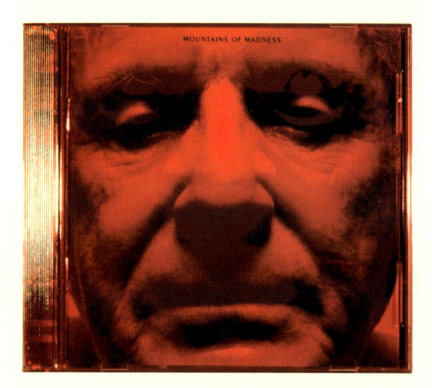

MOUNTAINS OF MADNESS

MANY LIBRARY SHELVES have been filled with books that commemorate the passing of the 12-inch record sleeve, each written with a tone of nostalgic lament. There are few books, if any, dedicated to the art of the CD cover, which, when it arrived to stay in the 1980s with its canvas a fifth the size of the old LP and a brittle, easily-scratched case, was welcomed by most designers like a consolation prize. The opposite was true for Sagmeister, for whom the CD package offered a new playground for optical trickery and invention.

The little plastic jewelcase not only had potential for exploring surprises, it offered the interplay of moving surfaces and materials. "Stefan actually welcomed the change from poster-sized album cover to CD," says Veronica Oh. "It has a book-like element, and its ins and outs can be a lot more surprising than pulling a big old record out. It becomes a toy that you want to cherish."

Having gained little feedback from record companies in response to his early marketing efforts, Sagmeister seized the studio's first CD opportunity—to design the packaging for *Mountains of Madness* by H.P. Zinker, his friend Hans Platzgumer's band—as a chance to show his studio's prowess with the little canvas.

Inspiration came from a disturbing and vivid interaction with a pedestrian on the streets of New York. Platzgumer had

mentioned that the lyrics for his songs were all connected to the idea that life in New York city made you "sick in the head," and Sagmeister recalled a moment during his first trip to the city: "I was on Sixth Avenue, and I saw this very distinguished-looking gentleman crossing 14th Street. He looked a little like my grandad. I stared at him, mostly because in Austria it's not bad manners to stare intensely at someone. He freaked out."

The abrupt transformation from placidity to freakish rage was captured during a Tom Schierlitz photoshoot with a model and re-enacted with a tinted CD jewelbox that doubled as a red filter. The placid man, printed in green, appears under the jewelbox. The angry man, printed in red, emerges as the booklet is slid from the case. "I had seen the technique in the subway," says Sagmeister. "I was sitting next >

> to a little girl with a math book who was using a red filter to see the answers. I thought it probably could work with photography too." The method was tested with endless color Xeroxes, while the studio developed other ideas for kinetically changing images on the inside pages of the booklet, including a shot of the band members who, under the filter, appear as skeletons.

Back in 1995, the standard CD jewel case came with a black opaque spine. The Zinker design, however, required a transparent spine for the band name, as well as a red tint that had to be Pantone-perfect to work. The record company was unwilling to fork out the extra cost for color corrections, so Sagmeister took the unprecedented step of paying the difference, sensing the project's potential as a promotional tool to secure the studio more CD work. The investment paid off, at least for the studio. The design was nominated for a Grammy award and yielded a slowly increasing stream of record company projects. In the design press, the CD put Sagmeister's name in lights, or at least in large point sizes. "No LP provides a comparable interactive experience," wrote Julie Lasky in *Print* magazine.

The news even made *Billboard* magazine, which reported that Sagmeister's name had "started to surface when labels were discussing designs for upcoming releases." The studio was so happy with the technique that it used it again six years later (*see cover of this book*).

For the back of the case, the band members were pictured, Beatles-style, crossing Sixth Avenue in line, a photoshoot that nearly ended with Tom Schierlitz under the wheels of a car. In fact, the only casualty of the project was the band itself, which broke up shortly after the release. Perhaps it was a fitting end: Everything in this project, it seemed, was about oxymorons, including the designer's success and the band's failure. Even the printing on the disk incorporated violent contrast, with two remarks Sagmeister had heard one morning in Manhattan's East Village, one of which appeared under the filter: "We get up at noon and go for a bite. Isn't our life just great?" and "I'll rip your fucking head off and shit down your neck."

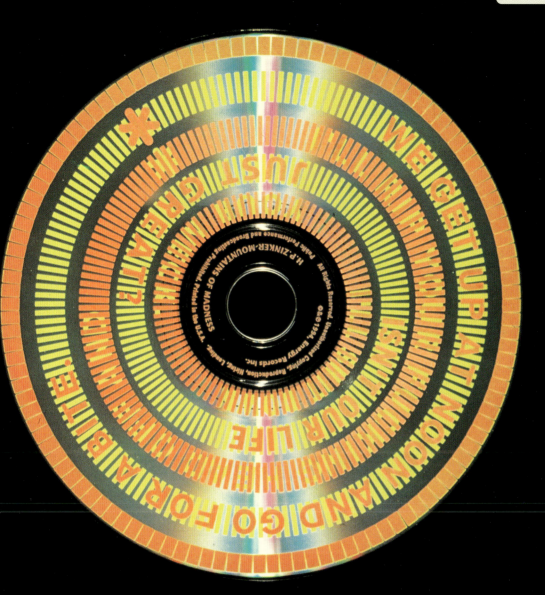

WE GET UP AT NOON AND WANT OUR LIFE GO FOR A BITE AND IT'S MNY WILL WE JUST GREAT IT'S

H.P. ZINKER·MOUNTAINS OF MADNESS

Funk Performance and Broadcasting Publishing, Printed in the U.S.A.

All Rights Reserved Unauthorized Copying, Reproduction, Hiring, Lending,

℗&©1994, Energy Records Inc.

Our masterpiece **Mountains Of Madness** *deserved a mastersleeve. Inspired by H.P. Lovecraft's title and our appropriate music Sagmeister came up with the 3D-box that was to win prizes even when the album turned out to be the band's last endeavor, due to erratic record companies and the final downcome of our rock 'n' roll behavior. I shall never forget the hot summer afternoon, when we had to cross Seventh Avenue about a hundred times, walking forward and backward like lunatics three times in one 'walk'-sequence, while photographer Tom Schierlitz took the pictures for the back sleeve, lying in the middle of the busy street about 20 meters away.*

Unfortunately I shall also not forget how members of the Academy were trying in vain to find the CD in any record store after it had gotten nominated for a Grammy Award. By that time our distribution had folded. The jury decided to vote for Patty Smyth's sleeve.

• **Hanz Platzgumer** H.P. ZINKER

SAGMEISTER FIRST WHET his appetite for adventurous CD booklets while he was working at Leo Burnett in Hong Kong in 1991. An old friend from school, Stephan Schertler, was playing with a Swiss jazz band called Songs of Maybe, which had recorded a session in a church in the Alps, and needed a package design. With the atmosphere of the church pervading the music, Sagmeister decided to print the booklet on the thin paper used for Bibles.

The translucent quality of Bible paper forced an appropriately improvisational approach to dealing with the images on each side of the leaves. A palm tree in black on the front side, for instance, reappears in white on the reverse side of the page with text accordingly reversed. The CD was titled *Moonmaids in my Garden*, and thus sprinkled with images of spheres and crescent moons, while each page featured a design to reflect the changing styles of the music, from bluesy to Be Bop. The thin, low-cost paper meant that for the same price as a regular CD booklet, a 40 page volume—practically a

tome, in CD terms—could be printed and squeezed into the CD case. A fabric bookmark was added so that readers could mark their place.

A happy printing accident occurred on the back page of the booklet: the printing of a line drawing of a sphere in gold left a ghostly imprint on the opposite page. It shimmered in the light like a divine apparition.

Songs of Maybe

but still I have wings to fly
to my new love in a silent night
and then we'll float in silver moonlight
till in the east the morning's in sight

never made it sense
never worked it well
now I'm in suspense
I feel I shouldn't tell

there's something I know
I guess you noticed too
the slightest breeze would blow
apart us, me and you

though a new love often bears an old one
I will say he's never to compare
to anything we've ever done
that danger in his eyes I'll not care

TIME

sun's left your eye
your heart is no more mine
after this good-bye
our words will never rhyme

the falling of your arm
the love that I was in
no longer will your charm
be there to make me sing

but still I have wings to fly
to my new love in a silent night
and then we'll float in silver moonlight
till in the east the morning's in sight

love a time
love a time
love a time

Monica Eggler – Voice
Pietro Tonolo – Soprano Saxophone
Lukas Kramer – Piano • Marco Micheli – Bass
Ettore Fioravanti – Drums • Marilyn Mazur – Percussion

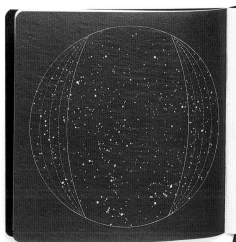

Monica Eggler – Voice
Hans Kramer – Trumpet
Pietro Tonolo – Tenor & Soprano Saxophones
Lukas Kramer – Piano
Nicodor Vrano – Solo Bass
Marco Micheli – Bass
Ettore Fioravanti – Drums
Marilyn Mazur – Percussion

WORDS OF A MOURNFUL SONG

all I have are words of a mournful song

that keeps going round in my mind

I will stay a-lone with my mournful song ..... and

still be-lieve in loves of your kind that

song remembers me of how your love made
me free but always sad I'll find that there's
another one to be with you this can't do
and I've no other words that'd be apt to
explain and leaving is a way that will make
me remain all alone with words of a mournful
song it can last maybe forever long all I
have are words of a mournful song that
keeps going round in my mind what I've
done were once-in-a-lifetime things all for

you unlike these normal springs everything
someday has to find its end many things
there are that you can't pretend now time
is running out and all remembering's in
vain there's nothing left of you that I would
like to remain with me this can't be for I
have sent these words right up to full
moon by 28 days they came back to me
soon so I stay with words of a mournful
song that keeps going round in my mind

In 1993, the New York artist Jenny Holzer was asked by Riuichi Sakamoto and YMO, Japan's godfathers of techno, to design their next CD cover. Holzer was not interested, but granted the group permission to use ten of her *Truisms* on the condition that her friend Tibor Kalman's firm M&Co be given the assignment of designing the cover. The *Truisms*, short, contradictory and provocative one-liners resembling maxims, were first developed by Holzer in the late 1970s as street posters, and reappeared variously in dot matrix signs and theater marquees. The assignment offered Sagmeister, then working at M&Co, another chance to try out a tricky packaging idea. "I was a big Jenny Holzer fan," he says. "So I was very happy."

Drawing on his thesis project experience, Sagmeister designed a system using a moiré effect to turn apparently abstract lines into words by sliding them behind the same pattern printed on the actual jewelcase. To incorporate all ten of the *Truisms* into the design, he developed a 20-page booklet without staples, each page serving as an alternative cover with an appropriate *Truism*. Sagmeister's boss, concerned that this elaborate scheme seemed to be taking up a great deal of studio time, would occasionally pass by and offer his opinion. "Tibor's only piece of advice," says Sagmeister, "was 'It's never going to work.'"

But work it did, and an additional kinetic bonus was reserved for owners of a CD player with a transparent window. On the CD, Sagmeister put a Benham pattern, an arrangement of black and white shapes from a series developed by a German physicist. When the pattern is spun around, the eye begins to see a variety of pale colors, a phenomenon that remains little understood.

riuchi sakamoto / ymo. technodon. cd packaging. prototype. japan

IN THE EARLY DAYS of the studio, Sagmeister and Veronica Oh, in lieu of a real project, would give themselves fake assignments. The idea behind a dummy package for a YMO remix album was to experiment with a CD design in which information was kept to the barest possible minimum. The booklet inside simply shows a series of abstract images (including two mysterious black squares, one blurred and one sharp) while all the information—title, band name and tiny pictures of the band members' faces—is printed on the spine. YMO are about as famous as the Beatles in Japan, reasoned Sagmeister, so the need for identifying text would be minimal. The package also quite effectively conveyed the ambiguousness and sparsity of the band's music. "This one we did just for fun," says Oh, "but Stefan kept a record of it, in case they came back and asked for it."

AUG 30 1994

THERE is not ENOUGH WORK FOR US TO DO.

SUSI IS CUTTING BOARDS FOR THE PORTFOLIO, VERONICA IS DESIGNING OUR BROCHURE THAT I DON'T REALLY NEED.

I DESPERATELY NEED A GOOD PAYING CLIENT. FAST.

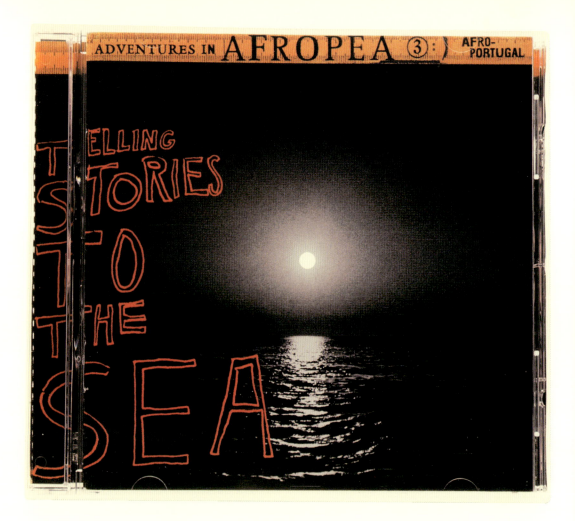

TELLING STORIES TO THE SEA, a collection of Afro-Portuguese music on David Byrne's Luaka Bop label, brought together a variety of artists from Angola, Cape Verde, Saò Tome, Principe and Lisbon, all thematically linked by the shared experience of Portuguese colonialism. The music has a melancholy flavor, born of the slave trade, described poetically on the liner notes to this compilation as "bittersweet sadness and rugged soul, tempered by a uniquely tropical funk, where moody melodies float above dreamy grooves." It is also considered an archetype for the Blues, and Brazilian and Cuban music.

The job was the studio's reward after a rather unglamorous assignment to lay out an advertisement for David Bryne. "Someone must have noticed that the ad was done carefully, and we got a call from his office," says Sagmeister. "The brief

was short and very nice. David played some of the music and said that the cover should be beautiful and shouldn't look like it's been produced in Africa—it could be clear that this is a compilation from a record company in New York. He gave me a video of the Cape Verde islands, which looked really depressive—stone islands with very little vegetation. The islands were always poor and the Portuguese used to go through there to pick up slaves on their way to Brazil, which is why so much Brazilian music sounds similar to this."

To link the several different artists and styles on the album, the studio had a hole drilled through the center of the entire booklet. The hole showed the "loss of center" as Sagmeister put it, suggesting the displacement of people from the islands. Each page of the CD booklet was given a

different treatment relating to the artist, which improvises on the punched hole theme. The sun was punched out of the cover, followed by an ear piercing, a record center, fish eye, target and so on. To evoke the sad, raw feeling of the music, all type and images had a rough-hewn hand-made feel. The cover type took the unprecedented step of running across from the spine to the booklet. "The whole feel was crudeness and unrefined beauty," says Veronica Oh. "Nothing is perfect, with all different typefaces, slightly skewed, mixed up handwriting and crude illustrations. We photocopied the type several times to give it the right look."

One rule of CD design, according to Sagmeister is that "if the music you package is crap, your cover is worth nothing." In this instance, happily, the cover graced a CD of evocative and powerful tunes.

1. Mona Ki Ngi Xiça *BONGA*

(The Child I'm Leaving Behind)

FROM the album *Angola '72* WRITTEN BY *Barcelo de Carvalho "Bonga"* ℗ 1972 VIDISCO

Attention! I'm in mortal danger And here I will go away ·
warned you · She will stay here and I will go away ·
This child of mine · Evil people are after her ·
This child of mine · On a tide of *M I S F O R T U N E*,
God gave me this offspring · That I brought into the
world · And she will stay here · When I am *G O N E*

② S A L A L É

(White Ant) **VUM VUM**

from the album *SALALÉ* Written by *Vum Vum* Produced by *Vum Vum* Licensed from *Voz de Cabo Verde*
Oh Salale my home · My true bosom friend · Only you really know · The suffering in this
life of mine · Salale, I beg you · When I die one day · Cry for my *M I S F O R T U N E*
beneath my roof · Don't take me to the church · Salale! Salale! · Salale, oh my star!
You're my mother who bore me · My deep peace and my refuge · In a world that is still
mine · Salale, I wish that life were a dream · And that my mother would give birth
dreaming · And would suffer no more · Salale, my wife · Twin child of Mother Nature ·
Day and night, every day · With patience and pain we were raised · Salale, we thought
that our land was ours · But she became the daughter of strangers · Salale, oh my God,
where are you hiding? · When I was still a child · We were always waiting for you · Salale,
we keep on waiting · Day after day · Come back tomorrow · We're tired of waiting · *THIS
IS ALL WE WANT*

3. SODADE

(Homesick)

Césaria Évora

Who leads you on · This long journey · Who led you on this long journey · THIS ROAD LEADS TO SÃO TOMÉ

IF YOU WRITE me · then I'll write you · if you forget me · THEN I'll forget you

HOMESICK, HOMESICK,

HOMESICK

For MY home island, SÃO NICOLAU until the day You RETURN

from the album *MISS PERFUMADO*
written by *Armando Cabral* and *Luis Morais*
produced by *Paulino Vieira* executive producer: *JOSÉ*
DA SILVA
published by *Les Éditions de Berthelève/*
Biska LUSAFRICA Sony Music Publishing Company from
Editions LUSAFRICA/BISKA LUSAFRICA and France

4. N'Zambi · (God) André Mingas [From
the album *Coisas Da Vida*] · Written by
Liceu Vieira Dias · Produced by
Roberto Sant'ana · ℗ 1991 BMI –
Valentim de Carvalho] · N'Zambi · God
My God draw nearer to me · Oh! My
shall praise me · My God · Oh God
of truth! · The truth of the world ·
The truth of hunger · The truth of
misery · and of the wretchedness of
slavery · Oh! My God · You shall
praise me · You shall praise me ·
Nb Legi Caçô Modá Bó · You Let the Dog
Bite You! África · [From the
album *Cosias Da Vida*] · África Negra
de Sab . . . ee · . . . EEN · Let you
yourself be . . . . . . bite by the
dog · And it's essential to know the
lcandoo . . . . the ocean
warned you not to . . . . observing the
without first · . . . observing the wave ·
You let the dog bite you · And only
afterwards did you tie it up · Oh Mama
oh Mama · life is essential to know · The
ground on which . . . . you walk

MAY 1 1995
MET UP WITH DAVID BYRNE TODAY
AND WE ARE GOING TO DESIGN A COVER
FOR HIS LABEL. YES! OH, IT ALL WORKS OUT
SO UNBELIEVABLY LIKE NEVER BEFORE:
HAVEN'T WORKED A WEEKEND IN AT LEAST
A YEAR AND GOT OUT EVERY NIGHT PRETTY
MUCH AT SEVEN.
THATS HOW IT SHOULD BE:
WORK HARD DURING THE DAY but
NO NIGHTS, — NO WEEKENDS.

WENT UP TO MIDTOWN, LOOKED UP,
SAW ALL THE BUILDINGS AND IT JUST
SCREAMED IN ME:
BOY, AM I GLAD TO LIVE IN NEW YORK.
AM I GLAD (AND THIS AFTER HAVING LIVED HERE FOR FIVE YEARS
— I COULDN'T STAND HONG KONG AFTER
TWO)

THE NIELDS, AN ALTERNATIVE FOLK
BAND made up of two sisters named
Nields and three men named David, came
to the Sagmeister studio with a pile of
lyrics for its album, *Gotta Get Over Greta.*
Since the songwriter Narissa Nields was
an English-literature graduate from Yale
University, Sagmeister felt obliged to pay
close attention to her words, and after the
Nields' had left, sat down underlining
memorable images in the lyrics. He then
made pencil drawings corresponding to
each underlined word or phrase, and
Xeroxed the result to increase the weight
of the pencil lines. The final design, influenced by the style of 1950s lottery cards,
appears with a short-width CD booklet to
draw attention to the printing on the CD.

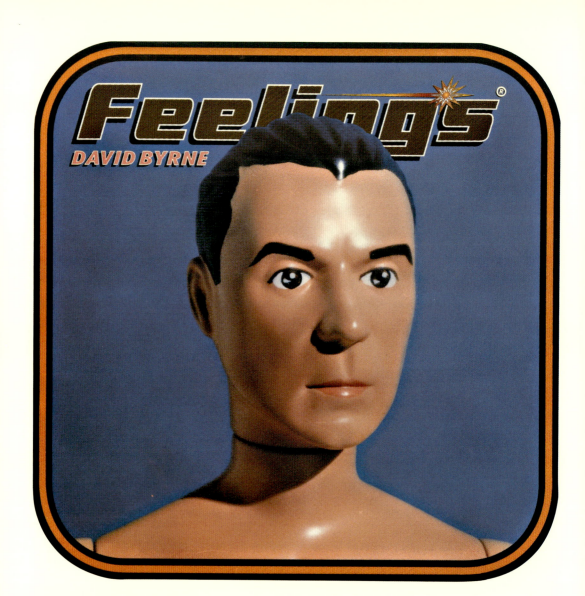

WAS AT the BIENNALE IN VENICE and REALLY ENJOYED IT. PROBABLY THE BEST ART EXHIBIT I HAVE EVER SEEN.
I WAS MOST SURPRISED BY HOW EXCITED I GOT ABOUT PURELY FORMAL PIECES, — HOW THE MORE IDEA/CONCEPT BASED WORK WAS, AT LEAST IN MY MIND, PUSHED TO THE BACKGROUND. THAT SHOULD KEEP ME THINKING ABOUT my OWN WORK (e.g.: MY SILLY LITTLE STYLE = FART THEORY, HA HA..)

THE ROCK—POP STAR RECAST as a plastic action figure was one of those ironic, off-beat David Byrne ideas that turned out to have considerable mileage. It played with the notion of a pop star as a commodity, and like, say, the early Talking Heads title *More Songs About Buildings and Food* offered a faux-naif response to the commercial nature of the music industry. Though Sagmeister's policy is not to accept CD packaging projects where a design idea is pre-set by the client, David Byrne was a worthy exception. "He is smarter than I am, and that makes an ideal client," says Sagmeister.

The original scheme, to create a computer-generated doll and position it in various places around the city, posed some problems, however. The production studio contracted to scan Byrne's head and digitally render the doll was unable to achieve a convincing look. "I was adamant that the doll had to be realistic and not computery," says Sagmeister. "If we weren't careful it would look like a Kraftwerk cover."

Salvation came in the form of Yuji Yoshimoto, a Brooklyn-based model-maker with a portfolio of work produced for advertising shoots, from giant strawberries to baseball player's heads. Yoshimoto was a David Byrne fan, and agreed to build four different model heads for a pinhead budget. The computer-rendered version of Byrne was scrapped and the project restarted with >

Feelings
DAVID BYRNE ®

I JUST COULD NOT BELIEVE THERE WERE MORE people ON EVERY SINGLE STREET OF VENICE THAN IN THE ACTUAL EXHIBITION AREA OF THE BIENNALE ITSELF. HAVING LIVED IN NEW YORK FOR SO LONG ITS EASY TO FORGET HOW MUCH CONTEMPORARY ART IS (IGNORED EVERYWHERE ELSE IN THE WORLD. (THE ONLY OTHER EXCEPTION MIGHT BE LONDON) - ITS A COMPLETE GHETTO. ITS HILARIOUS WHEN THE ART WORLD TALKS ABOUT THE "OVEREXPOSURE" OF ITS 'SUPERSTARS' LIKE HIRST OR SALLE, WHEN 99% OF THE POPULATION HAS NOT A CLUE ABOUT THEIR WORK. JUST TALK TO PEOPLE IN OHIO OR CAIRO OR MOSCOW →

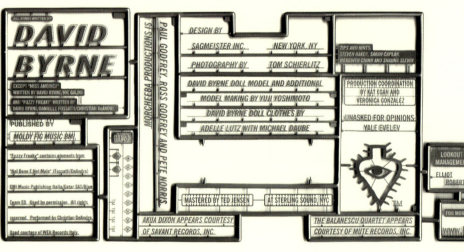

DAVID BYRNE

ALL SONGS WRITTEN BY

EXCEPT "MISS AMERICA"
WRITTEN BY DAVID BYRNE/JOE GALDO
AND "FUZZY FREAKY" WRITTEN BY
DAVID BYRNE/DANIELLE FOSSATI/CHRISTIAN DeANDRE

PUBLISHED BY
MOLDY FIG MUSIC BMI.

"Fuzzy Freaky" contains elements from
"Nel Bene E Nel Male" (Fossati/DeAndre)
EMI Music Publishing Italia/Gatar SAS/Blue
Team ED. Used by permission. All rights
reserved. Performed by Christian DeAndre
Used courtesy of WEA Records Italy.

MORCHEEBA PRODUCTIONS IS PAUL GODFREY, ROSS GODFREY AND PETE NORRIS.

DESIGN BY
SAGMEISTER INC.   NEW YORK, NY
PHOTOGRAPHY BY   TOM SCHIERLITZ
DAVID BYRNE DOLL MODEL AND ADDITIONAL
MODEL MAKING BY YUJI YOSHIMOTO
DAVID BYRNE DOLL CLOTHES BY
ADELLE LUTZ WITH MICHAEL DAUBE

MASTERED BY TED JENSEN   AT STERLING SOUND, NYC

AKUA DIXON APPEARS COURTESY
OF SAVANT RECORDS, INC.

THE BALANESCU QUARTET APPEARS
COURTESY OF MUTE RECORDS, INC.

TIPS AND HINTS, STEVEN HAKER, SARAH CAPLAN,
MEREDITH CHINN AND SHAUNA SLEVIN

PRODUCTION COORDINATION
BY KAT EGAN AND
VERONICA GONZALEZ

UNASKED FOR OPINIONS,
YALE EVELEV

LOOKOUT
MANAGEMENT

ELLIOT
ROBERTS

FOR MORE INFORMATION GO TO:
www.luakabop.com

I was touring recently and one of my shows took me to a little town in Austria, near where Stefan had grown up, and where he began his career. This was pointed out by some of the local club staff, who knew Stefan when he lived there, and knew we had worked together. I therefore began to take special interest in the surroundings, to gain some insights into my friend and collaborator. It was a fall holiday weekend, and in a field down the road from the club there had been erected a huge tower of logs, several meters high. A crowd was gathering and vendors were selling wursts and other tasty treats. Children ran here and there as darkness fell.

At the appointed hour the tower was set ablaze by large men, flames licked up the sides, the heat was immense and sparks flew into the air, threatening the surrounding houses and nearby forest. Children continued to frolic in the glow of the fire, running amongst the shower of falling sparks. I said to a fellow musician that in America there would be so many fire restrictions, barriers and regulations surrounding a spectacle like this that its power and dangerous beauty would be watered down and destroyed. Soon the flames reached the top of the tower, where a giant dummy of a witch was perched. All cheered as she went up in flames, bits of her rising to the heavens to set the pearly gates on fire.

This is what it's like working with Sagmeister Inc.

• David Byrne

I MEAN: THE COKE CAN HAS SO MUCH MORE CULTURAL IMPACT THAN - SAY - A WALTER DE MARIA.
PITY THE GUYS WHO DESIGNED THE FORMER ARE NOT AS TALENTED AS THE LATER. OR PITY WALTER DOES NOT GET AS MUCH EXPOSURE AS THE CAN. THIS, OF COURSE, IS AS MUCH THE FAULT OF THE ART WORLD AS ANYBODY'S, WITH ITS EXCLUSIVE OPENINGS, ART SPEAK BULLSHIT, ETC.

1. FUZZY FREAKY 4:58
2. MISS AMERICA 4:19
3. A SOFT SEDUCTION 3:00
4. DANCE ON VASELINE 5:07
5. THE GATES OF PARADISE 3:31
6. AMNESIA 3:26
7. YOU DON'T KNOW ME 2:28
8. DADDY GO DOWN 4:06
9. FINITE = ALRIGHT 2:24
WICKED
10. LITTLE DOLL 2:54
11. BURNT BY THE SUN 4:21
12. THE CIVIL WARS 3:41
14. THEY ARE IN LOVE 4:08

Luaka Bop, Inc.
©1997 Warner Bros. Records Inc.
Made in U.S.A.

I GUESS THE ONLY TWO 20th CENTURY FINE ARTISTS WHO HAD REAL IMPACT ON WORLD CULTURE WOULD BE PICASSO AND TO A LESSER DEGREE, WARHOL.
AND YET, IT IS POSSIBLE TO CREATE HIGH QUALITY WORK AND WIN THE ADMIRATION OF PRACTICALLY EVERYBODY:
JUST LOOK AT THE VIETNAM MEMORIAL, THE SIMPSONS, THE VOLKSWAGEN BEETLE, THE EIFFEL TOWER.

SURE IS, ITS MUCH EASIER TO CREATE SOMETHING GOOD FOR THE ENJOYMENT OF A SMALL GROUP OF PEOPLE THAN TO CREATE HIGH QUALITY FOR THE MASSES. IN MY LITTLE WORLD: ITS SO MUCH MORE DIFFICULT TO DESIGN A GOOD COVER FOR A HUGE BAND THAN FOR A TINY ONE.

On my Feelings CD package I knew I wanted to portray myself as a doll. It seemed a perfect image of contemporary consumerism, celebrity, blah blah blah. And I could look good, in a plastic-y sort of way. So it could be a gag, but with something to say. Something that sounds tedious in words, but hilarious in image. We went through various attempts at getting this look right, from me inserting my head into a 3D laser scanner to computer renderings. None of it worked, and we knew it. Stefan soon realized it had to be "real"…and found Yuji, a model maker, in Brooklyn, who made the final dolls.

Meanwhile, Sagmeister Inc. was taking the concept further, for example, developing type that would be made on a snap apart plastic model framework. Other refinements followed, one of the best, in my opinion, was the rounded corners Stefan proposed for the CD booklet (these were, sadly, only made on the initial run). To me, this tiny touch referred both to contemporary groovy cyber design and all its clichés, and to the rounded edges of toy packages hanging at Toys 'R us on 14th Street.

• David Byrne

WENT TO AN OPENING AT the Guggenheim WITH ANNI. WE RUN into a FRIEND, HE KNOWS US BOTH BUT HAS MET ANNI ONLY A couple of TIMES SO I make SURE TO INTRODUCE her AGAIN. MY FRIEND does NOT LISTEN SO WHEN HE INTRODUCES US TO HIS FRIENDS HE HAS TO ASK ANNI FOR her NAME. ANNI, HAVING JUST BEEN INTRODUCED, IS SURPRISED BY THE QUESTION AND ASKS: "WHO, ME?" PROMPTING MY FRIEND TO INTRODUCE HER AS "HUMI."

It's very difficult to describe our working relationship. To me it seems like a kind of telepathy. The vision, direction and attitude of a project are realized and apprehended very quickly by both of us. Poorly articulated verbal concepts become clearer as they are seen in sketch, mockup or layout. And we're ready to go. So there is very little talk or discussion at that point, except for some laughter and my constant griping about text legibility.

• David Byrne

WHEN I LAUGH HE gets INSECURE AND ASKS ANNI FOR HER NAME AGAIN.

"HE? ANNI!" MY GIRLFRIEND REPLIES, UPON WHICH SHE IS INTRODUCED AS "MEANNI". SHE HAS BEEN MEANNI EVER SINCE.

NOT FOR USE IN WATER

Relaxed	Relieved	Low	Comfortless	Angry	Irritated	Happy	Starry-Eyed
Contented	Undisturbed	Gloomy	Dismal	Mad	Furious	Satisfied	Cheerful
At Ease	Composed	Depressed	Sorrowful	Frantic	Provoked	Optimistic	Jubilant
Bored	Calm	Sad	Down	Uptight	Upset	Euphoric	Delighted
Snug	Cool	Miserable	Blue	Touchy	Crazy	Thrilled	Glad
So-So	Balanced	Discouraged	Dejected	Hysterical	Agitated	Tickled	Elated
Peaceful	Gentle	Heartbroken	Pathetic	Infuriated	Violent	Jolly	Upbeat
Rested	Melow	Unhappy	Somber	Pissed Off	Wild	Excited	Merry
Comfortable	Mild	Crushed	Crummy	Enraged	Turbulent	Enthusiastic	Pleased

> a Tom Schierlitz photoshoot of Byrne, who portrayed each of four emotional states—happy, angry, sad and content. Yoshimoto then modeled the four versions in clay, made corrections with Byrne present for reference, fabricated a mold, cast the dolls in plastic and hand painted them—all within ten days. Sagmeister was so impressed with the results that he decided to also have lyrics and song titles produced by Yoshimoto, in the style of a twist-and-snap toy kit. Though the results were equally impressive, in the final outcome, the packaging budget did not stretch to including color printing on all of the inner pages of the booklet, and the

extra detail was somewhat lost. "We might as well have constructed the type in Photoshop," says Sagmeister.

Under the CD itself, the studio designed a "Build Your Own David Byrne Mood Computer" chart, with instructions to break off the teeth of the jewel box hub and spin the disk, printed with a red arrow, to determine the user's current emotional state. The color codes in the computer chart were also applied to each song according to their emotional content.

Extra details included copyline parodies, such as "Parts are not interchangeable with other dolls." Curiously, turning under the glare of photographer Tom

Schierlitz's lighting, the "calm" version of the plastic doll seemed to come alive. "Tom took about ten shots of the content doll for the cover," says Karlsson, "and each expression was surprisingly different from the next. It was a strange effect from a plastic model." A horror movie serial may be in the works.

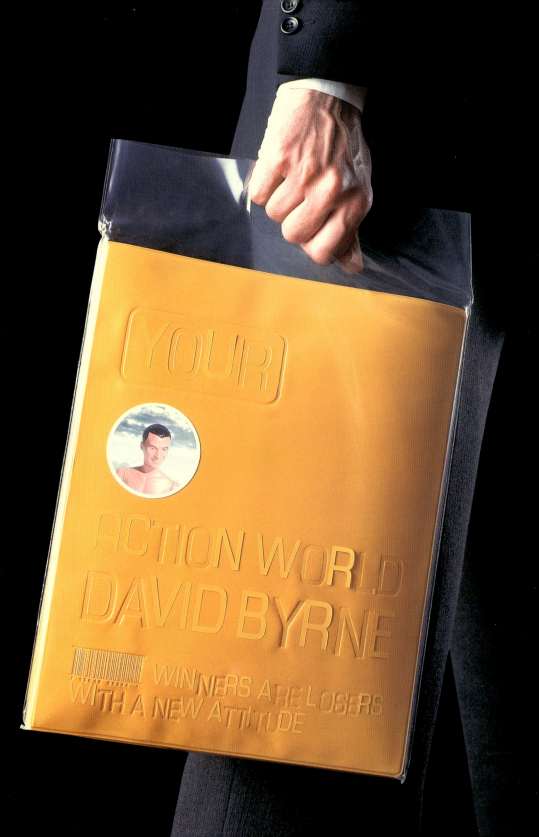

YOUR ACTION WORLD DAVID BYRNE was a book that grew out of a catalogue and mutated into a toy-like product, complete with floppy plastic cover and heavy matt varnish.

The first edition was sold in a clear shopping bag, incorporating an effect that established the unsettling tone of the book. Half the book's title was embossed on the actual book (the embedded letters "suggesting the impression that self-improvement has on your mind," according to Sagmeister) and half was printed on the clear plastic bag. Thus when the book was removed from the bag, the title—and its meaning—effectively came apart.

Inside was a disorienting mix of displaced images and messages drawn from the language of corporate and self-help movement America, together with Byrne's photography and exhibition artwork. The endpapers were devoted to corporate color combinations, chapter headings were indicated by corporate-style information graphics with familiar sounding, yet nonsensical maxims, and in the middle was a photocomic story. The images for the story were taken from stock photo books, with speech balloon text derived from Byrne's "Acoustiguide" soundtrack of rap lyrics, meditation tapes and business maxims. A beaming baby, for instance, is pictured commenting, "let me start with one major warning."

The resulting assemblage was a distinctive, if somewhat baffling publication. "It was an unusual project for me because of its ambiguousness," says Sagmeister. "I was not quite sure about it when we were working on it, but on the other hand I saw that if it came straight out and said 'this is this' it would be finger wagging and preachy."

After the pleasant CD experience I approached Stefan about working together more collaboratively on a book project that was scheduled to come out in time for a museum show of my photo-based art in Trieste. The Italians suggested a "catalogue" and I countered with "what if it were more of a stand-alone book?—a thing in itself, as they say". They liked this idea, loved Stefan's other work, and we were off on another nutty project.

The work that was being shown was inspired by advertising, motivational calendars, and corporate inspirational literature, so I suggested we use these kinds of things as models for this book. But Stefan soon pointed out that my idealized view of these materials outstripped the reality. In reality they were pretty boring, conservative and often very "tastefully" designed. We had to take it a step further, and create some kind of hybrid.

Other than the pieces that were the focus of the show, which look like ads, I wanted Stefan to "curate" the work that would be in the book. I brought piles of work prints, odds and ends, written and

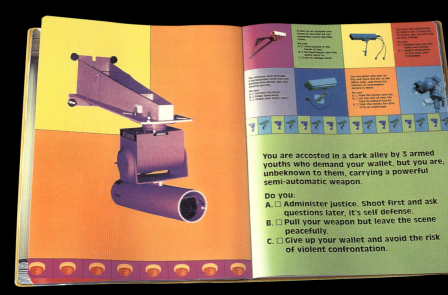

You are accosted in a dark alley by 3 armed youths who demand your wallet, but you are, unbeknown to them, carrying a powerful semi-automatic weapon.

Do you:

A. ☐ Administer justice. Shoot first and ask questions later, it's self defense.
B. ☐ Pull your weapon but leave the scene peacefully.
C. ☐ Give up your wallet and avoid the risk of violent confrontation.

Your Canceled Check Is Your Receipt. No Purchase Necessary. Employees And Their Families Are Not Eligible. Sanitized For Your Protection. Beware Of Dog. Contestants Have Been Briefed On Some Questions Before The Show. Limited Time Offer. Call Now To Ensure Prompt Delivery. You Must Be Present To Win. Slightly Higher West Of The Mississippi. Avoid Contact With Skin. Shading Within A Garment May Occur. Keep Away From Fire Or Flames. Replace With Same Type. Approved For Veterans. Price Does Not Include Taxes. No Solicitors. No Alcohol, Dogs Or Horses. Some Equipment Shown Is Optional. Reproduction Strictly Prohibited. Driver Does Not Carry Cash.

graphic, to his penthouse studio, and he chose, more or less, what would work...and then he, I assume inspired by what was happening, created his own work. The pages of corporate colors are all his, as are the "chapter headings" using motivational graphs and lingo. And likewise, I was inspired to create new work for the book and to write additional texts that would play off and link some of the images.

Then in a final perverse stroke, Stefan suggested it be sold in its own shopping bag, which would contain half of the cover text. Having worked with him before I knew that Stefan has a genius for charming clients (not me, in this case, but the publisher) into incorporating manufacturing innovations into the design.

Well, it worked, the Italians loved the bag idea. Even if their manufacturing of this element left something to be desired. Sadly, the stodgy Yanks opted to lose the bag...but did get much wider distribution than the Italians. So, the compromise, in my view, was worth it.

• David Byrne

AFTER LISTENING TO the hardcore thrash of Pro-Pain several times, Sagmeister began to hear what he called the "beauty in the noise," and found an image that seemed to represent the same contrast. Jeffrey Silverthorne's 1974 morgue photograph *Woman Who Died in Her Sleep* was both horrific and compelling, in no small part because of the dead woman's evident youth and beauty. The viewer's eye is immediately drawn to the surgeon's savage Y-cut—a standard procedure for autopsies—and crude stitches. Yet the uncannily restful pose creates a striking contrast. "I remember being very anxious about using it on the cover," says Sagmeister, "and was looking for a replacement photograph, for what seemed forever." In the process, Sagmeister went through the vast archives of police photography on New York's Center Street, and found a selection of images of crime scenes suitable for the inside of the CD booklet (next pages). Still nothing surfaced to match the power of the Silverthorne shot, and since the band's singer Gary Meskil was happy with it, Sagmeister decided to face the proverbial music and use this version of the cover. In order to invite feedback, he included the studio's

phone number on the sleeve.

The CD was titled *The Truth Hurts,* and the backlash came immediately. A European distributor refused to carry the sleeve, forcing the record label to issue the CD with a plain white cover in Europe, which fans could mail in to receive the original design. Several reviewers voiced criticisms of the cover, and one music magazine refused to review the album. More disturbing to Sagmeister, however, was an unexpected flurry of positive phone calls from Pro-Pain fans who thought "the cut-up chick was cool," as he paraphrases the reactions.

The final verdict for Sagmeister came a couple of years later, when press photos were circulating of the students responsible for the concurrent Columbine School massacre, wearing T-shirts for Rammstein, a German hardcore band known using for violent imagery in its CDs. Sagmeister realized that, knowing Rammstein's distributor, he might easily have worked for them too. "Since I don't know if violent imagery has an influence on their fans, I'd rather err on the side of caution," he says. "I learned that this is very much a matter of context. When the Silverthorne image is hanging on the

walls of the New Museum of Contemporary Art—which it has—that is perfectly fine. But I really think it is wrong to use it as a CD cover."

The record company has subsequently issued the CD with a replacement cover, using one of the interior images. "I am glad the woman is gone," says Sagmeister, "and that episode is over."

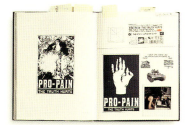

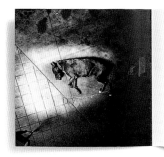

I AM TALKING
SO MUCH
ABOUT 'TOUCHING DESIGN'!

FUNNY, THOUGH,
THAT I STILL DO
ALL MY WORK
CONVENTIONALLY,
TRADITIONALLY,
WITHOUT REALLY BRINGING
IN TOO MUCH 'TOUCHING'!

I HAVE TO
CHANGE THAT,
- JUST TALK AND NO
ACTION IS JUST PLAIN SILLY.

223

INTO ANOTHER LIGHT

THE LAST RECORDINGS made by jazz guitarist Sonny Sharrock before he died were
compiled for release under the title *Into
Another Light*. The title's spiritual connotations and Sharrock's free-form, distor-ted,
wall of noise approach to jazz guitar suggested a non-figurative interpretation.
Sagmeister, commissioned to design the
sleeve by Enemy Records in 1994, found
what he considered a perfect match in the
cameraless photography of artist Adam
Fuss. Fuss's photograms and pinhole
photographs were evocative explorations
in the transmutative qualities of light.
"He had done these spirals of light which
always reminded me of what people say
they have seen when they are revived

from death," says Sagmeister.

Having been briefly introduced to the
artist at a restaurant, Sagmeister called
Fuss and asked if he would grant the
rights to use some of his images. After
seeing Sagmeister's comps, Fuss agreed
and the completed design was packaged
inside an opaque black jewel case. The
project was well received by all except
Sagmeister's accountant. In the studio's
early eagerness to design CDs, it had
taken on a project that paid a total design
fee of $250.

THE PHONE RANG: "This is Lou Reed. I saw your CD covers. Can I come over?" When Sagmeister received the call on a warm September day in 1995, he was afraid it might be a joke. Would the rock and roll legend, collaborator with Andy Warhol, writer of "All Tomorrow's Parties" and "Caroline Says" materialize in the humble little Sagmeister studio? The prospect seemed unlikely until the bell rang and the building doorman announced over the intercom that Lou Reed wanted to come up.

"Great building with great doormen," said Reed, walking in a minute later, "with excellent taste in music." The doorman reported subsequently that he had been listening to Reed's *Magic and Loss* on a Walkman when the artist walked in, and had seized the opportunity to ask the rock and roll animal to sign a copy of the tape.

The title of Reed's upcoming CD was to be *Set the Twilight Reeling*. Out of principle, Sagmeister pressed Reed on the direction of the music rather than his ideas for the packaging. Reed's response was unequivocal: "It's about the transformation of a dark prince character into a much more positive person," he said. Few rock music fans were unaware of Reed's career progression, from the founder of a New York underground art rock group to glam-rocker to junkie-rocker to poet-rocker and his recent coupling with performance artist Laurie Anderson. With this insight, the title, and Reed's zealous pronouncement, Sagmeister produced a cover concept: a bright, beaming portrait of Reed, shot by Timothy Greenfield Sanders inside a jewel case tinted in dark blue. As the booklet is removed from the case, the yellow filtered out by the blue is revealed, and Reed is effectively transformed by a golden light. Inside, the back of the booklet, the CD and the tray card form a diagram of an eclipse, "the ultimate twilight," according to Sagmeister. >

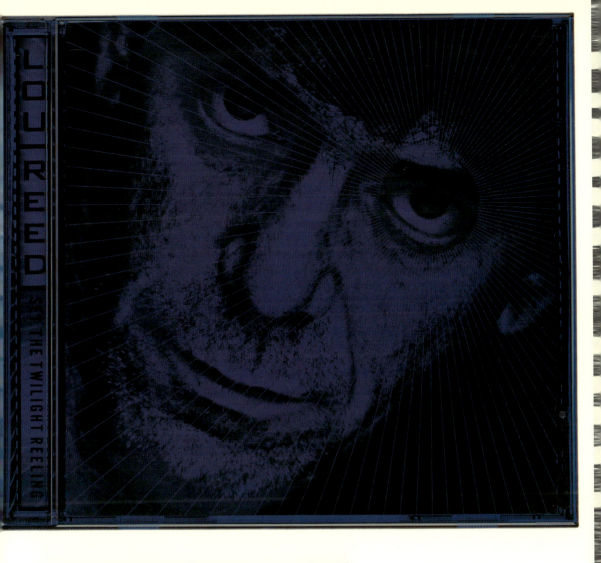

> Several ideas in the booklet were explored further in subsequent projects for Reed. The lyrics, for example, are designed in a way that reflects their content (an idea developed typographically in Reed's book of lyrics, pp.234-237). The lyrics to "Egg Cream," Reed's song about a particularly tasty version of the soda drink served at "Becky's" on King's Highway in Brooklyn, are set in the style of an old New York Coffee shop sign (p.227). The work of Middle Eastern artist Shirin Neshat inspired Sagmeister to hand-write the copy over a photograph of Reed's face. This idea was particularly popular with Reed and became the basis for a poster advertising the CD (right). The lettering effectively conveyed the personal, confessional nature of the songs on the album. It also looked good after eroding from a few days existence on bill-posting sites around New York, torn and buried among other fragments of wheat-pasted images (p.231).

The hue and opacity of the blue-tinted jewel case was particularly difficult. By testing the cover with photographers' light gels beforehand, the studio established that too much opacity would obscure the image beneath. If the color was slightly off, the yellow portrait of Reed would turn under the blue case into an ugly brown rather than black, "thus not transforming a black prince but a brown one," as Sagmeister puts it. >

Set the Twilight Reeling

IN THE POCKET OF THE
IN THE RUSHING
OF THE BLOOD HEART
IN THE MUSCLE OF MY

TAKE
ME FOR
WHAT
I AM
A STAR
NEWLY
EMERGING
LONG
SIMMERING
EXPLODES
INSIDE
THE SELF
IS REELING

A SOUL SINGER STANDS ON THE STAGE
THE SPOTLIGHT SHOWS
HIM SWEATING... HE SINKS TO ONE KNEE
SEEMS TO CRY
THE HORNS ARE UNRELENTING
BUT AS THE DRUMS BEAT
HE FINDS HIMSELF
GROWING HARD
IN THE MICROPHONE'S
FACE HE SEES
HER FACE
GROWING
LARGE

SEX
IN THE
MINDFULL
MINDLESS
LOVE

I ACCEPT THE NEW
FOUND MAN
AND SET THE
TWILIGHT
REELING

AT SAM THE MOON AND SUN
SIT SET BEFORE MY WINDOW... LIGHT GLANCES
OFF THE BLUE GLASS WE SET... RIGHT BEFORE
THE WINDOW AND YOU WHO ACCEPT
IN YOUR SOUL AND YOUR HEAD...

AND THE SWELLING
CRESCENDO NO LONGER
RETARDS
I ACCEPT THE NEW FOUND MAN
AND SET THE
TWILIGHT
REELING

WHAT WAS MISUNDERSTOOD... WHAT WAS THOUGHT
OF WITH DREAD... A NEW SELF IS BORNE...
THE OTHER SELF IS DEAD... I ACCEPT THE NEW
FOUND MAN AND
SET THE TWILIGHT REELING

SET
THE
TWILIGHT
REELING

AS THE TWILIGHT
SUN BURST GLEAMS
AS THE CADMIUM MAN IT SETS
AS I LOSE ALL MY REGRETS AND
SET THE TWILIGHT REELING
I ACCEPT THE NEW FOUND MAN
AND SET THE
TWILIGHT REELING

THE
NEW
ALBUM

LOU
REED

> Sagmeister advised the record company and midwestern manufacturer to match the color carefully, but two weeks after the artwork was shipped, the tinted cases returned with the wrong color match. "We were devastated," says Sagmeister. "We wailed, cried and complained, but just received the standard reply that this is the closest the tinting could get.

Unbeknownst to the designers, however, the international arm of Warner Bros. was meanwhile manufacturing the CD case with a different producer. The result was perfect. Immediately, the entire job was transfered to this plant, leaving the midwestern manufacturer with 100,000 next-to-useless blue-tinted jewel cases.

> *I feel that design affords another avenue into the imaginary field of the writer's concerns. Sagmeister's graphics are always blended effortlessly into the totality of the the original concept—his acute wit and style are a roadmap to the pleasures available to the viewer/listener.*
>
> **• Lou Reed**

The end result was a production success, but Sagmeister had a number of creative qualms to deal with. "I remember hating the cover for the whole time we worked on it, thinking it—among other things—too close to the H.P. Zinker concept," he says. The absolution came—as it had before—with public approval. "Immediately after its release, everybody seemed so positive about it. David Letterman called it the coolest cover he'd seen—on air—and Henry Rollins faxed us a congratulatory note," says Sagmeister. "I, like a flag in the wind, loved it too."

I grew up on a military base in the 1960s. Over my bed hung a poster that my father had brought home from Vietnam. It was a faux travel poster printed in dark greens and khaki, camouflage colors. It read "VISIT VIETNAM! See Exciting Places! Meet Interesting People! And Kill Them!" I am not sure why this poster he not the

17 IRVING PLACE AT 15TH
3RD AVE)
THE
THE NEW ALBUM
TAKE ME FOR WHAT I AM A STAR NEWLY EMERGING LONG SIMMERING EXPLODES INSIDE THE SELF IS REELING
TWILIGHT REELING
IN THE RUSHING THE BLOOD
SEX
FOUND
SUN
AT SAM THE MOON
SIT SET BEFORE MY WINDOW ... LIGHT GLANCES
OFF THE BLUE
RIGHT BEFORE
WHO ACCEPT

ALTHOUGH LOU REED'S 2000 album *Ecstasy* dwelled on the elusiveness of ecstatic moments, Sagmeister determined that the cover should attempt to capture him in the midst of one. Traditionally (before the drug was invented) referring to a moment of prophetic inspiration, or an exalted state of feeling that excludes thought, the word ecstasy has also gained more sexual connotations. After discussing the subject with Reed, Sagmeister returned with an idea: As an accomplished photographer, Reed could shoot images of himself at the moment of orgasm. "He looked at me and said it sounded like a great concept for somebody else," says Sagmeister.

Reed eventually came around to the idea, however, while he was working with Robert Wilson, the theater set

1 Paranoia Key of E • 2 Mystic Child • 3 Mad • 4 Ecstasy • 5 Modern Dance • 6 Tatters • 7 Future Farmers of America • 8 Turning Time Around • 9 White Prism • 10 Rock Minuet • 11 Baton Rouge • 12 Like a Possum • 13 Rouge • 14 Big Sky • Produced by Lou Reed and Hal Willner for Sister Ray Enterprises, Inc. • Reprise Records, a Time Warner Company, 3300 Warner Blvd., Burbank, CA 91505-4694, 75 Rockefeller Plaza, New York, NY 10019-6908. World Wide Web: http://www.repriserec.com/ ⓒ ⓟ 2000 Reprise Records for the U.S. and WEA International Inc. for the world outside the U.S. Made in U.S.A. All rights reserved. Unauthorized duplication is a violation of applicable laws. www.loureed.org www.loureed.com www.repriserec.com/loureed

designer and director, on another pro-ject. The photographs were to be taken with a giant format Polaroid camera, one of five in the country that produces poster-size images (20 by 24 inches).

Despite the sexual premise of the photoshoot, the portraits gained an unearthly quality more reminiscent of the mystical sense of the word ecstasy. Wilson's lighting and the backdrop, a heavy, velvet-like cloth with a glimmer-ing line of red light evoked an epic the-atrical setting in which Reed's head seems almost disembodied, his expression caught as an artist would paint a martyr. "We were all quite happy with the different overtones," says Sagmeister.

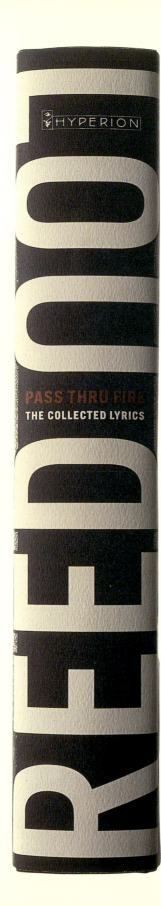

A peace poster designed by Tom Geismar for a 1985 American and Japanese exhibition called "Images For Survival." The poster was a simple photograph of a young person's hand, palm face-up, cropped to fill the vertical proportion. It offered friendship, and/or the statement "enough; stop the madness of war." I appreciated its effortlessness, simple on the surface, yet layered with nuclear overtones. But what to...

FOR THE 420-PAGE BOOK of Lou Reed's collected lyrics, the studio made an ambitious attempt at building an interpretive typographical voice that would emerge like a different character in each chapter. Given the weight of tradition in the art of book design, and accompanying reader expectations that type play the role of a neutral vessel, it was a difficult exercise to sustain over several hundred pages. The experiment nevertheless produced a number of successful moments, as well as some less successful, and meanwhile hurled the studio into a mire of technical problems.

The project began, simply enough, with the cover, which features a self-portrait photograph by Reed and embossed, hand-rendered typography resembling scars or hand-cut strips of clay. Sagmeister then discussed with Reed his recollections of the albums he had worked on, from the legendary 1967 Velvet Underground & Nico album (with the Andy Warhol banana cover) to the most recent CD, *Ecstasy*. With this insight, the studio began working up typographic treatments for each chapter (corresponding with a particular album).

At its best, the typographic voice has a flair and expressiveness akin to >

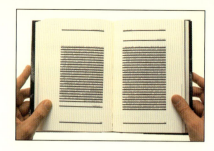

JUST SAW AN ALFRED HITCHCOCK EXHIBIT AT MOMA. THEY SHOWED HIS CORRESPONDENCE WITH THE STUDIO ABOUT THE TITLE FOR VERTIGO, HE WANTED TO CALL IT VERTIGO THE STUDIO WANTED SOME OTHER SILLY TITLE.

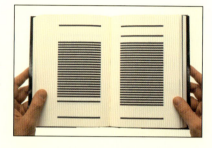

I JUST COULD NOT BELIEVE THAT EVEN GIANTS like HIM HAD to FIGHT ABOUT all THAT BULL SHIT. UNBELIEVABLE.

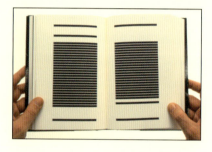

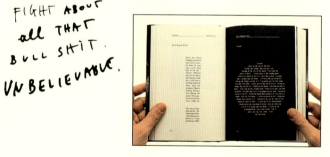

Something different every day. The photographs of Robert Frank. Reggae sleeves from 1970s Jamaica. Japanese chewing gum wrappers. The ads for galleries in art magazines. Old Penguin book covers. The work of Cy Twombly. German way-bill documentation. The work of Tadanori Yokoo. None of these things have been driven

> Robert Massim's famous typographic setting of Eugene Ionesco's surrealist play *The Bald Soprano*. The lyrics to Reed's first solo album, for instance, are subjected to eruptive distortions that begin as minor disturbances on "I Can't Stand It" and build into giant bulbous swells by the end of the chapter with the song "Ocean." The 1973 release "Berlin," which dwells on the divisions between men and woman and the subculture of the German city—then divided into Communist and Capitalist halves—begins with a thin black barrier spreading from the gutter. By the end of the chapter, the black barrier has spread to obliterate nearly half of the page. Subtler treatments are developed for the 1979 release *The Bells*, in which the ink fades away throught the chapter, and the Velvet Underground's *Loaded*, in which Reed's lyrics are spattered as if by rain or tears.

Unlike Massim's book, however, which was produced in 1964 with the help of manual distortion techniques such as printing type on rubber sheets, stretching it and photographing it, the Sagmeister studio had digital software—Adobe Photoshop—at its disposal. This made the project feasible within budget, but posed an unforeseen number of problems at the printing and publishing end. The publisher, it transpired, was not used to dealing with a

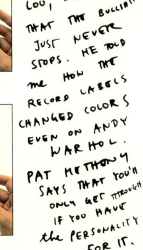

ALSO TALKED ABOUT IT TODAY WITH LOU, WHO SAID THAT THE BULLSHIT JUST NEVER STOPS. HE TOLD me HOW THE RECORD LABELS CHANGED COLORS EVEN ON ANDY WARHOL.
PAT METHONY SAYS THAT YOU'LL ONLY GET THROUGH IF YOU HAVE the PERSONALITY FOR IT.
IT WON'T HELP ME TO JUST RUN AWAY INTO A DIFFERENT FIELD
THE AMOUNT OF BULLSHIT WILL SURELY REMAIN the SAME.
(AT LEAST AS LONG AS MONEY IS INVOLVED).
INSTEAD OF GIVING UP ON graphic DESIGN, I SHOULD TRY TO REINVENT IT FOR myself.

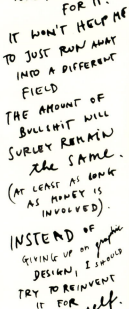

book interior designed in Photoshop, and, in addition, took a piecemeal approach to delivering text changes. Corrections then had to be made at the studio by retouching each character or rebuilding the entire file. Karlsson credits the studio intern, Jan Wilker, with the completion of this excruciating process, and rescuing him from nervous exhaustion. "Jan stayed in the studio most evenings and weekends—plus an extra week," says Karlsson. "On his

last day he brought his luggage to the studio and almost missed his plane home."

The finished files were finally sent back to the publisher (Hyperion), and the studio waited apprehensively for the page proofs. And waited. Fearing the worst, Sagmeister called the publisher. The pages, he was told, had been already sent to the printer: There would be no more proofs, just the finished book.

Astonishingly, the book arrived several weeks later with remarkably few errors. The studio had learned a lesson, however. "If you want to break out of the normal way of doing things," says Sagmeister, "you need a publisher who understands that, and is prepared to supply you with the necessary support." Experimental design, clearly, fares best when it is sanctioned from the top.

ACCORDING TO THE LYRICS, the "Modern Dance" in Lou Reed's first single from *Ecstasy* is both disorienting and difficult to learn: It is a dance "where roles are shifting" and "you don't know who you're with." As a metaphor for life and relationships in New York, it was potent, but not a particularly easy idea to visualize in a music video. A key ingredient was Reed's characteristically sardonic delivery, which immediately casts any earnestness in the song into question.

Sagmeister's first opportunity to direct a music video came about because the singer-songwriter Peter Gabriel, who had kept Sagmeister's materials on file after a meeting several years earlier, suggested to Reed that the designer, though inexperienced in directing, could take on the project. "I said that I would be happy to do it if I could collaborate with my friend Robert Pejo, a documentary filmmaker," says Sagmeister. Pejo was willing to co-direct.

The video came with a concept already attached. Reed—a figure firmly associated with black clothes and dark sunglasses—was to appear in a chicken suit. Few "modern dances" could be more difficult for the denizen of the New York underground than to appear in a stupid chicken outfit. Pejo and Sagmeister wrote five treatments, including an animated version, which was, unfortunately, not possible in the time allocated. The chosen narrative was simple: Reed the chicken

would stand on a small stage as if in a cheap burlesque show, with two women plucking feathers from his outfit. The final scene would have Reed sitting in a large cooking pot.

Pejo and Sagmeister, who had ten days to develop the video, and one day for the shoot, agreed that the video should be "as beautiful as possible," and be performed seriously, to avoid it coming out as a slapstick piece. The shoot was "scary," according to Sagmeister.

"There's an unbelievable adrenalin rush when you are shooting, which would be great if it could be somehow translated to graphic design." Particularly enlightening was the process of working with a team of 35 people at once. "You really have to learn to let go and trust them," he says.

The finished video was an odd mix, a vintage theatrical show, with cartoon content and deadpan delivery, which sat strangely amid the slick, energetic and sexually charged performances that fill

MTV. One of the determining factors is Reed's expression of bored distaste for the entire performance. This was not acting, according to Sagmeister: For the day of the shoot, Reed, generally a surprisingly easy person to work with, was distinctly grumpy. Apart from losing a day of tour rehearsals for the video, Reed was wearing a chicken suit that weighed nearly 30 pounds. He was, you might say, in a foul mood.

ODDLY SUGGESTIVE OF A KIND of psycho-
logical test, the full–empty rabbit–duck ad
for the band Judybats was redrawn from
a European book of brain teasers and
"topsy turvys"—the kind sold in highway
gas stations for parents to keep restless
kids quiet. The clean, crisp design was
intended to stand out on the densely
layered pages of music magazines like
Ray Gun, where the ad would be printed.

The Roses. Poster, invitation card and booklet cover by Werner Korn: I was in love with Werner at that time. I gave him a bunch of little roses for his birthday. It was November. When spring came, he gave me thousands of roses for my birthday. He put the November roses in his scanner and printed them on a poster, invitation card and program booklet for his new theater production. The roses hung all over the town for the whole of May and he said to me: Every time you see one remember: I love you. So many people started collecting these flowers. Even then it was a hit.

NIMBUS, A MANUFACTURER THAT had developed a method of printing holograms on the surface of compact disks, was introduced to Sagmeister by Marshall Crenshaw's record label, Razor and Tie. The company offered to provide the hologram technology for the price of a regular print job—its motive being to use the result for promotional purposes.

After some experimentation, Crenshaw's CD *Miracle of Science* was designed with a monochromatic pattern of diagonals over a hologram of the colors of the spectrum. To accentuate the hologram effect, Sagmeister created a half-sized booklet bearing Crenshaw's image and the same monochrome pattern. When several CDs were lined up in a record store, the hologram effect was quite impressive. "It was beautiful and reflected a great sense of fun," says Crenshaw. For the manufacturer, the scheme was a dazz-ling success: a subsequent report in *Billboard* magazine described how the firm had used the Crenshaw CD to secure an account with Lucasfilms for *Star Wars* merchandise.

"Indeed?" said Monte Cristo; "so this gentleman is an Academician?"

"Within the last week he has been made one of the learned assembly."

"And what is his especial talent?"

"His talent? I believe he thrusts pins through the heads of rabbits, he makes fowls eat madder, and punches the spinal marrow out of dogs with whalebone."

"And he is made a member of the Academy of Sciences for this?"

"No; of the French Academy."

"But what has the French Academy to do with all this?"

"I was going to tell you. It seems"—

"That his experiments have very considerably advanced the cause of science, doubtless?"

"No; that his style of writing is very good."

"This must be very flattering to the feelings of the rabbits into whose heads he has thrust pins, to the fowls whose bones he has dyed red, and to the dogs whose spinal marrow he has punched out?"

> *I remember seeing a big rack full of Miracle of Science CDs, with the rainbow hologram disk, on display at Tower Records. The disks were glowing, looking three-dimensional, and I thought, "this is unbelievable."*
>
> • **Marshall Crenshaw**

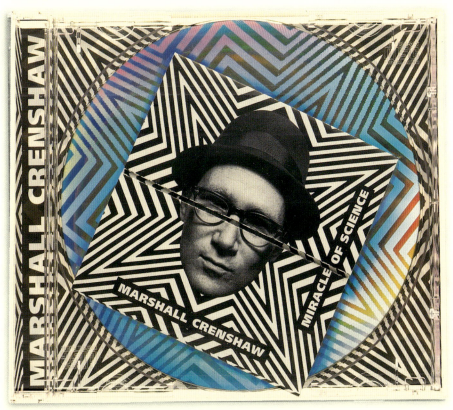

THE DISCOVERY THAT A CIGARETTE fit perfectly within the spine of a jewelcase was enough to convince Sagmeister that cigarettes held the only possible design solution for a CD by Jamie Block, a singer-songwriter and committed Rothmans Reds smoker. The smoking cigarette as a record of time passing became the central motif: On the cover, the Rothmans brand name is replaced on each cigarette with a word from the title, *Timing is Everything*, and inside, partially smoked cigarettes illustrate the length of each track. The effect was strangely profound. The cigarette, as the artist Damien Hirst has observed, is the perfect metaphor of life and, once smoked, death. "To smoke," says Hirst, "is somehow to admit how the world is."

Block's lyrics included some choice moments, such as the line, "I think a regular CD cover is not going to work for you. I think we should fly you guys to Iceland and take a picture on a glacier." The reference was not lost on the Sagmeister studio. "I called my good friend Gudmundur in Iceland," says Karlsson, "and he e-mailed us a shot of an Icelandic glacier photographed by his father. We then Photoshopped a picture of Mr. Block holding his guitar onto the glacier."

Sadly, U.S. laws and regulations governing the sale of cigarettes prohibited the studio from incorporating actual smokes in the spines of all but the batch of CDs sent out for promotional purposes. Otherwise, the project was refreshingly anxiety-free. Even the concept had come easily. "Maybe there is some truth to the thought that your first idea is your best," says Sagmeister.

One of the most frequently asked questions by reviewers, critics, and like, was: how did Sagmeister come up with that cool artwork. There were also quite a few DJs that confessed to breaking into the jewelbox in the dead of night and inhaling the little prize, thus derailing their self-inflicted "stop smoking" campaign. Some of them were a bit peeved. I think they must have been "ex-smokers" who just couldn't resist the little voice coming from inside the spine. Anyway, I told folks that after meeting with Sagmeister—an hour in which he peppered me with every kind of question: favorite music, colors, cities in Africa—on my way out the door, the last thing I said was, "I love to smoke Rothmans Reds." I remember seeing the light going off in his eyes and then a week later I came back and

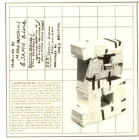

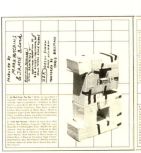

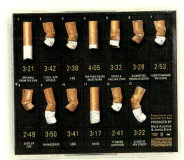

the artwork was done.
I wonder what the
CD would look like if
I hadn't mentioned
the smoking.

I had just come
back from L.A. where
they had just banned
smoking in all bars.
Completely overboard
and absurd to me.
Things seemed to have
calmed down a little
since, but at the time,
in late '98, being a
smoker in America
was about as low as
you could go—maybe
a small notch above
Nazis and child
molesters. Apparently,
the folks at the CD
plant, when they were
putting the artwork
together refused to
handle the cigarettes.
They literally
wouldn't touch them.
Capitol Records had
to purchase every
employee of the plant
two pairs of rubber
gloves. When I heard
that story I knew the
CD artwork was per-
fect, just perfect!

• **Jamie Block**

247

MAY 11 1997

WHEN I ACTUALLY MET with Mr. MICK JAGGER

I WAS SITTING IN THE TAJ MAHAL HOTEL IN BOMBAY WHEN A FAX COMES THROUGH FROM HJALTI STATING THAT THE MANAGEMENT OF THE ROLLING STONES HAD CALLED REQUESTING OUR PORTFOLIO. I FAXED HIM A LETTER BACK TO BE INCLUDED WITH THE PORTFOLIO, EMPHASIZING THAT WE DELIVER ON TIME AND WITHIN BUDGET.

TWO WEEKS LATER WE GET ANOTHER CALL FROM THEIR MANAGEMENT, STATING THAT THE BAND LIKED THE WORK AND WANTS TO MEET. THEY'LL SET UP THE TRIP. ON WEDNESDAY, A BRAND NEW AND EXTRA CLEAN STRECH LIMO PICKS ME UP AT THE STUDIO, WE ARE going TO NEWARK AIRPORT. THE DRIVER HANDS OVER BUSINESS CLASS TICKETS TO LOS ANGELES AND I HAVE A STUPID GRIN ON MY FACE ALL THE WAY TO THE AIRPORT LOOKING OUT OVER THE SUN-DRENCHED NEW JERSEY INDUSTRIAL LANDSCAPE WITH THE STATUE of LIBERTY IN MY BACK CONTEMPLATING IF THIS IS ONE OF THOSE "HAPPY" MOMENTS I HAVE ABOUT

ONCE A YEAR, - I ALREADY HAVE HAD A NUMBER OF THEM THIS YEAR! - I DONT KNOW IF MY STANDARDS OF WHAT CONSTITUTES A 'HAPPY MOMENT' GOT LOWER OR IF I'M JUST GETTING IN A HAPPIER MENTAL STATE.

THEY UPGRADE ME TO FIRST. I WATCH THE FIRST FUNNY AIRLINE MOVIE IN YEARS AND ARRIVE AT THE 4 SEASONS IN BEVERLY HILLS.

I GO UPSTAIRS AND SMOKE ON THE BALCONY, - NON SMOKING FLOOR. L.A. NEXT MORNING I GET A GOOD SUN BURN AT THE POOL, WATCHING CARTOONY L.A. TYPES WHEELING AND DEALING IN THEIR BATHING SUITS, SHOUTING LINES INTO PORTABLE PHONES LIKE: "YOU'VE GOT TO LAY it ON THE LINE FOR THEM." →

AT 2:30, JAGGER'S ASSISTANT LUCY MEETS ME IN THE BAR, GIVES ME A QUICK RUN DOWN ON MICK AND WE GO TO THEIR SUITE. IN THE ELEVATOR I'M NERVOUS. *Mick* OPENS THE DOOR, TURNS AROUND IMMEDIATELY WITHOUT SAYING HELLO AND I FEEL AWKWARD. LUCY INTRODUCES US, HE IS FRIENDLY BUT BUSY GOING THROUGH A SOTHEBY CATALOG WITH CHARLIE WATTS. THEY ARE CHECKING OUT A MONET PAINTING: "AT NINE MILLION THAT'S A REAL BARGAIN", MICK SAYS IN HEAVY BRITISH ACCENT. "PITY I HAVE NO WHITE WALLS LEFT TO HANG IT." →

THE PLAYWRIGHT TOM STOPPARD, known for a few surrealist moments, is said to have suggested to Mick Jagger the title *Bridges to Babylon*. No one seemed to know quite what it meant, but it became the title of the Rolling Stones' 1997 CD and world tour, and for the Sagmeister studio, the theme for a strange dream, set in a land where nothing quite made sense, but everything came together miraculously on the other side.

When it came to designing for an act otherwise known as the world's greatest rock and roll band, it wasn't easy for a small, two-man studio to dictate the terms. Two of Sagmeister's golden rules were to avoid CD projects with no title and never do presentations without a fee. Then he encountered the Rolling Stones' management. "They asked us to do early concepts on spec," says Sagmeister, "and I told them we don't do that. They told me that the Rolling Stones have always done that, and I told them that, come to think of it, we *do* do that."

Meeting with Mick Jagger and Charlie Watts in a hotel in Los Angeles, Sagmeister discovered that there was no title, either. It was hardly the time to take a stand on indecisive rock stars. He returned to New York elated and full of ideas for a design to match the Baroque stage set design that Jagger had shown him. He and Karlsson designed four variations, all Baroque in style, and sent them to London. They got the job, but by the time Sagmeister arrived in London for a second meeting with Jagger and Watts, all of the Baroque prototypes had been rendered useless by the new title, *Bridges to Babylon*.

The project took a stranger turn when Trudy Green, Jagger's manager, declared that Sagmeister could not leave London until a cover image had been agreed upon with the Stones. Sagmeister found himself living at the Stones' expense in a lavish, fusty old London hotel full of paper doilies and pot pourri, designing cover concepts with a blade, spray mount and curls of thermal paper faxes of background patterns sent by Karlsson in New York. Babylonian imagery was, thankfully, forthcoming in London. At Jagger's suggestion, Sagmeister had taken a trip to the British Museum, a treasure house of spectacular antiquities plundered from around the world, and encountered a 3,000 year old statue of a giant Assyrian lion with a square-shaped, bearded human head. It seemed like a divine revelation.

The idea was well received. Jagger was a Leo, and, equally important, the lion image could be easily attached to hats, caps and T-shirts for the Stones merchandising machine. (Sagmeister later received from a friend in Austria a *Bridges to Babylon* pencil sharpener and eraser bearing the lion image.) Several meetings followed in which Jagger approved a design concept showing the lion in a heraldic pose, and discussed with Sagmeister the idea of adding a silver element to the cover to match the silver curtain in the stage set designed by Mark Fisher.

Back in New York, however, the picture suddenly changed when Jagger called to request an alternative design based on a futuristic sculpture in the stage set. Sagmeister was confounded. He had already found an illustrator, Kevin Murphy, who had agreed to paint the lion on spec. The futuristic sculpture, which might have

I HELP LUCY OPEN THE WATER bottles, MICK GRABS MY PORTFOLIO AND STATES: "SO YOU ARE THE FLOATY ONE." "THE FLOATY ONE?" "YEAH, ALL YOUR COVERS SEEM TO FLOAT WITHIN THE PLASTIC BOX." HE LIKES THE LOU REED PACKAGE, LIKES THE ATTENTION TO DETAIL IN SOME OF THE OTHERS AND I CAN STOP BEING NERVOUS. HE DOES NOT HAVE A TITLE FOR THE ALBUM YET, BUT PROMISES TO SEND OVER THE music OF 3-4 SONGS NEXT WEEK.

looked great on stage, seemed like a terrible idea for a 5-inch CD cover.

The stress level in the studio began to reach mythological proportions. Dozens of cover variations, including ones featuring the dreaded sculpture, were designed and sent by email to Jagger's castle in France. Karlsson had developed carpal tunnel syndrome from using the computer for extended periods, and had switched to his left hand. He began having vivid dreams. "Two figures are walking on bright green grass. The sky is completely blue. I see them from behind—they are holding hands. They aren't really walking—it's like they are floating above the grass. After few seconds I realize it is Hjalti and Stefan. Scary monsters!"

For light relief, he and Sagmeister labeled the version of the ugly statue (above) with the filename "the worst." When Jagger called from France to tell them which of the various designs he liked best, Sagmeister and Karlsson watched as the chosen file opened up on the computer screen: It was "the worst." Sagmeister tried to hint that the statue didn't work too well, but Jagger was convinced. The statue was the one.

Sagmeister and Karlsson sat in the studio, aghast. Should they quit? They drew up a list of pros and cons. The pros—to have designed a Stones cover, to get paid, to have proven to themselves that they could do a very difficult job— won by a quarter point. (The cons were horrible design, loss of design integrity,

three more weeks of pain and the possibility of a flop.)

The project resumed with a desperate-looking Sagmeister and Karlsson standing outside Tower Records on Broadway with mockups of two covers: the lion and the worst, asking passers-by for their opinion on which was better. After two hours 65 percent said they prefer the lion, but it

wasn't quite the sweeping majority they'd hoped for.

A veritable miracle occurred, one stormy night at the studio. It had been raining for days, there were leaks in the studio ceiling, and Tony King, Jagger's assistant of 20 years, was sitting, surrounded by buckets of water, shouting to be heard over the noise of dripping water. He said that he too prefered the lion, and after hearing Sagmeister assure him the design could be resurrected and be ready to go in two days, put in phone calls to Jagger, Watts and Keith Richards. Within 15 minutes, the lion was alive and the original design was back on track. They had crossed the Bridge to Babylon and come out on the other side. The studio's sanity was intact.

The rest of the project was a relative breeze. The original lion design had incorporated a silk-screened filigree pattern (a representation of the silver curtain on stage) on the jewelcase exterior, but to meet the pressing print deadline, a custom-made transparent slip case was developed that could be printed separately. Finally, Sagmeister had all copyright problems and possible offensive overtones researched and checked by the Rolling Stones' lawyers. The lion survived the entire process unscathed.

Well, almost. In Dubai, the CD was refused entry: It is not legal to say "Babylon" in Dubai.

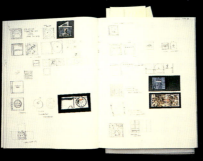

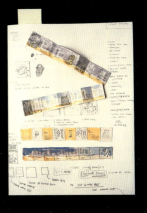

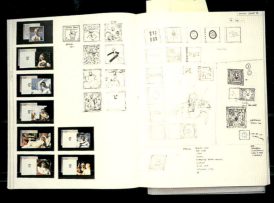

→ I ASK Mick ABOUT HIS FAVORITE STONES COVERS FROM THE PAST AND HE MENTIONS WITHOUT HESITATION: EXILE ON MAINSTREET, → STICKY FINGERS, → SOME GIRLS. THEY ARE MY FAVORITES AS WELL. "WE SHOULD HAVE AN EASY TIME WORKING TOGETHER SINCE I WOULD HAVE TOLD YOU EXACTLY THE SAME COVERS, ONLY IN A DIFFERENT ORDER: STICKY FINGERS, SOME GIRLS AND EXILE ON MAINSTREET."

CHARLIE WATTS (IN LOWERED VOICE) LEANS OVER TO MICK AND ASKS: "WHAT'S ON STICKY FINGERS?"

TO WHICH MICK REPLIES: "OH, YOU KNOW CHARLIE, THE ONE WITH THE ZIPPER, THE ONE THAT ANDY DID."

THE STUPID GRIN IS BACK ON MY FACE.

I TELL THEM I FEEL LIKE I'VE WON FIRST PRIZE IN THE "BIG ROLLING STONES MEET THE BAND ALL EXPENSES PAID" RADIO SHOW CONTEST. THEY LAUGH AND I AM OUT OF THERE. I MEET WITH THE STAGE DESIGNERS AND FLY BACK TO NEW YORK AT 9:30. I FEEL GOOD and AM ASLEEP before THE PLANE LEAVES the ground.

AUG 11 1997

I REMEMBER LOOKING AT SOME DESIGN ANNUALS WHEN I WAS 18 AND NOT THINKING much OF THEM. I THOUGHT THAT THAT STUFF CAN ONLY BE INTERESTING FOR DESIGNERS, FOR the general PUBLIC IT'S SIMPLY NOT EXCITING ENOUGH. EVERYTHING WOULD HAVE TO BE AT LEAST A COUPLE OF NOTCHES BETTER TO HAVE ACTUAL IMPACT. I THINK THAT THE LAST FOUR COVERS, SKELETON KEY, PAT METHENY, DAVID BYRNE AND THE STONES WERE ALL FINE COVERS THAT are good ENOUGH TO BE APPRECIATED BY OTHER DESIGNERS.

A DESIGNER'S INFLUENCES from outside the field of design are often the most revealing. Tibor Kalman often cited *Pizza Today* magazine, and for Sagmeister, the perennial schoolboy, it was the science exhibit. During the 1980s, while a student in Vienna, he visited a vast exposition in Zurich Switzerland called "Phenomena," where exhibits focused on scientific demonstrations and interactive marvels. Sagmeister walked around in a state of wonder: a giant, ten ton stone ball in a hemispherical cup which, because of the flow of water around it, could be pushed around by a child. A communication hose 1.5 miles long. A parabolic mirror that reflected objects so perfectly that it was impossible to tell which was the reflection. After spending a day with the designer of the exposition, Nicolaus Schwabe, Sagmeister had returned to Vienna with material for his thesis project. From then on, he made a point of seeking out science exhibits wherever he went.

The idea for Pat Metheny's *Imaginary Day* CD came directly from an exhibition at the London Science Museum. >

THE NEXT STEP SHOULD BE TO DESIGN SOMETHING THAT REALLY CAPTURES THE IMAGINATION OF THE general PUBLIC. I AM IN AN IDEAL SITUATION WITH my SMALL STUDIO - I SHOULD BE ABLE TO TAKE ADVANTAGE OF it.

> Metheny had asked the studio for a collage, reasoning that his music was too complex to be represented by one image. Sagmeister found the music "precise, composed and accomplished," signaling to him the need for a more planned and orderly collage than the random compositions that had graced Metheny's previous CDs. During a trip to London, Sagmeister had seen a collec-

tion of decoding devices on display at a Science Museum exhibition of World War II encryption and decryption equipment. "They were round, even," he says. "I would have been an idiot not to think of CDs."

The code employed on *"Imaginary Day"* would not require a team of cryptologists to crack: one picture symbol would simply be allocated for each letter

of the alphabet, in three separate, color-coded systems. By turning the CD on its hub so that an arrow pointed to one of the three colors, the Metheny fan could swiftly find the key to decoding that block of text. The benefit of pictograms was that each could also represent a significant theme, working title, or important location in Metheny's music. For example, a train-crossing symbol

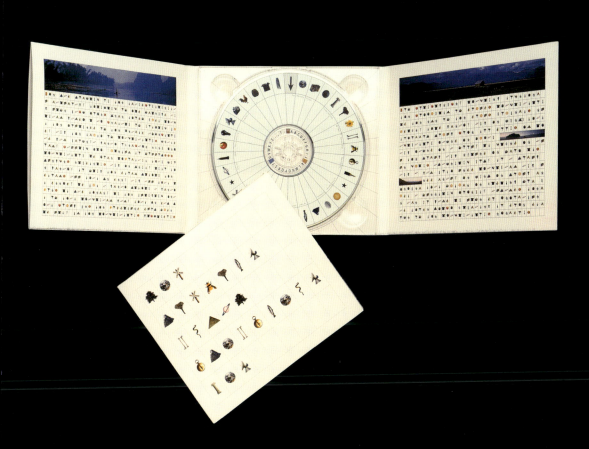

was introduced by Metheny to signify references in the music to Chinese railroad workers in the U.S.—as well as the letter T. The formal constraints on each symbol dictated that the images chosen should be legible at a small point size, with some volume, and not too bright a color. "If we had more than three really colorful ones, it began to look very childish," says Sagmeister.

Metheny wrote a poetic text to accompany the CD, which the studio also encoded. An extraordinarily diligent proofreader at Warner Bros. then undertook the task of proofreading the code (with 12-page booklet) and triumphantly came up with a number of extra spaces and missing commas. Any concerns that the whole encryption system would fly over the heads of Metheny's audience

were swiftly dispelled: Within 24 hours of the CD's release, an equally diligent Metheny fan had translated all the text and posted it on the Internet. This was particularly handy for lazy music critics, including a writer for the Web-based *All Music Guide*, who described the system indignantly as "some kind of strange Esperanto alphabet."

01 (Go) Get It 02 Giant Steps 03 Just
Like The Day 04 Soul Cowboy 05 The
Sun In Montreal 06 Capricorn 07 We
Had A Sister 08 What Do You Want?
09 A Lot Of Livin' To Do 10 Lone Jack
11 Travels Pat Metheny: Guitar Larry
Grenadier: Bass Bill Stewart: Drums
Barcode no. 0 9362-47632-2 2

PAT METHENY'S RETURN to a trio line-up for a 1999 recording of jazz standards and originals warranted a back-to-basics sleeve design. Metheny's initial request had been to put the disk in an "O-card" type cover. Sagmeister saw in this notion an opportunity to haul out of storage a design that had been waiting for an opportunity to be born. It was a simple,

relatively inexpensive scheme to create a near-infinite array of variations on a design. By die-cutting a small hole in the cardboard sleeve so that the CD showed through, and printing a blend of gradually changing hues on the disk itself, each CD design would appear to be different, the hole varying in color according to the position of the disk inside.

The design was at its most impressive during the album's release, when stores would display several variations in a row. It was at its worst a year later, when the record company ditched the die cut and put out the CD in a conventional jewelcase with a trompe-l'œil of the hole: each design looked exactly the same as the next.

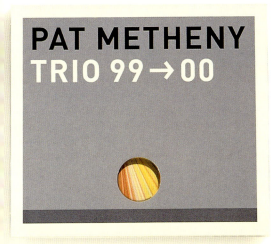

KNOWN FOR ITS ANTHEMIC ROCK with Eastern spiritual overtones, Live had discussed with Sagmeister the idea of using a mandala on the cover of its fourth album, *The Distance to Here*. The mandala, a Hindu term for a circle, represents a microcosm of the universe and the divine forces at work within it, and is used as a focus for meditation. Several design varia-tions were developed for the CD, but the favorite was one Sagmeister had commissioned from designer-illustrator Motoko Hada, who based her design on images suggested by the lyrics. "When you see a mandala it's just a flat picture, but the original concept is three dimensional—you are seeing it from the top," she explains. "You enter it from one of 12 directions and meditate. When you feel OK, you come out."

Hada constructed the packaging as if it were a dimensional mandala, with the sequence of imagery representing the passage through, from turbulence at the center, to a calm point of self-knowledge (the back of the CD). The record company was concerned that the cover should not

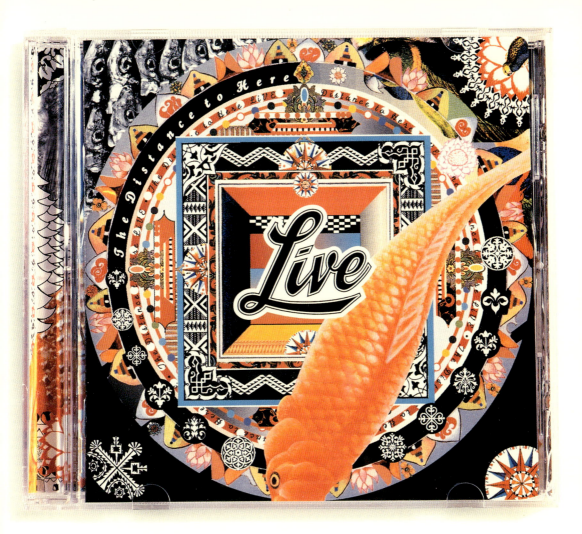

appear too Eastern, so Hada added a number of Western motifs, including Native American figures. The fish, a religious symbol in the West and sacred good fortune symbol in the East, became a predominant feature in the collage. The result was a giant, 800 megabyte file with hundreds of separate elements that had computers screaming for mercy, and a satisfied illustrator. "It was fun to combine manual and digital elements," says Hada, "it came out looking very handcrafted."

Hada's near-obsessive attention to detail was a good match for the studio. "One day she came by to show us all the art that was used in the package—we were double-checking that all of it was copyright free," says Karlsson. "She brought in this huge stack of neatly cut boards. Pretty much every single piece of art that you see on the CD—all those tiny ornaments and dingbats—she did as small paintings, ranging from 2 to 7 inches in size. I was totally blown away by all the work she put into it." >

> For Live's 1999 promotional single "Dolphin's Cry," Sagmeister and designer-illustrator Motoko Hada chose to avoid the obvious solution of putting a dolphin on the cover in favor of a symbolic approach more in keeping with the lyrics. The dolphin is a symbol of salvation—legends depict it as a friend of man—which she chose to portray as a force of energy represented by fire. "You can find a fire everywhere in a mandala," she points out. A similar theme was developed for a follow-up single, "Run to the Water."

THE ETHEREAL ELECTRONIC MUSIC of Mimi, a New York-based techno artist, was a popular choice on the Sagmeister studio hi fi. After Mimi asked the studio to design her CD, to be called *Soak*, inspiration of an appropriately aqueous variety struck Sagmeister during a trip in 1999 to a special jellyfish exhibit at the Baltimore Aquarium. Jellyfish echoed the music's unearthly quality, and, as Sagmeister noted, having witnessed these creatures before visiting an art show, "Nature blows art away. There were jellyfish there that

looked like three-quarters of your stomach had somehow got out of you, and were swimming happily through the water. There were tanks with clusters of tiny jellyfish, 10,000 all tangled together, moving as a cloud. And the see-through ones were a light show— jellyfish who really thought they were Las Vegas."

The sting in the tail of experience was that the aquarium would only let the studio photograph its specimens for an extortionate location fee. Having tried negotiation, to no avail, the studio asked a

selection of nature photographers to send in their work. Images were chosen, and one particularly colorful and circular image was set aside for the CD itself. Frustratingly, the record label was unwilling to pay the additional cost required to print the image in full color, and unable (for bureaucratic reasons) to permit Sagmeister to foot the bill. The result was a two-color label, a disappointed Sagmeister and a school of crestfallen Vegas jellyfish.

Mimi "Soak"

JAN 10 1998 → THIS IS REALLY GETTING ON MY NERVES, IT'S EXACTLY HOW I THOUGHT IT WOULD BE: THE EXCITEMENT TO DESIGN ANOTHER CD COVER DECREASES WHILE THE LEVEL ✝ BULLSHIT STAYS EXACTLY THE SAME.

When we first began construction of the Soak cover, I gave Sagmeister lyrics, visuals I found inspiring and a list of my favorite things: insects, beetles, Bruce Lee, floating, nature, dreams, outer space and the inside of the body. We also had the music which was sparkly, dense, emotional and more inclined to technology than most rock music at the time.

To me, Stefan's stroke of brilliance was the idea of using jellyfish. It encompassed all of my favorite things and the heart of the music in a single metaphor. Jellyfish are so otherworldly—underwater and outer space at the same time (especially these photographs which are lit glowingly with a black background). They are insect-like and human X-ray-like, they have a gentle, graceful quality with no apparent threat (except we all know they carry a poisonous sting) and there is something about them that looks very futuristic, which mimics the modern sound in the music.

Another dilemma per-

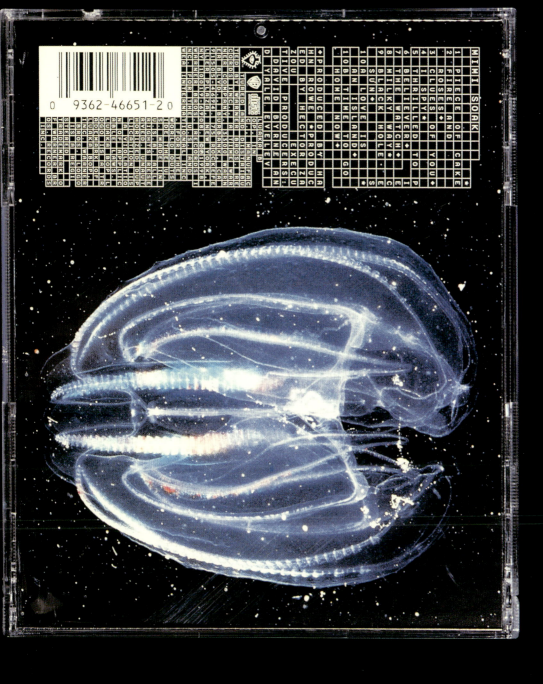

MIMI SOAK

1 ● PIECE OF CAKE ●
2 ● FIRE AND ●
3 ● ROSES ●
4 ● CLUES OF YOU ●
5 I ● SPY ●
6 THRILLED TO P
7 ● BELIEVER I
8 ● THE WATCH ●
9 ● THE MILKY WAY ● E
10 ● BLACK HOLE ● S
10A LOVE IS
10B TIME TO GO
● HOME NOW ●

PRODUCED B HA
ZOU EXECU
TIVE PRODUCERS:
DAVID BYRNE AN
D YALE EVELEV.
PRODUCED
BY HECTOR ZA
JOHN ROWE

fectly presented was the
layout of the lyrics. I felt
awkward about putting the
lyrics on my sleeve because
I felt it could be interpre-
ted as pretentious. But I
had spent a lot of energy
working on them and
wanted to share them.
Instead of just presenting
the lyrics, Sagmeister made
the reader have to work
very hard to read. Each letter of every word is separated into its own box, so
you read it as a stutter.
This is not just devilish
though, it also echoes the
digital aspect of the music.
The Joseph Cultice pho-
tographs were the icing on
the cake. The inside photograph makes me look like a
jellyfish and the ones on
the front make me look
more attractive than I
really am, which is always
a boost. Seeing a visual
interpretation of the music
was completely inspiring
and has made me a better
artist. I only have one
regret. I wish sometimes
Sagmeister had no finan-
cial restrictions on his work
and that would be able to
follow an idea to its far-
thest reach.

● mimimimimimi

WITH A MUSIC SCENE perhaps unrivaled in any other city, New York rewards intrepid music lovers with occasional gems. Skeleton Key, known for its energetic shows in downtown clubs and a percussionist who plays scrap metal and junk found in dumpsters, had a signifi-

cant following at the Sagmeister studio. "I had seen them two or three times and they were definitely my favorite unknown band," says Sagmeister. "When Tommy Steele from Capitol called and asked if we'd like to design the cover for this band they'd just signed—Skeleton

Key—it was quite a coincidence."

The Skeleton Key connection had also yielded a side project to design the band's CD single, for which the guitarist and vocalist Eric Sanko brought in a Mexican stamp commemorating the Day of the Dead. The studio worked out a

system whereby an illustration based on the stamp—by Sanko—could be turned into a cartoon sequence showing a grinning skeletal man in cowboy hat. As the flaps holding the CD in its cardboard case are opened, the skelecowboy's head pops off.

My ex-girlfriend once said of Skeleton Key's music that it made her "want to get violent in a really funny way." We have always embraced the manic-hysteria that falls between complete terror and complete comedy. The cover for the EP captured that sensation perfectly.

• **Eric Sanko**
SKELETON KEY

FOR THE SKELETON KEY ALBUM, which was to be called *Scratch*, the studio came up with several ideas, including an ingenius scheme in which the CD booklet would be covered with sandpaper, so that removing it several times would scratch up the jewelcase. Naturally, when the bandmembers changed their minds about the title, Sagmeister was upset. "I swore to myself I'd never take on a project without a firm title again."

The replacement title, *Fantastic Spikes Through Balloon*, was derived from a magic trick one of the band members had mastered as a child in which spikes are pushed through a balloon without popping it. The initial thought was to incorporate the actual trick in the CD package, but after establishing that this was prohibitively expensive, Sagmeister and Karlsson tried the studio-favored brainstorming method of

list making (see p.118). This time, the mystical creative process revealed to the designers a line up of balloon-like objects, from a German sausage to a blowfish. To complete the picture, the booklet would be riddled with holes representing those left by the magical spikes.

The idea won the Skeleton Key vote unanimously, leaving only the problem of the lyrics: band vocalist Eric Sanko hated

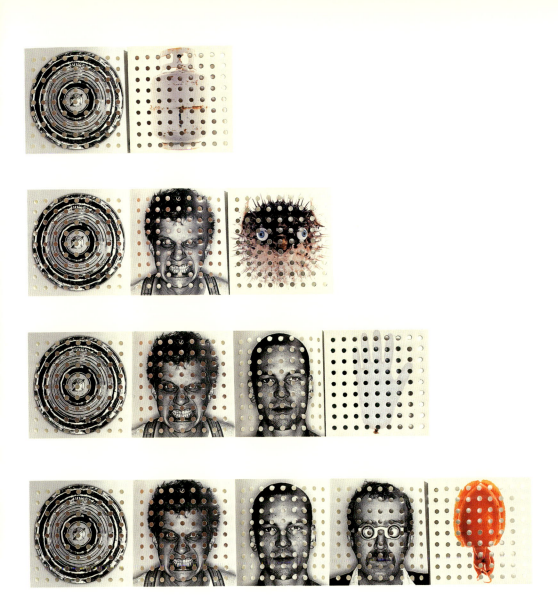

the fact that people read lyrics while the music was playing. Much of the text would be obliterated by the holes anyway (with the careful exception of the design studio credit, as Sagmeister points out) but to make the process more challenging for the reader, it was decided that the lyrics should be printed in reverse, so that the viewer would need to use the CD itself to read them, in reflection—impossible while the music was playing.

Since the CD package was looking increasingly crammed with images, text and holes, the studio decided to fill every last corner—including a blank area on the inside of the spine. In a moment of mindless brilliance, Karlsson filled the blank with dummy copy of his own invention, and sent off the prototype for the band to review. His filler text, a surreal free association story improvising on the album title theme was so popular

with the band that they insisted it should stay.

Karlsson subsequently left the studio to form his own design firm. For readers unable to wait for Karlsson's collected writings to be published, the tale is included, unabridged, as follows:

"I bought a donut from the donut store. Normally they have fantastic donuts. I took one bite and realized it was a cheap imitation donut from >

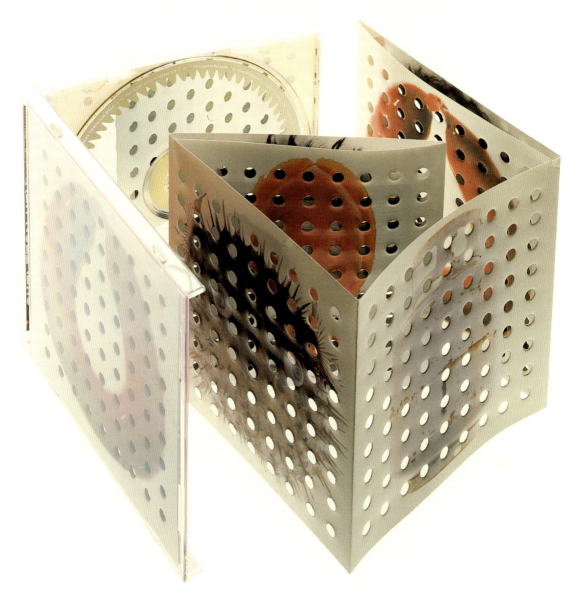

OCT 18 1994

I ALWAYS HAVE TO REMEMBER
HOW INCREDIBLY PRIVILEGED
I AM TO BE ABLE TO TAKE
these 1-2 YEARS OFF FOR
EXPERIMENTATION.
ITS REALLY COMPARABLE
to my TIME AT GRAD
SCHOOL AT PRATT.
I JUST REALLY HAVE TO MAKE
THE BEST OUT OF IT!
ALWAYS KEEP IN MIND: THIS is my LIFE. I AM GOING TO DIE, EVENTUALLY.
I HAVE TO MAKE THE BEST OUT OF IT WHILE I'M HERE.

Fantastic Spikes Through Balloon was originally the name of a magic trick in which the magician delicately skewers a balloon with a long knitting needle without breaking the balloon. We liked the idea of something hard and unyielding and pointy coming together with something soft and maleable and dopey. The packaging reflected that combination—in one way very sophisticated and sleek, but also served like a large dollop of goofiness to balance things out. And the holes— absolute genius!

• **Eric Sanko** SKELETON KEY

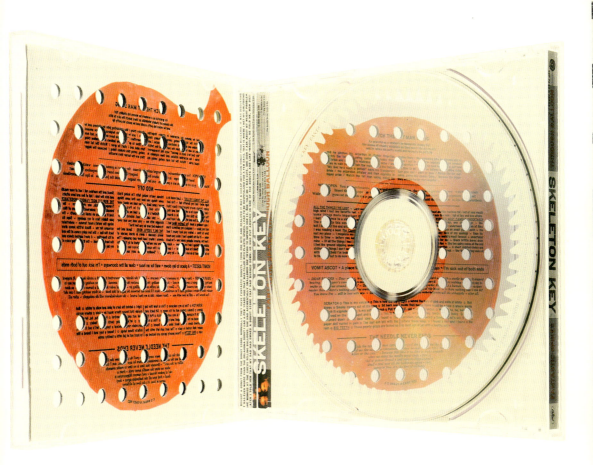

> Bulgaria. It was disgusting, it was even worse than the Oklahoma donut I had a few years ago that was filled with plastic spikes. I had to be hospitalized for a few days. That is where I met my girlfriend, she worked at the circus selling balloons. She had accidentally swallowed one trying to impress her ex. She told me I was cute. She didn't ask about my weight problem and later I told her that my dad had owned a donut store that

had burned down. He had put arsenic in one of the donuts and like magic, he told me, mom died."

The ambitious design passed through the record company intact largely thanks to Capitol's chief design director Tommy Steele. Confronted with the extra cost of drilling the holes, Steele persuaded the promotions department at Capitol to forsake some of the advertising budget to meet the print budget. "You need some-

body like that at a label," says Sagmeister. "The disadvantage of working outside of the record labels is that some of these avenues are normally closed to you."

is it possible to touch somebody's heart with graphic design?. lecture. aiga national confereence. las vegas

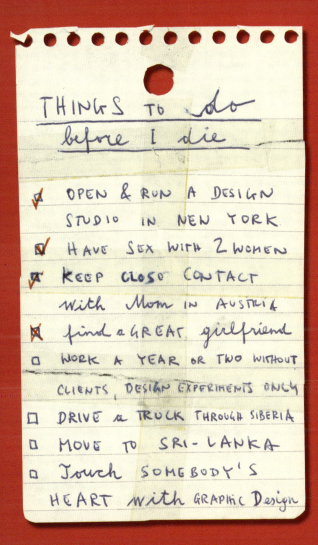

IS IT POSSIBLE TO TOUCH SOMEBODY'S HEART WITH DESIGN?

I FIRST STARTED TO THINK about this subject at the 1997 AIGA National Conference in New Orleans. Each and every one of us received a big black canvas bag, stuffed with goodies, conference programs, party invites and paper sample books, all designed by big-name designers especially for the big conference.

And it was all fluff. Well-produced, tongue in cheek, pretty fluff. Nothing that moved you, nothing that made you think. Some was informative, but still all fluff. And there were tons of New Orleans clichés: Jazz, striptease dancers, voodoo, crawfish, Mississippi steamboats.

Or combined clichés: Jazzy striptease dancers performing voodoo on a crawfish while going down the Mississippi in a steamboat.

I think one reason for all this fluff is that we as designers don't really believe in much. We are not much into politics or religion and don't have much of a stand on any important issues. I guess when our conscience is so wishy-washy, so is our design.

At that conference it was refreshing to hear Kyle Cooper talk about the much heralded titles he

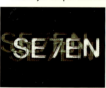

designed for the movie *Seven* and to find out that he is a Born Again Christian. That does give him a strong perspective on evil things. Which might just be why his title sequence for *Seven* stood out so much in this sea of well-produced, professional mediocrity.

I've seen movies that moved me, read books that changed my outlook on life and listened to numerous pieces of music that influenced my mood. Somehow, I never seem to be touched quite the same way by graphic design. I know, the comparison is

not all that fair, after all, movies do have 90 minutes to do all that heart touching, books have several days, while most graphic design has to connect in seconds.

However, a piece of graphic design that did touch me when I was six years old was this little story of Konrad, the little boy who

sucked his thumb. His mother tells him not to suck it while she goes out of the house, or else the tailor with the big scissors will come and cut it off.

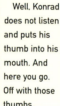

Well, Konrad does not listen and puts his thumb into his mouth. And here you go. Off with those thumbs.

Here you see poor Konrad, sad because both his thumbs are missing.

I was very impressed. And touched.

Let's look at our poster of the last AIGA

conference. You can obviously see the Konrad influence. It helped bring a lot of people to New Orleans, a record at the time. I still like some of the detail.

But did it touch people's hearts? I don't know.

I TRIED TO TOUCH SOMEONE'S HEART

Of all the hundreds of pieces I completed in the last 20 years, there were only a couple of projects where I can say for sure that I touched somebody's heart with design. Right after we completed the Stones' CD there was quite some media interest in the studio and a number of TV crews, among them an Austrian news show, came by. My mom's 70th birthday was

coming up and we designed a little T-shirt (that I wore during the interview) congratulating her. The news crew agreed to air the segment right on her birthday.

Mom was touched.

DESIGNERS TOUCHED MY HEART

So ever since I got that black canvas bag at that conference in New Orleans, this touching thing has been on my mind, and I've looked for design pieces that cut through to my heart. Here's something of a personal favorites list:

This image just captivates me, its an almost 30-year-old album cover for King Crimson. When I was 14, I drew a 40 x 40 inch version of it in pencil and then I got addicted to staring at it.

I remember being very impressed with

those bulging pants and the actual, real zipper that was featured on this 1971 *Sticky Fingers* Rolling Stones album. I was touched by the unexpectedness as well as the obvious commitment of the designer and the record label to getting through such a production nightmare.

"This is a record cover. This writing is the design upon the record cover. The design is to help sell the record. We hope to draw your attention to it and encourage you to pick it up. When you have done that maybe you'll be persuaded to listen to the music—in this case XTC's *Go 2* album. Then we want you to buy it." …and so on, it might look familiar to you just because it's been ripped off so often.

I was incredibly touched by Art Spiegelman's story about his Jewish father, a survivor of Hitler's Europe and how, as a car-

toonist, Spiegelman tries to come to terms with his father's story. It's a project that illustrates very well the importance of choosing the right subject, the right content.

Art obviously knows his subject inside out.

I think it was Katherine McCoy who said that graphic design can never rise above its content.

If I have nothing to say, the best design won't help me.

Designer Ellen Shapiro has a son who had difficulties learning reading and writing so she worked on a solution: Instead of leaving this for the teachers to sort out, she saw it as a classic design problem and

developed a set of cards and flip books that teach letter sounds and reading.

In the meantime she founded a company, Alphagram Learning Materials, which offers a whole range of materials to help kids read.

She proudly reports that her

son just came back from a summer session at Cornell having read Kant and Freud.

The one piece of graphic design that truly touched me was a campaign by a New York designer, illustrator and artist who calls himself True.

It's a project that took place within the New York

subway system. There is a whole slew of official signs and stickers in the subway train that tell you what you should and should not do.

True printed up an entire range of additional stickers imitating the look of the official ones but rather more philosophical in content.

I've met people who mentioned that when they read the "strive to be happy" sign it actually made them feel better.

True met every Wednesday at midnight with 15 to 20 friends at the same subway stop and they divided up the different subway lines among them. One group would do the A line, another the F and so on.

He equipped all of his helpers with fake transit authority I.D.s and even made up

fake authorization letters so his friends would not get arrested.

ARTISTS TOUCHED
MY HEART

You might have noticed that all these projects are fairly old. I've seen very few design projects lately that touched me in the same way. However there are a number of contemporary fine artists who blow me away:

Walter DeMaria installed his "Lightning Field" in New Mexico, close to Albuquerque. He arranged hundreds of highly polished stainless steel poles in one

of the most thunderstorm-intense areas in the world. As a visitor you can rent out a hut on a nearby hill, wait and anticipate lightning striking the poles.

New York artist Janine Antoni went into an apprenticeship with a Hollywood special effects make-up artist for a year in order to be able to do this piece about her parents.

This is her Dad as her Mom and her Mom as her Dad.

Then she shows her Dad as her Dad and her Mom as her Dad.

And finally her Mom as her Mom and her Dad as her Mom.

In her catalog she includes photos of the "making of" of this piece showing her and her mom making up her dad, which leads to great captions like: Me and Mom as Dad making Dad into Mom.

Adolf Wölfli is a Swiss artist from the turn of the century who developed these

intense notebooks in the mental hospital.

Just this stack by itself touches my heart.

WHAT HAS ART GOT
TO DO WITH IT?

Most of the visual heart-touching examples I just showed are from fine artists and we, of course, are just graphic designers. So, what is art, what is graphic design? Is there a difference?

My favorite art definition comes from Brian Eno: He says, not to think of art works as objects, but as triggers for experiences. That solves a lot of problems: We do not have to argue about whether photography is art, or whether performances are art, or whether Andres Serrano's piss is art, or whether graphic design is art, because, Eno says, art is something that happens, it's an experience, not a quality. And of course, you might have a different art experience in front of a Rembrandt than I do, it might be art to you but not for me.

He says there is nothing absolute about the esthetic value of a Rembrandt or a Mozart or Neville Brody for that matter.

I think this book, a collaboration of the designer Jonathan Barnbrook and the artist Damien Hirst, itself is a work of art.

I spoke to a number of artists who thought it was the best thing Damien ever did. They preferred the book as an object over his paintings and sculptures, even though the book is about his paintings and sculptures.

I do think that in England the mental gap between design and fine art is smaller than in the U.S.. There is a larger design avant garde in England: Tomato, Me Company, Peter Saville, Designers Republic, Fuel, etc. Experimentation seems to be part of their daily practice.

And you do notice it in the publications: Compare *Eye* magazine to *Print;* Compare D&AD to the One Show.

Or in book publishing: Compare Booth Clibborn to Rockport.

Why is that?

I found this quote by Marcello Minale in a book by the British corporate identity firm Minale Tattersfield:

"In my experience, every designer whose prime aim in going into business was to make money while at the same time producing good design, failed on both counts. I believe that designing is something that you have to do for love. If you are commi-ted first and foremost to producing good design then you'll make money as a by-product because good design is something people are willing to pay for. But that financial reward will be a bonus, a gift."

That from a very mainstream design company.

But what qualities do the pieces that CAN touch my heart have in common? What do they need to touch my heart? Is it possible to create a list?

Well, I tried.

1. NEW PERSPECTIVE

They have to have the ability to make me see things in a new way.

If you go out to PS 1 in Queens, New York you'll see on the top floor a sculpture by James Turrell. It's basically a square room with a retractable ceiling that opens every day at dusk. The space is completely open but still feels enclosed. The sky is framed and you sit on these long benches observing very subtle color changes in the sky.

When I visited this room I noticed how I automatically reduced my voice to a whisper. There is an almost sacramental feeling in there.

2. TRIGGER OF MEMORIES

Somehow they remind me of an experience, maybe of my childhood.

Also at PS 1, I saw on the site map there was an Ann Hamilton sculpture on display. So I went to check out the spot, but I couldn't see anything other than a white wall. So off I went to the information desk, where they assured me that it was in fact there. I went back again, and all I saw was the white wall. Only this time I noticed the wall was wet. When I looked really close I discovered tiny little holes in the wall. Small droplets of water would slowly develop out of these holes, grow bigger and bigger until they were big enough to run down the wall, wait until another droplet caught up with them and then run further down the wall. Some would stop, some would pick up speed.

Only afterwards I learned the title of this sculpture: Crying wall

3. PASSION AND GUTS

They show passion and commitment.

On 57th Street I visited an exhibition by Anselm Kiefer, probably the most famous German artist of his time and certainly the most expensive: His work sells for mil-

lions of dollars.

A number of years ago I had seen a retrospective of his work at MOMA where he had shown huge canvases, as big as 60 x 15 feet in size.

So at the Marian Goodman gallery in New York, Anselm Kiefer showed ALL of his work that he owns. He piled it up 20 feet high, rolled up canvases mixed with canvases on stretchers, all the work literally destroying each other through its own weight.

On the white walls he wrote with a piece of chalk:

20 Jahre Einsamkeit: 20 years of loneliness.

4. SURPRISE

There is an element of unexpectedness.

When I was 16, Chancellor Kohl had just been elected in Germany and another right-wing politician called Strauss was ex-tremely popular in Bavaria. They had a slogan "Germany for the Germans" and their goal was not only to curb the influx of immigrants into Germany but also to coax German people into having more kids, so as to secure a German Germany for the future.

At the same time a number of German writers published a brand-new magazine and they ran this photo story under the headline: "Let's save the Germans from extinction."

These guys are helping the cause, done in the days before Photoshop.

Save the Germans.

5. VIRTUOSITY

There is virtuosity of craft or technique—or simply just the astonishment that somebody can be so good at something.

I met the designer of Swiss currency a couple of weeks ago in Switzerland. The virtuosity here does not really lie in the design (even though it's good) but in the printing. They designed their own printing dot: Every dot consists of several Pantone colors that are printed in register with each other.

They have to match to a 1/25 000 of an inch. Every note has eight security features, plus another four features only known to banks, plus another four features only known to the government. I'm sure all

this security is bullshit: I just like the obsessiveness of it all.

6. BEAUTY

And then there is beauty or whatever I see as beauty.

As in this case, a great poster by Makoto Saito for a Buddhist Temple.

HOW TO TOUCH SOMEBODY'S HEART

If I just follow that list, if I check all my design pieces against these six points and make sure they conform, will I automatically wind up with a touching visual piece?

I guess the list has the same problem as all those "How do I make other people love me?" books. If I want to touch somebody's heart with a piece of design, it has to come from my heart, it has to be true

and sincere. Mere list-following won't do.

The audience of my design piece will feel if I'm honest, if it comes from my heart. Just like the way my friends know instinctively if I'm being authentic. If I'm true, if I have the guts, if I have the passion, my message will get through.

Then I thought: If I'm so eager to touch somebody's heart, why does it have to be with graphic design?

I mean: Why not touch somebody's heart by running a hospital in Calcutta? Why not write a really sweet letter to my mom?

Well: "How to Write a Sweet Letter to my Mom" does not sound like a particular interesting subject for an AIGA talk. And I think that I'd like to touch somebody using a medium that I'm comfortable in.

Strangely, I also suspect that in ten years' time this touching design is going to be the only kind of design that's going to be done by actual designers.

All that professional, good-looking, well-produced pretty fluff is going to be generated by sophisticated computer programs. You type in the client, select a format and a style, the program lets you chose from a vast list of visual clichés, downloads a picture selection, aligns everything and sends the files to the printer.

And I think I simply don't have the guts for the hospital in Calcutta.

While I was working for the ad agency Leo Burnett in Hong Kong, my managing director there was always hanging out with local policemen, so I got to hear quite a number of crime stories.

The Hong Kong police had finally captured the youth leader of the triads, the Hong Kong version of the Cosa Nostra. They locked him in a holding cell in the 20-story police headquarters in Kowloon and questioned him for days without being able to extract any kind of information out of him. After hours and hours of unsuccessful questioning they completely lost it, grabbed him by his feet and hung him out of an 18th-floor window. Still, he would not talk. They had to set him free. The triad leader turned around and sued the police department for applying torture during questioning. At the trial, it was his word against that of five policemen, who all denied the charges. But he said he had proof: While they hung him out that win-

dow, he had signed his name on the wall. And sure enough when the court went to check, there was his signature on the wall, written upside down, 18 stories up in the air.

I would LOVE to create a piece of type, a visual, any design piece that has as much guts as this one.

So far I just haven't figured out how.

Credits

> "I'm an amazing person," she said, without a trace of irony. "I am truly fascinating."

We graded all projects (from 1–5, 1 being highest) and included this grade in parentheses following most project titles. Our opinion is very much influenced by reactions we get from clients, audiences and friends (like wet-finger politicians*).

The most frequently asked question after lectures "Do you still have scars?"** is often followed by: "How long do you actually work on a CD cover?" and: "How much do you get paid?" Although we are not particulary interested in either, in an effort to render this book informative to our readers, we included, wherever possible, the design hours it took to complete the projects as well as the design fees (including handling, excluding expenses) paid. Starting from 1993 onwards (no earlier time sheets and billing info available) these pieces of information appear at the end of each credit block.
Stefan Sagmeister

cover:
Xeno (2)
art direction: Stefan Sagmeister
design: Hjalti Karlsson
photo: Kevin Knight
Booth Clibborn, 2000

inside cover (underneath flaps)
Xeno (2)
art direction: Stefan Sagmeister
photo: Kevin Knight
2000

pp.2-9
timeline
art direction: Stefan Sagmeister
design: Franziska Morlok
2000

p.11
CD cover sketch
design: Stefan Sagmeister
2000

p.17
underwear
art direction: Stefan Sagmeister
photo: Michael Grimm
2000

p.19
Otto Sagmeister invoice
design: Otto Sagmeister
Otto Sagmeister Fabrik Feiner Liqueure
around 1900

p.20
Liederlenz poster (4-5)
design/illustration: Stefan Sagmeister
Jeunesse 1981

Bewegung 81 poster (4)
design/illustration: Stefan Sagmeister
Jugendhaus Bregenz 1981

Harry Pierron Trio poster (4)
design/illustration: Stefan Sagmeister
Spielboden Dornbirn 1981

Alexander Goebel, Schraeg Oben
unpublished record cover (2)
design: Stefan Sagmeister
1982

p.21
Children's Book Fair Bologna poster (5)
Paris ist starker Tabak poster (3-4)
Zoo Schönbrunn poster (3)
Vitamin B poster (3-4)
all unpublished
design/illustration: Stefan Sagmeister
Hochschule für Angewande Kunst
1982-1986

p.22
Bottle, Self Portrait, Typewriter,
illustrations (3-4)
Wolgang Bauer poster (3-4)
all unpublished
Hochschule für Angewande Kunst
Hackenmörder sticker (2)
design/illustrations: Stefan Sagmeister
1982-1986

p.23
Elias Sagmeister
birth announcement (3)
illustration: Simon Sagmeister
design: Stefan Sagmeister
Heidrun & Gebhard Sagmeister 1984

p.24
Über die Dörfer poster (2-3)
design: Stefan Sagmeister
© Schauspielhaus 1984

p.25
Brüder poster (4)
design: Stefan Sagmeister
© Schauspielhaus 1984

p.26
Clara S. poster (3)
design: Stefan Sagmeister/Jurislav Tscharijsky
photograph: Jurislav Tscharijsky
© Schauspielhaus 1984

p.28
Bruder Eichman poster (3)
design: Stefan Sagmeister
© Schauspielhaus 1984

p.29
Combat poster (4)
design: Stefan Sagmeister
photograph: Jurislav Tscharijsky
© Schauspielhaus 1984

p.30
Abendrot poster (3)
design: Stefan Sagmeister
© Schauspielhaus 1985

pp.32-35
Ronacher posters (2)
design: Stefan Sagmeister
Hans Gratzer 1984

pp.36-37
Sagmeister im Scala
invitation and poster (3)
design: Stefan Sagmeister
Hannes Rothmayer 1985

p.39
Mirrored pyramid postcard (3)
design: Stefan Sagmeister
thesis project
Hochschule für Angewandte Kunst
1986

p.39
Sundial postcard (1-2)
design: Stefan Sagmeister
thesis project
Hochschule für Angewandte Kunst
1986

pp.40-41
Record player postcard (1-2)
design: Stefan Sagmeister
thesis project
Hochschule für Angewandte Kunst
1986

pp.43
Ointment jacket (2)
design: Stefan Sagmeister
sewing: Tina Budewig
1993

pp.44-45
Cairo perfume packaging (4-5)
unpublished
design: Stefan Sagmeister
Pratt Institute 1988

p.45
Memphis brochure (3-4)
unpublished
design: Stefan Sagmeister et al
Pratt Institute 1988

pp.46-47
Guggenheim identity and posters (4)
unpublished
design: Stefan Sagmeister
Pratt Institute 1988

pp.48-49
Little Gold business card (2)
design: Stefan Sagmeister
Tony Goldman 1988

pp.50-59
Socko (2-3)
design: Stefan Sagmeister
Pratt Institute 1988
full version published in
Everlast, Comic Kunst aus Vorarlberg
many of the symbols appeared
originally in Modley:
Handbook of Pictorial Symbols,
reprinted with permission from
Dover Publications, Inc.

p.60
Armin Schneider badminton (3)
business card
design/illustration: Stefan Sagmeister
1989

* forefinger up high in the air, checking which direction the wind blows.
** No.

MORE CREDITS

pp.130-133
Schertler identity, packaging
brochure and campaign (3)
art direction: Stefan Sagmeister
design: Eric Zim, Patrick Daily, Veronica Oh
photo: Tom Schierlitz
© Schertler Audio Transducers
1992-1995
81 hours / $ 4,850 (brochure only)

pp.134-135
Talk to a Stone book (3)
art direction: Stefan Sagmeister
design: Hjalti Karlsson, Veronica Oh
photo: John Bigelow Taylor
© Mikio Shinagawa 1996-1997
374 hours / $ 12,935

pp.136-137
Toto identity (3)
art direction: Stefan Sagmeister
design: Veronica Oh
photo: Michael Grimm
© Toto Ltd 1995
265 hours / $ 33,750

pp.139-147
Stories photo comix
art direction: Stefan Sagmeister
design: Jan Wilker
photo: Barbara Gentile
2000

pp.148-149
DeathDrome (5)
art direction: Stefan Sagmeister
design: Veronica Oh, Hjalti Karlsson
Illustration: David Schleinkofer
© Viacom 1996
239 hours / $ 24,897

pp.150-155
Anni Kuan identity and brochure (2)
art direction: Stefan Sagmeister
design: Hjalti Karlsson, Martin Woodtli
photography: Tom Schierlitz
Anni Kuan Design 1998-1999

p.156
Quantum Weirdness poster (3)
creative director: Janet Froehlich
art direction: Joel Cuyler, Stefan Sagmeister
design: Veronica Oh
Illustration: John Kahrs
© The New York Times Magazine 1996
48 hours / $ 1,000

p.158
The Shock of the Familiar magazine cover (3-4)
creative director: Janet Froehlich
art direction: Stefan Sagmeister
design: Hjalti Karlsson
photo: Tom Schierlitz
paintbox: Dalton Portella
© The New York Times Magazine 1999
121 hours / $ 1,000

p.159
The Shock of the Familiar magazine cover
creative director: Janet Froehlich
art direction: Jennifer Morla
© The New York Times Magazine 1999
reprinted with permission of
Morla Design

pp.160-165
Aiga National Conference New Orleans poster
(1-2)
art direction: Stefan Sagmeister
design: Hjalti Karlsson
photo: Bela Borsodi
Illustration: Peggy Chuang, Kazumi Matsumoto,
Raphael Rüdisser
paintbox: Dalton Portella
Aiga 1997
pro bono

pp.166-167
New York State quarters (3)
(not realized)
art direction: Stefan Sagmeister
design: Hjalti Karlsson
The New York Post 1999

pp.169-173
Move our Money identity and campaign (2)
art direction: Stefan Sagmeister
design: Hjalti Karlsson
inflatable sculptures: George York
© Business Leaders for Sensible Priorities
1998-1999
1265 hours / $ 39,520

pp.174-175
Kunsthalle Tirol business card (2)
art direction: Stefan Sagmeister
design: Hjalti Karlsson
© Kunsthalle Tirol 1999

pp.176-179
Whereishere spreads (2-3)
art direction: Stefan Sagmeister
design: Hjalti Karlsson
photo: Tom Schierlitz
illustration: Kevin Murphy
Gingko Press 1998

pp.180-183
Unavailable perfume packaging (2-3)
art direction: Stefan Sagmeister
design: Hjalti Karlsson
copy: Karen Salmansohn
© Blue Q 2000

pp.184-185
Idea magazine cover and inside page (2-3)
art direction: Stefan Sagmeister
design: Hjalti Karlsson
photo: Tom Schierlitz
Idea magazine 1998

p.186
Sagmeister 5 years anniversary party invites (3)
art direction: Stefan Sagmeister
design: Hjalti Karlsson, Regine Stefan
Sagmeister Inc. 1998

p.187
Print magazine cover (4)
art direction: Stefan Sagmeister
design: Veronica Oh
photo: Tom Schierlitz
Print magazine 1996

pp.188-189
American Photography book (2)
art direction: Stefan Sagmeister
design: Hjalti Karlsson
© Amilus Inc. 1999
263 hours / $ 5,500

p.190
Aiga Detroit poster (1-2)
art direction: Stefan Sagmeister
cutting: Martin Woodtli
photo: Tom Schierlitz
Aiga Detroit 1999
pro bono

pp.192-193
Studio SGP CD Rom packaging (2-3)
art direction: Stefan Sagmeister
design: Veronica Oh
Studio SGP 1994
41 hours / $500

pp.194-197
H.P. Zinker CD package (1)
art direction: Stefan Sagmeister
design: Veronica Oh
photo: Tom Schierlitz
© Energy Records 1994
220 hours / $ 1,800

pp.198-201
Songs of Maybe CD package (2-3)
art direction: Stefan Sagmeister
design: Mike Chan
photo: Bela Borsodi
The Design Group, Hong Kong
© Ubu Records 1992

pp.202-203
YMO CD package (2)
creative director: Tibor Kalman
art direction/design: Stefan Sagmeister
illustration: Eric Zim
photo: Ed Lachman
M&CO. New York
© Toshiba/EMI 1993

pp.204-205
YMO CD package (3)
(unpublished)
art direction: Stefan Sagmeister
design: Veronica Oh
1993

pp.206-207
Afropea CD package (2-3)
art direction: Stefan Sagmeister
design: Veronica Oh
photo: Tom Schierlitz
illustration: Indigo Arts
© Warner Bros. Records/Luaka Bop 1995
268 hours / $ 4,900

pp.208-209
The Nields CD package (3)
art direction: Stefan Sagmeister
design: Veronica Oh
illustration: Stefan Sagmeister, Carola Pfeifer
photo: Michael Halsband
© Razor & Tie 1996
99 hours / $ 1,050

pp.210-215
David Byrne Feelings CD package (1-2)
art direction: Stefan Sagmeister, David Byrne
design: Hjalti Karlsson
model making: Yuji Yoshimoto
photo: Tom Schierlitz
color advice: Anni Kuan
illustration: Indigo Arts
© Warner Bros. Records/Luaka Bop 1997
392 hours / $ 12,736 (including poster/ads)

pp.216-219
David Byrne book (2-3)
art direction: Stefan Sagmeister, David Byrne
design: Hjalti Karlsson
photo: David Byrne/stock
© David Byrne 1998
262 hours / $ 20,640

pp.220-223
Pro Pain CD package and poster (n/a)
art direction: Stefan Sagmeister
design: Veronica Oh
photo: Jeffrey Silverthorne,

Municipal Archives, New York
© Energy Records 1994
135 hours / $ 8.300

pp.224-225
Sonny Sharrock CD package (3)
art direction: Stefan Sagmeister
design: Veronica Oh
photo: Adam Fuss
© Enemy Records 1996
76 hours / $250

pp.227-231
Lou Reed Set the Twilight Reeling CD package
and poster (2-3)
art direction: Stefan Sagmeister
design: Veronica Oh
photo: Timothy Greenfield Sanders, Pete Cornish
illustration: Tony Fitzpatrick
© Warner Bros. Records 1996
429 hours / $19.850

pp.232-233
Lou Reed Ecstasy CD package (4)
art direction: Stefan Sagmeister
design: Hjalti Karlsson
photo: Lou Reed
© Reprise Records 2000
155 hours / $ 12.500

pp.234-237
Lou Reed Pass thru Fire book (2-3)
art direction: Stefan Sagmeister
design: Hjalti Karlsson, Jan Wilker
photo: Lou Reed
© Lou Reed 2000
347 hours / $ 11,672

pp.238-241
Lou Reed Modern Dance music video (3)
direction: Robert Pejo, Stefan Sagmeister
© Warner Bros. Records 2000
still photo: © Clifford Ross 2000

p.243
Judybats ad (3)
art direction: Stefan Sagmeister
design: Veronica Oh
© Sire Records Company 1994
15 hours / $ 1,880

p.245
Marshall Crenshaw CD package (3)
art direction: Stefan Sagmeister
design: Veronica Oh
photo: Tom Schierlitz
© Razor & Tie 1996
88 hours / $ 1,800

pp.246-247
Block CD package (3-4)
art direction: Stefan Sagmeister
design: Hjalti Karlsson
photo: Susan Stava
additional photo: Barbara Ehrbar, Gudmundur
Ingolfsson
© Java Records/Capitol Records 1998
173 hours / $ 7,150

pp.248-255
The Rolling Stones CD package
banners and prototypes (3-4)
art direction: Stefan Sagmeister
design: Hjalti Karlsson
photo: Max Vadukul
illustration: Kevin Murphy,
Gerard Howland (Floating Company), Alan Ayers
© Promotone B.V. 1997
797 hours / $ 53,000

pp.256-259
Pat Metheny Group Imaginary Day
CD package (1-2)
art direction: Stefan Sagmeister
design: Hjalti Karlsson
photo: Tom Schierlitz, Stock
© Warner Bros. Records 1997
298 hours / $ 8,485

pp.260-261
Pat Metheny Trio CD package (2-3)
art direction: Stefan Sagmeister
design: Hjalti Karlsson
photo: Latifa
© Warner Bros. Records 1999
114 hours / $ 14,100

pp.262-265
Live CD package and singles (3)
art direction: Stefan Sagmeister
design/illustration: Motoko Hada
photo: Dan Winters, Danny Clinch
© Radioactive Records 1999
248 hours / $ 47,000
(including extensive campaign)

pp.266-267
Mimi CD package (3-4)
art direction: Stefan Sagmeister
design: Hjalti Karlsson
photo: Joseph Cultice, Carl May, Stock
© Luaka Bop/Warner Bros. Records 1998
182 hours / $ 6,500

pp.268-269
Skeleton Key EP CD package (3)
art direction: Stefan Sagmeister
design: Veronica Oh
Illustration: Erik Sanko
© Motel Records 1996
40 hours / $800

pp.270-273
Skeleton Key Fantastic Spikes through Balloon
CD package (1-2)
art direction: Stefan Sagmeister
design: Hjalti Karlsson
photo: Tom Schierlitz
© Capitol Records 1997
286 hours / $8,800

p.275
Aiga Atlanta invitation
art direction: Stefan Sagmeister
Aiga Atlanta 1999
pro bono

p.276
Seven movie titles
title direction, design: Kyle Cooper
studio: New Line
director: David Fincher
reprinted with permission
from Imaginary Forces

The story of little Suck-A-Thumb
from Hoffmann, Heinrich
Struwwelpeter
Dover Publications 1996

Aiga National Conference New Orleans poster
see page 160-161

Liebe Mama T-shirt
design: Stefan Sagmeister
1997

King Crimson In the Court of the Crimson King
album cover

The Rolling Stones Sticky Fingers
album cover
reprinted with permission
from Promotone b.v.

XTC Go2 album cover
courtesy of Virgin Records Limited

p.277
Art Spiegelman Maus book

Alphagram Learning Materials
reprinted with permission
from Shapiro Design

Subway stickers
1994
reprinted with permission
from True

Janine Antoni Mom and Dad
materials: mother, father, makeup
1994
reprinted with permission
from Janine Antoni

Adolf Wölfli
Santta-Maria-Burg-Riesen-Traube:
Unitif Zohrn Tonnen schwer 1915
Zinsrechnung 1912
stack of note books 1908-1930
reprinted with permission
from Adolf-Wölfli-Stiftung
Kunstmuseum Bern

p.278
Damien Hirst book
Booth-Clibborn Editions 1997

Zwei Männer der Tat
Nikolaus Jungwirth, Paul Taussig
Titanic magazine 1979

p.279
Switzerland bank notes
reprinted with permission
from Schweizerische Nationalbank

Makoto Saito
poster for a Buddhist temple
reprinted with permission
from Makoto Saito

p.286
Lunch
photo: Stefan Sagmeister

pp.288-290
Before/After
Business 1995

inside back cover (underneath flaps)
laundromat
photo: Stefan Sagmeister
1998

back cover
Stefan Sagmeister
photo: Kevin Knight
2000

We tried very hard to come up with complete
credit information. If we missed you, please
e-mail stefan@sagmeister.com and we'll make
sure to include you in future editions.

Practically all photos of our designs have been
taken by Tom Schierlitz. Some additional ones
were shot by Michael Grimm, Bela Borsodi and
Zane White.

Thanks

OVERCAST

SUNNY

THANKS A WHOLE LOT TO MY FAMILY who supported me always, paid my way through school, allowed for a very cushy adolescence, listened to my stories and looked at all my pictures: Mama Sagmeister, Gebhard, Simon, Clemens, Elias and Heidrun Sagmeister, Christine (extra thanks for helping me to get out of HTL Bregenz engineering school and saving my life) Carolin and Juliane Schneider, Martin, Victoria and Susanne Sagmeister, Andrea, Raphael, Gabriel, Valeria, Lucia and Bernhard Rüdisser, Veronika, Jonas and Günther Sagmeister Hrazdjira.

THANKS TO MY LOVELY Anni.

THIS BOOK WOULD HAVE NEVER seen the light of day without my collaborators Hjalti Karlsson (who stuck with me through many years in the studio and through many changes in the book) and Veronica Oh. Many, many thanks to Peter Hall for accepting the gargantuan task to write this sucker. And to lovely Matthias Ernstberger.

AN ENORMOUS THANK YOU to Chee Pearlman, Paola Antonelli and Andrea Codrington for for reading the entire manu-script, marking it up and giving great tips.

A VERY BIG THANK YOU goes to my friends Tom Schierlitz (who not only photographed most of the projects but also many of the samples), Arthur Schulten, Ulrika Janosch, Reini Ehrenboeck, Edgar Fontanari, Lisli Kopf, Michael Grimm, Kevin Knight, James Victore and Robert Wong.

AND OF COURSE TO ALL FRIENDS without whom we'd be nothing: Christoph Abbredis, Janet Abrams, Demi Adeniran, Ed & Maura Albers, Gerry Amann, Sirikit Amann, Siegrun Appelt, Nancy Arnold, Corinne Auge, Lucia Belci, Paul Belci, Peter Belci, Uday Benegal, Gerald Benesch, Laura Benko, William Bevington, Florian Birkmayer, Ayse Birsel, Frazer Brosnahan, Bettina Budewig, Christian Bühner, Claude Cafengiu, Cindy Chang, Allan Chochinov (and hello Victoria), Hope Cohn, Michael Conrad, Paul Corcolon, Stuart D'Rozario, Werner Dauter, Bill Dean, Lynda Deppe, Marlaina Deppe, Julie & George Dermansky Steinboeck, Ilona Drozdzik, David Easton, Balz & Elisabeth Eggimann, Jessica Ellner, Andy Eigner, Judith Eisler, Jessica Enert, Eva Engel, Janet Eusebio, Hans Falb, Judith Fink, Mark Fisher, Alberto Foyo, Dina Fragale, Alexandra Gaspar, Rheinhard Gassner, Werner Geier, Reinhard Geiger, Paul Goebert, Itai Goral, Alexander Gröger, Roland Güttler, Philip Hämmerle, Thomas Häusle, Kayo Hayashi, Mary Healy, Wolfgang Hermann, Hugues Hervouet, Christian Hochmeister, Klaus Hoeller, Max Hollein, Michael Hübl, Ilona, Raimund Jaeger, Reinhard Johler, Anni Kim, Marlene Kindhauser, Jutta Knoeller, Barbara Kowatz, Bernd Kräftner, Patricia Kunkel, Kirk Lancaster, Peter Langebner, Waltraud Langer, Lilli Licka, Renate Lindlar, Olaf Lingenhöle, Johannes & Anja Linhart, Shirley Liu, Katie Liu, Janet Lo, Mark Lukas, Mary Luria, Lisa Lurie, Diana Ma, Gerlinde Manz-Christ, Lorraine Massey, Heinzi Matuschek, Falko Mätzler, Raymond Mayer, Brandon & Julie McCormick, Michael Mellinger, Edith Merz, Arno Miller, France Morin, Sigward Moser, Aimee Mullins, Katja Nussbaumer, Theresa & Bona Ok, Robert Pejo, Regina & Meinrad Pichler, Dalton Portella, Jessica Ragaza, Elena Reeves, PippiLotti Rist, Nina Ritter, Gregory & Kate Roll, Günther & Rainer Roppele, Laurie Rosenwald, Hannes Rothmayer, Michele Rowbotham, Christoph Rucker, Wolfgang Rüscher, Ulf Ryberg, Rudolf Sagmeister, Theresia Sagmeister, John Salvati, Monika Sandri, Thomas Sandri, Stoff Sauter, Andrea Scabo, Tomi Scheiderbauer, Andreas Schneider, Didi Schobel, Hubert Schober, Walter Schönauer, Lisa Schreiner, Bobby Siems, Maggie Silverman, Nancy Skolos, Peter Slodczyk, Gary Smith, Debbie Stein, Clemens Steinboeck, Al Stolzer, Chrissie Stott, Maria Stürz Feuerstein, Christina Sun, Andrea Szabo, Lita Talarico, Todd Tarhan, Janna Thür, Alexander Tinti, Sng Tong Bang, Jurislav Tscharijsky, Katharina Uschan, Christine Wagner, Vicky Walter, Katharina Weingartner, Fritz Westenberger, Helmut Wiener, Michael Williams, Albert Winkler, Mary & Kacey Wong, Howard Wood, Tia Wou, Isabella Wunderl, Canan Yilmaz, Vera Yuan and Lauma Zemzare

AN ENORMOUS THANK YOU TO ALL OUR CLIENTS who not only put up with our shit but also paid for everything: Mahmut T. Birsel, R.O. Blechman, Dave Boonshoft, Craig Braun, David Byrne, Chuck Caronia, Christopher Cheeney, Ben Cohen, Marshall Crenshaw, Joel Cuyler, Paula Doyle, Joost Elffers, Yale Evelev, Tom Evered, Gary Ferdman, Diane Fish, Peter Freedman, Janet Froehlich, Laurie Gerber, Peter Geubels, Hans Gissinger, Judy Glassman, Mimi Goese, Tony Goldman, Hans Gratzer, Trudy Green, Andrew Greenblatt, Dennis Hayes, Martha Hayes, Mick Jagger, Tony King, Mike Knuth, Edward Kowalczyk, Lukas Kramer, Wendy Laister, Kirk Lancaster, Lori Megown, Mitch Nash, Katryna Nields, Nerissa Nields, Lyle Mays, Pat Metheny, Thomas Nussbaumer, Kara Orr, Paxton, Hans Platzgummer, Alfred Polczyk, Michael Pollock, Hans-Jürgen Rabe, Mike Ragogna, Lou Reed, Hubert Salden, Larry Sato, Ryuichi Sakamoto, Erik Sanko, Stephan Schertler, David Sestak, Anthony Schneider, Bridget Shields, Mikio Shinagawa, David Sholemson, Deborah Sims, Peter Steele, Tommy Steele, Diana Stirling, Chad Taylor, Yohanes Teja, Naomi Uesaka and Katsuyuki Yamabe.

THANKS TO EVERYBODY IN THE MUSIC INDUSTRY, especially: Tina Agnello, Lucy Aubree, Chris Austopchuk, Dave Ayers, Steve Baker, Evan Balmer, Stefanie Barn, Richard Bates, Nancy Berry, Richard Bishop, Gary Borman, Laurie Burke, Carol Chen, Cliff Chenfield, Raymond Coffer, Gary Cohen, Art Collins, Tim Collins, Paul Craig, Roger Crammer, Kelly Curtis, Jerry Cutler, Clare De Graw, Ron Decker, Andrea Del Regno, James Diener, Jerry Dorn, Bertis Downs, Marc Droescher, Stacy Drummond, Skye Edwards, Peter Freedman, Peter Gabriel, Steve Gerdes, Jeff Gold, Margery Greenspan, Beth Grobert, Arlene Grzesnak, Michael Hausman, Jeri Heiden, Peter Herbert, Doug Isaac, Jerry Jaffe, Karyn Kaplan, Howard Kaufman, Gary Kurfirst, Ira Lippy, Kathy Malloy, Gail Marowitz, Paul McGuiness, Peter McQuaid, Peter Mensch, Melanie Nissen, Dennis Oppenheimer, Xilonen Oreshnik, Len Peltier, Matt Pierson, Mike Ragognia, Tom Recchion, Marc Reiter, Henry Rollins, Debbie Samuelson, John Silva, Susan Silver, Randy Skinner, Robin Sloan, Norika Sora, Tim Stedman, Steve Stewart, Bonnie Sugarman, Alli Truch, Stacy Valis, Marsha Vlasic, David Wasik, Nat Weisse, Scott Welch, Alan Wolmark and Jon Zazula.

THANKS TO ALL THE PHOTOGRAPHERS, many of whom endured tight lay-outs, nit-picking and shitty deadlines: Jaime Ardiles-Arce, Adolf Bereuter, Bela Borsodi, Barbara Gentile, Andy Goldsworthy, Timothy Greenfield Sanders, Jonathan Hillyer, Rainer Hosch, Günther Parth, Toby Richards, Ashkan Sahihi, John Sexton, Ringo Tang, Jurislav Tscharyiski, Tom Vack, Max Vadukul, Bob Wagner and Ray Charles White.

THANKS TO ALL THE ILLUSTRATORS who made our bad sketches look fantastic: Alan Ayers, Motoko Hada, Steven Hagg, Hungry Dog Studio, Kevin Murphy and David Schleinkofer

A TON OF THANKS TO OUR INTERNS who worked their asses off for no pay (!): Ulli Bayer, Peggy Chuang, Sabine David, Barbara Ehrbar, Friedericke Gauss, Stephan Hans, Stefanie Heiliger, Mathias Kern, Janice Kim,

Isabell Klett, Kazumi Matsumoto, Franziska Morlok, Nina Pavicsits, Carola Pfeifer, Tom Phillips, Susanne Poelleritzer, Alexander Pohl, Heike Reinsch, Regine Stefan, Bradley Theodore, Franz Tschol, Anke Wagner, Janet Wagner, Robert Wagner and Jan Wilker.

THANKS TO ALL THE PEOPLE WHO HELPED US WITH COLOR SEPARATION AND PRINTING, especially Howard Bromberg, Angela Cousins, Fran Griffin, Dave Haas, Debbie Kara, Elmer Ketler, Robert Kushner, Jim Ladwig, Tim Linn, Michael Marolda, Tom Mustapich, Rob Schroeder, Pat Seeholzer, Peter Simpson, Mike Stevens, Rob Thatcher and Craig Wenrich.

THANKS TO EVERYBODY IN THE SEQUOIA INCLUDING: Ramon DeArmas, Henry Diaz, James DePesa, Vince Occhipinti, Joe Rodriguez, Tony Roopnarine and Clara Valencia.

THANKS TO EVERYBODY WHO GRANTED US THE RIGHT TO SHOW THEIR WORK, especially Janine Antoni, Daniel Baumann, Anouk Fundarek, Rosa J. Lopez, Rick St. Maurice and Art Spiegelman.

THANKS TO Sherri and Ted for improving the narrative on page 36.

I'D LOVE TO THANK THE ENTIRE DESIGN PROFESSION IN THE U.S. for not being bitchy, not being backstabby but being genuinely supportive. After we started our little studio and slowly began turning out projects we could reasonably be happy with, calls from other designers started to come in. And these were not just any designers: Paula Scher, Milton Glaser, Steff Geissbuhler, Seymour Chwast, Michael Bierut and Emily Oberman all called in the first couple of years to say how much they liked this or that piece. I don't think there are many professions (certainly not fashion, advertising or fine art) where the practitioners are that supportive of each other.

SO MANY THANKS TO ALL THOSE DESIGNERS who always had an encouraging word for us, specially to those who answered our question: "Which piece of graphic design touches your heart" in this book: Sean Adams, Cordula Alessandri-Ebner, Cathy Altieri, Jürgen Altzhieber, Charles Anderson, Ian Anderson, Philippe Apeloig, Dana Arnett, Neil Ashby, Eric Baker, Aubrey Balkind, Jonathan Barnbrook, Richard Bates, Anthon Beeke, Gerald Benesch, Craig Bernhardt, John Bielenberg, Kim Biggs, Lisa Billard, Nicolaus Blechman, R.O. Blechman, Irma Boom, Bob Bowen, Laurene & Constantin Boym, Neville Brody, Steven Brower, Stefan Bucher, Ken Carbone, Martha Carothers, David Carson, Ken Cato, Vladimir Chaika, Allan Chan, Art Chantry, Ivan Chermayeff, Hyun Sun Alex Cho, Young Jae Cho, Ann Coffett, Kyle Cooper, Peter Corriston, Mark Cozza, Moira Cullen, Roger Dean, Doris Dell, Alfons Demetz, Mary Domowitz, Michael Donovan, Stephen Doyle, Spencer Drate, William Drenttel, Gert Dumbar, Michael Erlhoff, Peter Felder, Ed Fella, Louise Fili, Marc Fisher, Tobias Frere

Jones, Janice Fudyma, Frank Gargiulo, Paul Geczik, Tom Geismar, Alexander Gelman, Peter Gerardi, Michael Gernike, David Gibson, Barbara Glauber, Marc Gobe, Carin Goldberg, Jeanne Greco, Bob Greenberg, Steven Guarnaccia, Christian Guth, George Hardie, Daniela Haufe, Laurie Haycock Makela, Carla Hall, Steven Heller, Jessica Helfand, Hendrik Hellige, Ursula Hiestand, Christian Hochmeister, Drew Hodges, Paul Holden, D.K. Holland, Gerard Howland, Millie Hsi, Richard Hsu, Kent Hunter, Mirko Ilic, Melk Imboden, Alexander Isley, Dakota Jackson, Andy Jacobson, Dave Johnston, Maira Kalman, Craig Kanarick, Carolin Kavanagh, Karin Kautzky, Michael Ian Kaye, Jeffrey Keedy, Kan Tai Keung, Chip Kidd, Markus Kiersztan, Robert Kneitschel, Gary Koepke, Jacques Koeweiden, Kai Krause, Lisa Krohn, Patricia Kunkel, Steven Lavaque, Dominic Lippa, Uwe Loesch, Andrew Logvin, Elaine Louie, Reinhold Luger, Ellen Lupton, Robyn Lynch, Lisa Lurie, John Maeda, Shin Matsunaga, Sigi Mayer, Brandon & Julie McCormick, Petra Mercker Reichenbach, Noreen Morioka, Natalaya Mikheeva, Jennifer Morla, Miao Moy, Allison Muench, Lars Müller, Jackie Murphy, Hideki Nakajiama, Andreas Netthoevel, Christoph Niemann, Frank Olinsky, Vaughan Oliver, Taki Ono, Brent Oppenheimer, John Parham, Ander Pecher, P. Martin Pedersen, Rosanne Percivalle, Joe Perndl, Michael Peters, David Plunkert, Neil Powell, Uli Prugger, Karim Rashid, Phil Risbeck, Michael Rock, Gabriela Rodriguez, Laurie Rosenwald, Rhonda Rubinstein, Paul Sahre, Makoto Saito, Mike Salisbury, Maruchi Santana, Emily & Scott Santoro, U.G. Sato, Clemens Schedler, Walter Schönauer, Ralph Schraivogel, Nikolaus Schwabe, James Sebastian, Carlos Segura, Adrian Shaughnessy, Jim Sherraden, Marc Shillum, Gary Smith, Leonardo Sonnoli, James Spindler, Jamie H. Stedman-Novo, Henry Steiner, Scott Stowell, Lita Talarico, Lucille Tenazas, Rick Tharp, Tam Thomsen, Janna Thür, Michael Toomey, True, Niklaus Troxler, Rick Valicenti, Erik Van Blokland, Rudy Vanderlans, Tucker Viemeister, Massimo Vignelli, Kamil Vojnar, John Warwicker, John Waters, Alexander Wiederin, J.P. Williams, Wang Xu, Tadanoori Yokoo, Xiao Yong, Eric Zim, Kai Zimmermann and Jörg Zintzmeyer.

A BIG THANK YOU TO EVERYBODY WHO WROTE AN ARTICLE ON THE STUDIO, included our work in their book or said otherwise nice things about us: Alexa Agnelli, Sarah Ameer, Jong Won Baik, Dan Barron, Herbert Bauernebel, Claudius Baumann, Lewis Blackwell, Liz Brown, Max Bruinsma, David E. Carter, Heidi Christian, Brooke Comer, Darcy Cosper, Ken Coupland, Patrick Coyne, Melissa Dallal, Susan Davis, Ann Diaz, Christa Dietrich, Antje Dohmann, Clare Dowdy, Spencer Drate, Andreas Dressler, Juanita Dugdale, Genevieve Duris, Andrea Eschbach, Barbara Fernandez, Anne Fink, Cathy Fishel, Chris Foges, Martin Fox, Michael Freund, Teiji Fujii, Werner Geier, Amy Goldwasser, Doris Gordon, Takaya Goto, Lynn Haller, Laurel Harper, Talita Harper, Toru Hayashi, Lu Hua Heng, Ben Hunter, Takenobu

Igarashi, Irene Jancsy, Don Jeffrey, Terry Kattleman, Maya Kishida, Etsuko Kitagami, Robert Klanten, Katerina Kojoukhova, Uschi Korda, Manabu Koseki, Doris Krumpl, Julie Lasky, Jeremy Lin, Walter Lürzer, Melissa Milgrom, Anistatia Miller, Arno Miller, Franz Muhr, Kiyonori Muroga, Jutta Nachtwey, Tomoe Nakazawa, Marty Neumeier, Stefan Nink, Brigitta Nitsch, Heike Oberleitner, Annabel Pilgersdorfer, Matthew Porter, Rick Poynor, Anzgar Rau, Alice Rawsthorn, Hans Dieter Reichert, Kathleen Reinmann, Lynda Relph Knight, Margaret Richardson, Uwe Richter, Therese Rutkowski, Tom Samiljan, Katharina Sand, Herbert Saringer, Bettina Scherer, Andreas Schneider, Bonnie Schwartz, Ellen Shapiro, Leslie Sherr, Caori Shibata, Clarissa Stadler, Carol Stevens, Cyndi Stivers, Michelle Stone, Anne Telford, Gerrit Terstiege, Michaela Ulmer, Bettina Ulrich, Anthony Vagnoni, Udo van Kampen, Stefan Wagner, Roger Walton, Ann Weber, Timothy White, Liliane Wlassikoff, Fabian Wurm, Yuko Yoshio and Stefanie Zellmer.

A HEFTY THANK YOU TO ALL THE PEOPLE WHO ORGANIZED LECTURES, invited us to present our work in front of designers and in colleges and took us out to dinner afterwards: Patrick Baglee, Mike Bash, Hon Bing Wah, Kelly Bjork, Peter Borowski, Giorgio Camuffo, Erica Clark, Gavin Cooper, Kerry Crossen, Mary Domowitz, Martha Dunn, Alice Drueding, Martha Garguis, Reinhard Gassner, Ferko Goldinger, Rick Grefé, Einar Gylfason, Stephen Hinton, Phil Jones, Susan Kacapyr, Amos Klausner, Kathrin Kluge, Laura Laitham, Stuart McBride, Allison Millar, Gabriela Mirensky, Bill Moran, Margaret Morton, Gabriela Perez, Jennifer Philips, Kate Rader, Elizabeth Resnick, Hank Richardson, Paul Rustand, Heather Scarbrough, Serge Serov, Ame Simon, Lanny Sommese, Clif Stoltze, Alice Twemlow, Bernard Uy, Carol Wahler, Richard Wilde and Richard Saul Wurman.

I AM VERY GRATEFUL TO MY TEACHERS Paul Schwarz, Tino Erben, Barbara Markstein and Hans Hofman in Vienna and Elisa Zamir, Tony DiSpigna, Kevin Gatta in New York.

THANKS SO MUCH TO ALL MY STUDENTS.

THANKS TO ALL THE PEOPLE AT LEO BURNETT HONG KONG AND THE DESIGN GROUP specially Mike Chan, Eric Cheng, Gary Conway, Patrick Daly, Tom Hartje, Kenneth Lau, Basil Mina, Andrew Pogson, Peter Rae (very, very much so) and Sng Tong Bang.

THANKS TO STORM THORGERSON AND TIBOR KALMAN FOR BEING MY IDOLS.

AND VERY LAST BUT OBVIOUSLY NOT LEAST a hearty thanks to everbody at our publisher Booth-Clibborn specially Edward Booth-Clibborn, Phil Ashcroft, Denny Hemming and Rachel Scott.

(SOMEWHAT) SELECTED BIBLIOGRAPHY

Antonelli, Paola. *Surface*, USA, March 2000.
pp.104-108, p.188.

Baik, Jong Won. *Design net*, Korea, March 1998.
pp.78-83.

Baumann, Claudius. "CD-Hüllen für David, Lou und die Rolling Stones." *Neue Vorarlberger Nachrichten*, Austria, 31 August 1997.

Brown, Liz. *Zoo*, UK, Issue 4, January 2000.
pp.214-229.

Carter, David E.. *Cool Cards*, New York: Hearst Books International, 1998.
p 72

Carter, David E.. *Letterheads in the Third Dimension*, New York: Hearst Books International, 1997.
p.52, p.60, p.80, p.114, p.124.

Codrington, Andrea. *I.D. Magazine*, USA, March/April 1995,
pp.72-73.

Comer, Brooke. "Persistence And Timing Lead To Success In Music Business." *Artist's & Graphic Designer's Market '99*, USA,
pp.632-634.

Coyne, Patrick. "Great Ideas Produced On Limited Budgets." *Communication Arts*, USA, May/June 1995.
p.84, p.91.

Davis, Susan E.. "Ninety Percent Image." *Step-by-Step Graphics*, USA, January/February 1995,
pp.70-83.

Dietrich, Christa. "Als Film hätte er fünf Sterne." *Vorarlberger Nachrichten*, Austria, 15 November 1997.

Drate, Spencer. Salavetz, Jütka. *Cool Type 2wo*, Cincinnati: North Light Books, 1999.
pp.128-131.

Dressler, Andreas. "Austria goes New York." *Diners Club*, Austria, May 1995,
pp.28-29.

Fishel, Catharine. *Paper Graphics*, Gloucester: Rockport Publishers Inc., 1999.
p.8, pp.12-13, p.57, pp.67-68, p.85, p.92.

Foges, Chris. *Letterheads & Business Cards*, Crans-Près-Céligny: Roto Vision SA, 1999.
p.18, p.20, pp.64-65

Goto, Takaya. *+81*, Japan, Volume 5, Spring 1999.
pp.74-79.

Graphic Design New York 2, Rockport: Rockport Publishers Inc., 1997.
pp.157-162.

Graphic Design USA 19, New York: AIGA, 1999.
p.103, pp.107-109, p.191.

Hall, Peter. "Pushing Through Innovative CD Package Designs Can Be Difficult, If Not Impossible."

Upper and Lower Case, USA, Volume 24, No 4, Spring 1997.
pp.18-20.

Hall, Peter. "Box Clever." *Creative Review*, UK, April 1997.
pp.49-50.

Hall, Peter. Printed Matter. *I.D Magazine*, USA, March/April 1999.
p.50.

Haller, Lynn. *Fresh Ideas in Letterhead and Business Card Design 3*, Cincinnati: North Light Books, 1997.
p.23, p.28, p.95, p.115, p.137.

Harper, Laurel. *Radical Graphics*. San Francisco: Chronicle Books, 1999.
pp.198-201.

Hayashi, Toru. Nakayama, Yukika. *Business Card Graphics 2*, Tokyo: P.I.E. BOOKS, 1992.
pp.80-81, p.87, p.154, p.156.

Heller, Steven. "Budget Buster." *Print*, USA, November/December 1999.
pp.88-91.

Heller, Steven. Fink, Anne. *Less is more*, Cincinnati: North Light Books, 1999.
p.9, p.83, p.92.

Heller, Steven. *Design Literacy*, New York: Allworth Press, 1999.
pp.149-152.

Heng, Lu Hua. *Package Design Magazine*, China, No 4, 1998.
pp.10-13.

I.D. Magazine, USA, Annual Design Review 1995.
pp.108-109.

I.D. Magazine, USA, Annual Design Review 1997.
p.111, pp.124-125.

I.D. Magazine, USA, Annual Design Review 1998.
p.123, p.144.

Igarashi, Takenobu. *3-D Greeting Cards*, Tokyo: Graphic-Sha-Publishing Co. Ltd., 1993.
p.13, p.27, p.114.

Intro. Contemporary Music Graphics, New York: Universe Publishing, 1999.
pp.54-57.

Jancsy, Irene. "Ein Löwe für Mick Jagger."
Profil, Austria, No. 41, 6 October 1997,
pp.132-133.

Jeffrey, Don. "Hot Designer Matches
Concepts To Music."
Billboard, USA, 8 November 1997.

Kattleman, Terry. "Style Counsel."
Creativity, USA, July/August 1995,
pp.14-15.

Kishida, Maya. *Private Greeting Cards*,
Tokyo: P.I.E. BOOKS, 1998.
p.19, p.26, p.68, p.75, p.77, p.124.

Kitagami, Etsuko. *New Business Card
Graphics*, Tokyo: P.I.E. BOOKS, 1996.
p.119, p.121, p.133, p.141, p.151, p.161, p.173,
p.178.

Klanten, Robert. Hellige. Hendrike.
Mischler, Michael. *Trigger*,
Berlin: Die Gestalten Verlag, 1999.
pp.84-85, pp.153-155.

Krumpl, Doris. "Vertraute Zeichen."
Standard, Rondo, Austria, 25 February
2000,
pp.13-14.

Lürzer's Archive, Design for Music 1, 1999,
p.106, pp.128-129, pp.147-149, pp.160-161,
pp.178-179, pp.185-186, pp.202-203, p.210, p.217.

Lupton, Ellen. *Design Culture Now*.
New York: Princeton Architectural Press,
2000.
p.18, pp.84-85, p.212.

Milgrom, Melissa. "Campaign With a
Conscience."
I.D. Magazine, USA, November 1999,
p.25.

Muhr, Franz. "Vorarlberger ist Top-
Designer in New York."
Vorarlberger Nachrichten, Austria,
16 December 1998.

Nakazawa, Tomoe. *One & Two Color
Graphics*. Tokyo: P.I.E. BOOKS, 1997.
pp.44-45, p.117, p.179, p.196.

Neumeier, Marty. *Critique*, USA, Winter
1998,
pp.26-28.

Nink, Stefan. "Der Designer Ihres
Vertrauens."
Rolling Stone, Germany, February 1998,
pp.9-10.

Reichert, Hans Dieter. "Perception and
Reality."
Baseline, UK,
pp.4-8.

Relphknight, Lynda. "Cover Star."
Design Week, UK, 3 March 2000,
pp.16-17.

Richter, Uwe. "A Natural Born Creative."
Novum, Germany, June 1998,
pp.60-65.

Roppele, Günther.
C.A.R.L., Austria, April 1998.
pp.68-77.

Sagmeister, Stefan. "Brief aus New York."
Form, Germany, No.152, April 1995,
pp.17-18.

Sagmeister, Stefan. "What Does
Typography Mean To Me?"
IDEA, Japan, No.275, July 1999,
pp.92-96.

Samiljan, Tom. "Our Motto is Style=Fart."
Time Out New York, USA, Issue 140,
May/June 1998,
p.158.

Sand, Katharina. "Zwischen Avantgarde
und Megastars."
Horizont, Germany, No.49, 3 December
1998.

Saringer, Herbert. "Der Mann ohne Stil."
Bestseller, Austria, October 1995,
pp. 24-25.

Shapiro, Ellen. *Communication Arts*,
USA, September/October 1999,
pp.58-67.

Sherr, Leslie. *Graphis*, USA, May/June
1996, No.303,
pp.54-65.

Sherr, Leslie. "Shaking it up."
Print, USA, March/April 1996, cover,
pp.28-37.

Sherr, Leslie. "The frontiers of visual
images."
IDEA, Japan, No.266, 1998-1, cover,
pp.26-31.

Sherr, Leslie. Katz, David J., *Design for
Response*, Gloucester: Rockport Publishers
Inc., 1999.
p.48, p.119.
Shibata, Kaori. *Business Stationery
Graphics 2*, Tokyo: P.I.E. BOOKS, 1994.
pp.46-47, p.144.

"Hannar geisladiska-umslög fyrir fræga
tónlistarmenn."
The Sunday-paper, Iceland, July 1999.

Terstiege, Gerrit. "Stefan Sagmeister",
Form, Germany, No.171, January 2000,
cover,
p.4.

The Best of Business Card Design 3,
Gloucester: Rockport Publishers Inc.,
1998.
p.25, p.28, p.36, p.49, p.53, p.67, p.77, p.93.

Twemlow, Alice. *Graphics International*,
UK, No.52, February 1998,
pp.12-15.

Twemlow, Alice. *Graphics International*,
UK, Issue 45, July 1997,
p.27.

Ulmer, Michaela. "Just do it."
Trend, Austria, July 1996,
pp.72-74.

Ulrich, Bettina. "Cover Designs by Stefan
Sagmeister."
Novum, Germany, November 1999,
pp.40-41.

Walton, Roger. *Sight for Sound*, New York:
Hearst Books International, 1997.
p.82/3.

Walton, Roger. *Printed Matter*,
New York: Hearst Books International,
1999.
pp.124-125.

Weber, Ann. "Decoding music."
HOW, USA, April 1999,
pp.110-113.

Wlassikoff, Liliane. Signes, Versailles:
SARL Mithra-Editions, 1997.
p.70, p.128, p.142.

Xu, Wang. "Box Clever."
Hi-Graphic, China, 1998.
pp.52-59.

Xu, Wang. *Stefan Sagmeister*,
Guangzhou: China Youth / Press, 1998.

Yoshio, Yuko. *1, 2 & 3 Color Graphics Vol.2*,
Tokyo: P.I.E. BOOKS, 1996.
p.99, pp.171-173.

Zellmer, Stefanie. *Art Direction*, USA, May
1995,
pp.30-31.

INDEX

This headline is solid, but it would sooner attract someone who's already a piano student.

The ad needs to convey that Home Conservatory makes piano lessons fun.

BEFORE:

The musical notes in this ad give it some pizazz, but there's not enough of a theme or strong visual focus to hook the passing reader.

Why drive to
PIANO LESSONS
When piano lessons
Will come to you?

PIANO
Instruction in
the comfort and
convenience of
YOUR HOME
• Qualified Teachers
• Adults & Children
• All levels
• Piano Rentals Available

HOME
CONSERVATORY
410-263-2628
301-261-2121

MORE

INDEX